Jani Tully Chaplin

The Swallows Have Landed

Other people's lives are so much more interesting than one's own.
It's like going to a dinner where I almost feel like I'm a psychiatrist.

Her Majesty Queen Camilla

Cover image © Jani Tully Chaplin:
A Cornish Beach

ISBN: 978-1-3999-6306-0

Enquiries to: jani@janitullychaplin.com
www.janitullychaplin.com/books
www.themanorhousestories.com

Printed and bound in the UK by Gomer Press Ltd, Ceredigion

Typesetting and design by JS Typesetting Ltd, Porthcawl, Mid Glamorgan
jstype@btconnect.com

Cover layout by Rory James Christopher Chaplin
RJCC Events, Oxfordshire
rjccevents.com

FSC
www.fsc.org
MIX
Paper | Supporting
responsible forestry
FSC® C114687

Contents

The Nearly Home Trees

*A distinctive spinney on top of a knoll that tells
drivers returning to Cornwall that the border on
the River Tamar is only minutes away.*

Pencil drawing © Jani Tully Chaplin

Author's note

I must apologise to all my readers of the first two books in this Corfu Trilogy: there is not quite as much about Corfu and the Ionian Islands in this third book – the clue is on the cover. However Corfu and our many dear Corfiot friends are forever in my family's thoughts; I can hardly write more than a few lines without some memory of Corfu popping into my head, which then has to be included. I hope you will bear with me and enjoy these reminiscences and others amidst the tale of our lives since we returned to England.

Once again my long suffering husband has struggled to edit this book and organise my chaotic writing into a semblance of sensible orderliness. There was a dreadful moment last summer when I was happily ensconced in my pretty little summer house at the top of the garden, when for no reason at all my laptop suddenly lost the first word of every single line and began putting paragraphs into boxes. I thought little of it and just carried on typing with two fingers. When Jeremy arrived with a tray of afternoon tea, I casually mentioned it to him and he nearly passed out, telling me I had lost the whole thing. At the time there were 80,000 words on the manuscript.

I have never got on with anything remotely technical; I only learn how to do something by trying it over and over until I've got it firmly embedded. I have a 'need to know' attitude and only use computers to send emails, use Facebook, search the internet and buy things online. Rory has tried to teach me how to use my laptop properly and has despaired. Miranda is equally computer savvy and also knows far more about car engines than most men. Jeremy is convinced I would master the laptop and the remote controls if only I would cut my fingernails, which tend to hit the wrong key, or occasionally the self-destruct button. The funny thing is I love doing anything repetitive and would have been very happy working on a production line. I don't know exactly what I will do after this book is published, but as Emma Fellowes assured me last year, 'I am certain your next adventure is just around the corner.'

And by the way, I don't *really* want to work in a factory…

Chapter One

Surviving

Just when the caterpillar thought the world was over, it became a butterfly.

Chuang Tzu

April 2015, North Cornwall

Beyond a rise where the track of an ancient coach road curves away towards Jamaica Inn over the wilds of Bodmin Moor, we turned off the main road. An uneven lane wound its crooked path for several miles between blankets of unkempt bracken and gorse; ancient standing stones defiant on the skyline and granite quarries taken back by nature provided the only signs of human activity. Eventually the lane passed over a quaint old clapper bridge, where shaggy longhorn cattle drank contentedly from a shallow river, completing a scene of perfect bucolic tranquility. Approaching our destination we pulled over to the verge to find our bearings and stepped out of the car onto closely grazed moorland turf. Butter yellow gorse blossom surrounded us, filling the air with its sweet scent of coconut; above us the cerulean sky seemed to continue far below our high vantage point as we slowly absorbed the views from the top of the ridge. Before us an ancient church tower stood proud in the middle distance, keeping vigil over a cluster of cottages and farm buildings; to our west the Cornish Alps, the pyramids and artificial hillsides of spoil from the old clay mines, stood dark against the skyline; to our north the Camel Estuary led like a sparkling ribbon towards the bluff headlands between Port Isaac and

Mawgan Porth, above which a thin horizon of sapphire sea shone enticingly. Behind us, dappled in the bright midday sunlight, the two highest tors in the county rose from the distant moor; their peaks, we already knew, acted as beacons for the first swallows of spring to arrive exhausted from their long migration. Perhaps we too had found a place to settle at last.

Four long years had passed since we left Corfu, yet that day was still etched indelibly in our minds.

* * *

March 2011, The Adriatic
The first glimmers of dawn stretched tentatively above a quilt of cloud shrouding the high peaks of Greece and Albania as the *Europa Palace* set course up the Adriatic for Venice. In the ferry's wake our beloved island faded relentlessly into the grey. We had made the same journey dozens of times over the years, but on this occasion Jeremy and I were unsure if we would, or ever could return. Relief at our successful escape from Corfu with the Jeep soon faded as the last fourteen magical years of our contented lives in the sun began to evaporate into the mists of a half-remembered dream.

Our drive through Italy was fast and furious; having endured several robberies and even an attempted hijack along the road between Venice and Milan, we decided discretion was the better part of valour and only stopped when we had crossed the border into the comforting safety of Switzerland. Hours later as darkness fell, snow had blanketed the quaint little village high in the Vosges, where we had booked one final night at a favourite hotel. Rifling through our holdalls for warm coats that hadn't seen the light of day for several years, Dash snuffled around in the snow until I picked him up and carried him inside. Luckily all the shops, hotels, restaurants and cafés in Europe welcomed him with open arms and warm hearts, unlike our own ostensibly dog loving nation. Once inside our room Dash investigated every corner, nose to the carpet like an anteater, as he familiarised himself with the scents of any previous canine occupants, before curling up on his travelling bed for a refreshing nap until we ventured out to savour one last supper at a simple French restaurant. Later as we picked our way back to the hotel through the snow, a host of high chimneys jutted into a clear night sky, each one adorned with its own untidy stork's nest. Long since vacated, yet still perched precariously like outsize chimney brushes, we wondered if we would ever pass through Alsace again in Spring to see their inhabitants return.

At Calais the following afternoon we took the Channel Tunnel to Dover. I could never get used to the idea of being so far under the sea, but it was the only way we could keep Dash with us – the Channel ferries never allowing dogs above the car deck, despite the Royal Decree allowing all Cavalier King Charles Spaniels to pass wherever they pleased. Given our many disasters over the years Jeremy and I had been married, my furtive imagination was always on the lookout for the next one. I played out a scenario in my mind in which our ferry would collide with an oil tanker and catch fire; the order to abandon ship would be given and I would be unable to rescue Dash from beyond the locked steel doors of the car deck; inevitably I would be obliged to go down with the ship. As Dash slept peacefully on my lap, I reclined my seat, put in my earphones, closed my eyes and listened to *The Sound of Music* as the train rumbled its way beneath the Channel to England.

Emerging into the grimy daylight at the Folkestone railway terminal had rarely been an uplifting experience for us; crossing the divide without a single glimpse of the English Channel, we always felt strangely cheated of a journey. Bill Bryson's description of his first arrival in England resembling 'being inside a Tupperware box with the lid on' never seemed more apt; we were definitely inside that box, both mentally and physically. I tried to shake myself out of this despondency and think of all the things which could cheer us up; seeing Rory and Miranda again was top of the list of course, for we had not been together since Christmas. There was Oxford to look forward to: this ancient city of dreaming spires and willow-lined rivers, where louche young orators would be reciting Byron's sonnets to their sweethearts as they reclined in the cushioned comfort of elegant punts; there were art galleries and theatres, the Ashmolean Museum and the Bodleian Library. The venerable colleges with their hallowed quads would be populated by those alluringly enigmatic students, so fondly remembered from *Brideshead Revisited* – surely they would all resemble Sebastian and Charles.

Somewhere between Folkestone and Oxford, Jeremy and I resolved to be cheerful, to put on a brave face and generally pull ourselves together. Suddenly finding ourselves most unwillingly separated from our funds was the very opposite of winning the lottery jackpot; our lives had changed dramatically, lean times beckoned and it was only to be expected that we felt a little down in the mouth. But we had to remember our lives had been incredibly and some might say undeservedly rosy until now. Ours was by no means the worst lot in the world.

Eventually reaching Rory's leafy cul-de-sac in Summertown I focused on the ranks of daffodils nodding gently in the shade of mature lime trees, their branches already full of tight buds that promised so many sweetly scented bunches of cream flowers to come. Rory and Miranda greeted us with hugs and kisses and helped us to unload the Jeep. Dash was overjoyed to see them again and you could tell he was so happy to have his family complete once more. As he raced around the garden and the men took our substantial luggage into the house, I tried not to think of Corfu; instead, amongst all this unsettling confusion, I took a moment to be thankful we were all safely reunited and to appreciate my new, unfamiliar surroundings. The first lines of William Henry Davies' evocative poem, *Leisure*, came to mind.

What is this life, if full of care,
We have no time to stop and stare.
No time to stand beneath the boughs
And stare as long as sheep or cows ...

Miranda had done her best to make the house as welcoming as possible for our arrival; there were fresh lilies in the sitting room and another vase of narcissi in our bedroom, where sun poured in through a bay window. After lunch I decided to take Dash for a well-deserved walk after so many days spent travelling through Europe in the car, while Jeremy, Rory and Miranda were busily trying to shoehorn our bags and boxes into the little house. Less than a couple of hundred yards down the road there was a convenient park, where the tree lined and tranquil River Cherwell ran though its meadow.

It sounded like a godsend in the middle of such a suburban jungle, so I put Dash on the lead and set off for the park in plucky mood until I noticed a sturdy dog of the pit bulldog variety, prowling unsecured ahead of his pit bulldog variety owner. Within a few seconds the brute had spotted Dash and flown across the road towards us. I scooped little Dash into my arms as the beastly dog attacked us. I am not very tall and the ravaging beast could easily reach Dash in my arms; he was obviously going in for the kill. I screamed for help as loudly as I could but there was nobody around except the owner. I kicked out at the dog, all the time holding Dash as high as I could from the reach of snapping jaws. The owner made no move to help, so I screamed at him to call off his dog.

"He ain't gonna kill yer!" he shouted back.

Poor Dash was yelping in fear and panic as I held him for dear life. The man sauntered across the road, attached a chain and dragged the dog away as I stood there shaking like a leaf and feeling quite sick. I ran back to Rory's house, slammed the door behind me and told the family I was never going out alone with Dash again. Only when Miranda was cuddling him did she notice a puncture wound on one of his hind legs and tufts of white hair missing from his beautiful long tail – the only thing the misbegotten animal had been able to grab. So much for the River Cherwell and punts, I thought.

Nevertheless a stranger had actually spoken to me! Even such an extremely unpleasant altercation was proof that human interaction was still possible. After so many years in Greece I couldn't understand why people in England never greeted one another or spoke a single word of acknowledgement, preferring instead to walk past with downcast eyes and glum expression. Were they all searching the pavements for coins? My offerings of a 'Good morning' I remembered, had invariably gone unanswered in England.

If this incident discoloured my rose-tinted opinion of Oxford, a visit into town the following morning settled the matter once and for all. Recalling the excellent cafés in most of the London museums and galleries, Jeremy thought it would cheer me up to go to the Ashmolean Museum for coffee and cake at their restaurant in the cellars; the bar in the Randolph, where we used to stay when visiting Rory, would have been more congenial, but for now those days of affluence were over. We were in the city centre early and had managed to park in St. Giles, not far from Balliol College. I had dressed carefully in smart court shoes, skirt and jacket, imagining for some unknown reason that I was visiting Corfu Town and remembering Coco Chanel's advice about keeping your heels, head and standards high. After all I would be stepping onto the set of *Brideshead Revisited.*

Within a few yards of the car I almost stepped in a pool of something yellow with orange lumps in it – unmistakeably vomit. Leaping in very unladylike fashion over the mess, I wondered if these elegant leather shoes had been such a good idea. By the time we reached the imposing entrance to the Ashmolean I had avoided several more festering puddles and was feeling decidedly queasy. On our way up to the Troodos Mountains in Cyprus we often used to see cautionary signs warning drivers to beware of roads slippery with grape juice, but here we needed warnings about pavements slippery with excreta. I began to imagine filling in an insurance claim form:

Slipped on vomit, shattered hip, caught exotic disease when face hit pavement, broke heel of shoe. Suggest sue Oxford City Council.

From now on I would wear my wellies into Oxford, I vowed as I complained bitterly to Jeremy.

"Well it's Monday morning in a university city," he replied, seemingly unconcerned.

"What's that got to do with it?" I asked furiously as we reached the grand façade of the Ashmolean..

"It's the students," he continued, with an unmistakable flicker of guilty reminiscence in his expression. "They always drink far too much at weekends and nobody's cleaned the streets yet."

So *that* was the reason everyone walked the streets of Oxford with permanently downcast eyes. Of course it's not just Oxford and not just England: Jeremy and I had been forced to do the same in Lille not so many years earlier. The attractive city's streets were so pickled with dog mess that walking along the pavements required the agility of a hopscotch champion. *Vieux Lille*, the magnificent city centre, certainly carried away the prize for *Nouvelles crottes de chien*.

I wish I had seen some reviews of the café before we had gone in and waited in a queue for twenty minutes to reach the self-service checkout. There, we were charged a king's ransom for a piece of cardboard shortbread and two lattés served in cups unworthy of the tiniest *skéto* Greek coffee. We couldn't find a single table that wasn't littered with previous occupants' detritus and I ended up clearing one myself. An entry at the time in one of the leading review sites read:

Forget the Ashmolean cafe. If you want to eat, go and find somewhere else. First of all, the cafe is filthy. There is rubbish everywhere you look. All the tables and chairs have used tissues, crumbs and all sorts. So after we spent a quarter of an hour cleaning our table and chairs, we went to order. £1.60 for a tiny bottle of water?! Theft!! They have maybe two staff working in the entire place and the counter is really dirty. There's also the atmosphere to consider. It's dim and the lights don't make a bit of difference. Waste of time and money.

Ah well, that was another one off the list.

Our English bank accounts were virtually empty and we had only been able to get our hands on a few hundred euros from Corfu, where currency was becoming scarce. The Greek bond crisis and a sleight of hand of epic proportions had well and truly skewered us; but our own misfortune was nothing compared to the misery that was about to be inflicted upon the Greeks by the hypocritical torture of the detestable European *troïka*. Needs must when the devil drives, so our faithful Jeep was sold within the week to an armed response police driver, who obviously needed lots of luggage space for all his guns. Four years would pass before we could afford another car of any sort, but in the meantime the proceeds of the sale would give us the wherewithal to fund a couple of years' rent.

A week after our return to England, as luck would have it, two bits of apparent bad luck and bad timing struck our family; in the eventuality both would make life much easier for us all. First, Rory's landlords casually informed him they were selling up and duly gave him the obligatory two months' notice. It was actually the perfect opportunity for Rory and Miranda to suggest we might all pool our resources and share a property – rents in Oxford being as high as London at the time. Jeremy and I remonstrated with them that living with their parents was the very last thing they would want to do, but they insisted it would help them too; together we could afford to rent a much larger property.

They both disliked living in a city as much as Jeremy and I would have, so our search took us to the villages and countryside within a fifteen mile radius of Oxford. Rory had been working very long hours in the theatre, including at weekends, so it was left to Miranda, Jeremy and to me to scout for possibilities. And what a grim selection they were! It slowly dawned on us that we had all been thoroughly spoilt by the various homes we had enjoyed in our lives. Photographs in the agents' particulars often looked vaguely promising, carefully cropped and taken with a wide-angle lens, but in reality they turned out to be much smaller and hemmed in on a scruffy estate, or set beside a fume-laden commuter route.

It was also at this time that Rory's theatre was reclaimed by Oxford City Council. They would be closing it for a year while the entire building was refurbished and converted into a 'space' for the homeless and deprived of Oxford, complete with café and studios. A redundancy payment would serve as a springboard for Rory to start his own events company, which had been many years in the planning. Through contacts made whilst moonlighting from the theatre he was able to get bookings almost immediately, so a name was needed. I suggested *Roars* – a nickname from schooldays that had a suitable connotation of the sound produced by his megawatt loudspeaker systems, which I thought rather clever. He didn't care for it and eventually decided on the initials of his full name and RJCC Events was born. Rory bought a small Jeep and a sizeable van, both in silver, to which smart branding logos were applied with the help of Miranda's hairdryer.

Rory and Miranda were angels and suggested we share their cars until we could afford to buy something for ourselves; we could use one or other of them when they weren't required for work. I got some strange looks whenever I drove Rory's branded Jeep to nearby Burford for shopping, but I was used to that – I can't imagine why. Some were even admiring glances, until the day came when I received a parking fine and a caution from a particularly beastly traffic warden. I had berated him after a disagreement, shall we say, about the merits of parking in the middle of a pedestrian crossing. Well how else was I supposed to collect my heavy bags of groceries in such a crowded high street? Unfortunately my antics were recorded on my persecutor's lapel camera. Thereafter I was in disgrace and Rory forbad me to use the car by myself again, as my cavalier attitude to parking, and for that matter to driving, would bring his company into disrepute. I had definitely spent too many years driving on Corfu, where such behaviour would have attracted cheers of support for me, ribald jeers for the traffic warden, followed by a spontaneous outbreak of applause and offers of free drinks.

(Miranda, on the other hand, is an excellent driver. But when she arrived in Corfu with her new Golf, having successfully driven all the way through Europe at the age of nineteen, she was perplexed and not a little offended to see every other Corfiot driver conspicuously crossing themselves as soon as they saw her car approaching.

Eventually her Greek boyfriend worked out that one of our local priests owned a new Golf in the very same colour; wherever she drove she was treated with the courtesy and deference due to an Archbishop, until closer inspection revealed her long blonde hair and lack of beard.)

In the summer of 2010, while Jeremy and I were still settled in Corfu, Miranda had telephoned me from Oxford, where she had moved into a house with her brother.

"Hi Mummy, I've answered an advert for a resident beauty therapist in Zante and they want me to go to London tomorrow for an interview! What do you think … and where is Zante anyway?"

I was delighted and urged her to take the opportunity, adding that Zante was the Italian name for Zakinthos and that she had often been within spitting distance of the island on many of Sarava's cruises past the south of Kefalonia. Forays along its coasts had revealed it to be the only large island in the Ionian to lack enticing and tranquil anchorages, so we had never been tempted to drop anchor. Miranda sounded apprehensive about the job but we both thought it was a terrific opportunity for her, Jeremy having immediately looked online to scrutinise the company she would be working for. The Peligoni Club, an exclusive bijou beach resort boasting many facilities including pools, restaurants, a beauty spa and a range of watersports, sounded highly respectable.

"Well, go along for the interview and if you're successful you can decide whether to take the position or not," I advised her. "After all, you would be closer to us in Zakinthos than you are in England. We could even pop down to see you in the RIB!"

I often have premonitions about things, usually quite insignificant but occasionally more disturbing. My mother was exactly the same, so I had grown up respecting these intuitions. The worst one she had experienced occurred the night before my brother was drowned in Torbay at the age of fifteen. Chris, a strong swimmer and a natural seaman, sailed his canoe almost every day of the Easter and summer holidays. My mother had a terrible premonition and begged him not to venture out that April day; but it was the last day of the holidays and in typical Arian fashion, he wouldn't listen. The day had dawned sunny and calm until a vicious squall blew up out of nowhere. Despite the best efforts of the lifeboats, local fishermen, tourist boats and all the private craft that joined the search for the two boys, my brother and his best friend were never found. Chris was well known and liked at the harbour, where my father and two uncles had kept boats since before the war. Mummy told me later the Bay resembled Dunkirk, with an armada of boats scattered from Hope's Nose to Berry Head as they searched for the boys.

My premonition was equally strong regarding Miranda and Zakinthos, albeit at the positive end of the spectrum; I was convinced she should go, but I didn't really know why. The next phone call we had from our daughter was to let us know she had immediately been offered the position; her expensive training at Champneys and a summer as resident beautician at the Rothschild estate in Corfu had paid a dividend. However there was a hesitancy in her voice as we congratulated her.

"But they want me to fly to Zakinthos the day after tomorrow!"

"Then go out and buy a few holiday clothes to celebrate and pack your suitcase!" I reassured her, knowing the thought of clothes shopping would get her in the right frame of mind and distract her from any worries.

A very excited young lady called us from the Peligoni Club two days later.

"Mummy, Daddy, it's fabulous here! Everyone's so friendly! I'm sending you a photo of the Peligoni crew giving me my welcome drinks when I arrived; they're a really nice crowd. I'm wearing a long black beach-cum-evening dress I bought at Zara in Oxford. Do you like it?"

Miranda spent the rest of that summer in Zakinthos, working with another beautician and spending her free time with the young guests and staff during their summer holidays from universities and public schools. Miranda had flown to us in Corfu at the end of her contract and we heard an awful lot about her new circle of friends during the couple of months until we returned to England together for Christmas with Rory. Millfield had provided a very diverse selection of friends for both our children, but many of them lived and worked overseas; many more spent their leisure time – in other words their entire lives – jetting from one celebrity gathering to the next. One amongst Miranda's friends from Zakinthos featured large in her life. I began to sense a wedding in the air, until Jeremy reminded me of the apocryphal story of a son informing his parents he was about to get married, whereupon the father had replied 'Against whom?'

This delightful young man became a frequent visitor to Oxford whenever he could escape from university for the weekend. I will always remember a particularly damp and dismal Sunday afternoon, all five of us silently scanning the property websites on our phones and laptops in front of the sitting room fireplace.

"Jani, look at this one. I think it looks rather promising," said the young beau as he passed me his laptop.

The particulars showed an attractive traditional Cotswold cottage of local stone with a slate roof, surrounded by woods on two sides in a small hamlet west of Woodstock. The layout would be perfect for us with its two front doors and two staircases leading to four bedrooms. One side of the cottage would be ideal for Rory to come and go to work at odd hours without disturbing the rest of us; on that side a dining room on the ground floor would serve Rory as an office. Miranda could have the middle bedroom and Jeremy and I could have the larger en-suite bedroom at the far side, which had French doors leading onto a raised terrace surrounded by mature beech and conifer trees – little did we know at the time they were the favourite homes to the most enormous spiders I had ever seen in England; nor did we fully appreciate how its partially glazed roof would make it colder than a fridge in winter and hotter than a greenhouse in summer.

There were two sitting rooms both with wood burning stoves, the cosier one with windows overlooking the front garden and private lane; but it was the other sitting room that was really impressive. An extension had been added to the simple cottage, with double aspect windows and a glass apex at one end that flooded the room with light on the dullest of days. At the centre of this forty-foot long room was an enormous freestanding stove, its chimney ascending through the ceiling high above. Thinking of it merely as an attractive feature, we couldn't have known at the time how ineffective this would be against the ravages of a Cotswold winter in a cottage bereft of proper insulation and double-glazing.

The following afternoon we all went to view the cottage and were comforted to find it beautifully warm on such a chilly April day, blissfully unaware that all the radiators had been turned up to full bore and both wood burning stoves had been stoked up for our benefit. Charmingly quaint and for once even more spacious than photographs suggested, it provided enough room for the remains of our furniture that was still in storage in Devon. The gardens consisted of a pretty paved courtyard at the back of the cottage, with raised beds of mature shrubs; the remaining side of the cottage was laid to lawn with an apple tree and a large bay tree. No part of it was overlooked and the surrounding trees made the area totally sheltered, flowerbeds planted with peonies, roses, rosemary, oregano and thyme providing privacy from the lane. Most importantly there was a very large double garage and an equally spacious covered carport that would be very useful for Rory's growing bulk of sound and lighting equipment. Miranda had wandered down the lane to where it gave way to a narrow, oak-lined path leading to open countryside. She was back in minutes.

"Mummy, come and look at this!" Miranda called excitedly. "Wait 'til you see where this leads – it will be perfect for Dash and you'll never have to take him in the car for walks!"

The overhanging branches of oak and horse chestnut trees formed a leafy green tunnel that abruptly opened onto a vista of grassy fields, distant woods and the Evenlode river, where the fields joined the Blenheim Palace estate. A lesser spotted woodpecker called urgently as we disturbed it from its perch in one of the trees, rising and dipping in its distinctive flight across the fields towards the woods. That did it for me. Here we could feel we were in the middle of the countryside and would not feel enclosed and stifled by living in a town or city, something completely alien to Jeremy, Dash and me. We settled on the cottage there and then, although the monthly rent was five times as much as we had been paying for the last few years in Corfu. We had just given up a very spacious three bedroom, three bathroom, two storey house surrounded by mature lemon and olive trees; its long balconies overlooked the delightfully picturesque harbour of Kassiopi and the shimmering Straits of Corfu, thence to the dusty pink hills and misty mountains of Albania across the sea … Ah me.

Only when winter set in with a vengeance seven months later would we discover some distinct disadvantages. Black mould would grow vigorously on our bedroom walls, ice would form inside the windows every night and the gargantuan spiders would happily seek refuge in our beds. Blissfully unaware, having had the famous Cotswold sheep's wool firmly pulled over our eyes, we signed the contract for a rolling lease on the cottage. Our furniture arrived from Devon on the same day as Rory's belongings and equipment were delivered from Oxford; and as it was placed in the rooms, the cottage suddenly transformed itself into a home. It felt better than Christmas as we unpacked boxes containing so many memories of our married life, some of which we hadn't seen in over seven years since we had sold our last home on Dartmoor to move permanently to Corfu; more poignantly many of the boxes were still labelled The Lion House, Liondari, 49100 Corfu. The beds were made and for the first time in many years Jeremy and I spent the night in our treasured Georgian four-poster, hidden amongst stacks of boxes we were too tired to unpack. In bed that night it occurred to me that the proceeds from the sale of the Jeep would not last forever, now we were paying such serious rent. I racked my brains for some ways to generate an income.

I constantly felt guilty about what had happened to us in Corfu. After all much of it had been my fault. I was the one who had persuaded Jeremy to buy the land at Liondari in the first place; he had fought against the idea tooth and nail, but I had insisted. Only years later did he tell me how a sudden feeling of trepidation had washed over him as he stood on the land the day before we had completed the purchase. He didn't know how such an uncharacteristically paranormal moment had overtaken him, but he sensed everything was telling him not to buy it. Certainly the slope of the site was steeper than he would have liked, but there was something darker that made his blood run cold; an indistinct glimpse into the future perhaps.

Long before we lost our beloved Sarava to the devastating fire that destroyed her, so nearly taking the lives of my husband and daughter in the process, even Jeremy had come round to the idea that the building project would turn out well in the end. We had been assured the house would be ready for our occupation before eighteen months had passed; thereafter we would continue to live on Sarava during the long summer months and let The Lion House for the high season; this income would easily cover all our living expenses, including the considerable cost of running a yacht such as Sarava. The traditional three-bedroom house, connected by an Italianate loggia to the four-bedroom annex we had originally planned, with its large pool and irresistible views over the Corfu Straits, could command a very high rent in the days when larger luxury villas were few and far between. But two years had spun into six before the house became a completed shell; building costs had doubled during that time – ours had more than tripled – but property prices had not kept pace. Worst of all Jeremy's original, beautiful triptych design had been lost to the laziness and negligence of our architect, Spiro, and his poorly chosen teams of incompetent builders. Many among the Albanian craftsmen in Corfu were first class tradesmen, but Spiro never had been able to spot a bad apple in the basket.

In our wildest nightmares we could never have imagined losing Sarava in such a terrifying manner; nor could we have foreseen the many 'wrong place, wrong time, wrong trust' events that were ultimately responsible for our losses. I was carrying the weight of guilt around like a heavy rucksack on my back; no matter how many times my best friends told me it wasn't my fault, I couldn't accept it. One kind friend suggested that Jeremy could have refused to have anything to do with the idea; but I had been persuasive to the point of divorce, so utterly convinced had I been that buying the land and building our dream house was exactly what we should do.

My mother would probably have called it yet another of Mr Toad's 'poop poop' ideas, to which I had so often been prone.

A Greek friend had once asked me how long I wanted to stay in Corfu, to which I answered without pausing to think, 'Forever, I want to die here' – quickly adding 'but not yet, obviously'. So I felt it was totally up to me to recoup whatever I could of our lost money; I still feel the same to this day and I doubt the guilt will never leave me. I simply can't dump the rucksack and leave it behind – as my reflexologist friend Christine suggested. It has driven me for sixteen years and I don't think it will ever disappear, unless I manage to earn enough from my different schemes to replace everything our Corfu venture has cost us.

On the other hand would I ever have accomplished all the writing and design work I have done over the last few years without this driving force? I don't think so. Jeremy and I would have still been living an idyllic life in Corfu, free from financial worry, with constant summertime visits from our children and friends on board Sarava. I had even imagined decorating every room in The Lion House for Christmas and knew exactly where I would place the tree; I could see the garland of olive branches decorated with silver painted cockleshells I would make for the traditional Corfiot double front doors. I had planned our house warming party and made an invitation list of all our friends on the island and from overseas; I had even bought a gorgeous pure silk long dress for the occasion, with a misty design of lions and leopards in the African Savannah, in soft tones of gold and brown. Sadly I never got to wear it, as it was amongst the countless possessions lost on Sarava.

Very few of our friends had been able to grasp the scale of our plight. We should splash out and take a long, exotic holiday to recover from our little setback, they suggested. Surely we still had stocks and shares, pension funds and some property to fall back on;

surely we had a Swiss bank account isolated from the ravages of the financial crisis. Jeremy found it too painful to keep explaining how we had mistakenly moved all our assets into one basket while we took time to consider the next chapter of our lives – it had widely been seen as quite a clever move at the time, given the prevailing economic climate. In the past we had willingly helped friends who had found themselves in tricky positions, but Jeremy was far too proud to consider any such approach now. In any case he would need a substantial sum if he were ever to return to the stock markets – just like his father, the only form of livelihood he had ever known.

I searched for something else to bring in some money quickly. Jeremy had promptly sent all his family silver, paintings, rare books and the 'good' furniture to a well known auction house; it was sad to see such heirlooms leave the family after so many generations, especially the solid silver Georgian candlesticks, tureens and warming dishes I had so enjoyed seeing on our various dining tables; I would not miss cleaning them however. Jeremy agreed we should keep the antique silver canteen of cutlery inherited by my parents and given to us as a wedding present. The canteen had been to India and back during the last glory days of the Raj and had survived the fire that destroyed our home in 1983, although the beautiful walnut case had been burnt to a cinder. Without its case the set would have fetched very little, much of the cutlery remaining tarnished where the heat-encrusted tar had been removed.

But I still wanted to do my bit so I arranged for a highly recommended dealer to assess my gold jewellery. He bought everything I showed him – not a vast amount and mostly items I no longer wore – many of which had been given to me years ago by a boyfriend who called them 'rainy day presents'. He must have been psychic because it was absolutely pouring now.

In 1989 my parents had secretly bought me a Mikimoto two-string pearl choker for Christmas, knowing I had admired one worn frequently by Princess Diana. In December that year Mummy contracted double pneumonia and was taken by ambulance to Torbay Hospital where she remained over Christmas. At her bedside on Christmas Eve, she and Pop told me they had something special for me that year but would keep it until Mummy was out of hospital. We decided we would do the same with our presents to them and theirs to Rory and Miranda, who were then seven and two. A few days later Mummy died of dehydration caused – as her specialist admitted – by the negligence of the nurses who had not monitored her fluid intake; Pop and I were with her until the end, which came peacefully. She was only 69. At home a couple of days later Pop gave me the surprise present and told me how Mummy had been so excitedly looking forward to seeing me open it, and we both cried. I had worn the choker on many special occasions, including Rory's 21st party, so it held only happy memories. Pop had died in his sleep in his bedroom at our house exactly a year after my mother; I think he died of a broken heart. They would have celebrated their Golden Wedding anniversary that August and Pop had already written his speech for the occasion.

The pearls were valuable and I felt it was time to make a sacrifice. With a heavy heart I reluctantly took the choker to Bonhams, where a pretty young lady took it to a senior valuer while we waited in her small office. A few minutes later she returned with the box and laid the pearls on the desk in front of her.

"The pearls are top quality and very beautiful," my heart stopped, I was so hoping she was going to say they were of little value. "But the choker is for a very small neck so it would be difficult to sell and this style is not the current fashion."

I could have hugged her. I think she had realised the sentimental value of the piece and as I took the box from her she gently put her hand over mine.

"Now you can keep it," she said quietly.

Long before we had even dreamed of moving to Corfu, I had designed a bespoke notecard for the Royal National Lifesaving Institution. Featuring a puffin dressed as a lifeboatman, it proved extremely popular and I was immediately commissioned to design a Christmas card in the same vein for the charity. For eight consecutive years thereafter I had designed a new RNLI Christmas card; they sold in the millions altogether and helped raise very considerable funds for the charity. Perhaps it was time to renew my association with the good folk at the lifeboat charity. One call to a young and newly appointed Artistic Director got me an invitation to meet her at the RNLI headquarters in Poole, Dorset, the following week. I made a couple of detailed pencil drawings of designs for her to consider, hoping that one would be chosen. My appointment at ten o'clock meant a very early start from Oxfordshire and an even earlier start for me to make myself presentable for the meeting. With Dash sleeping soundly on a rug on my lap, I slept all the way there until Jeremy thoughtfully nudged me to let me know we had arrived and that I might want to wake up.

It was a cool day for June, a vigorous easterly from the sea taking the edge off the strong sunshine. I had worn my best coat, retrieved from storage in Cheltenham, but the high heels I had chosen hurt my feet, which were still unaccustomed to structured shoes after years of living in flip-flops in Corfu. The young woman met me in the smart reception area of the very swanky building; I thought she must be straight out of art college but refrained from saying so. I hobbled painfully up a long flight of stairs to a conference room and opened my portfolio to show her the new drawings and the cards I had previously painted for the charity.

Amongst the many folders was a design featuring several sea-horses I had painted for my own pleasure in Corfu; it wasn't supposed to be there at all, but the young lady alighted on it like a bird of prey. Stupidly I agreed to let her take a photocopy of the design for 'future reference,' reasoning that I might get another commission out of it. I thought no more about it as she returned my original painting and began scrutinising my new 'Puffin Lifeboatmen' designs.*

"Oh I love that one!" she said, pointing to the drawing of three Puffin Lifeboatmen wearing a variety of RNLI headgear and Wellington boots from different eras.

Each puffin carried a present variously labelled *Gold, Frankincense*, and *Myrrh*. The puffins were gazing at a bright 'Star of Bethlehem' hanging conveniently over a lifeboat station, copied from the contemporary building at Mother Ivey's Bay near Padstow; the star's glow illuminated snow falling over the sea in the background and an ivy and snow covered signpost behind the puffins proclaimed 'AFAR'. The title, naturally enough, was *We Three Puffins*.

"I'd like to commission this one and keep the other design for next year," she said to my great delight. "But there's just one little problem. In the past we've paid you for the design alone and produced the card ourselves. Nowadays we only buy in finished cards directly from publishers. Can you do this? We would want an initial delivery of 150,000 by the last week in August when our autumn catalogue goes to print, with an option for repeat orders in the run-up to Christmas".

---

*The following Spring the RNLI bought out an extensive new range of giftware featuring a seahorse design that was strikingly similar, if not absolutely identical, to the painting I had allowed to be copied. I was furious with myself, but even more dismayed at such underhand behaviour. It's not only at sea one must be aware of sharks!

"Of course, that's fine," I replied, swallowing hard and trying to forget it was already June.

We were living in a Cotswolds cottage with no extra room to collate and store 150,000 cards and 150,000 envelopes, moreover we didn't even know if a suitable printer could be found to produce them in time. More importantly, I wondered if I could paint the design, then have the cards printed, collated into packs of ten and delivered in just eight weeks; equally I could not let the chance of such a lucrative and prestigious order slip away. Back at the car I decided not to tell Jeremy the entire truth, as it would send him into a state of panic during the long drive home. Instead I simply said which design had been chosen and that they would like us to produce the cards, leaving out any mention of the lead time and quantity.

I handed Jeremy a sandwich and settled down with Dash curled up on my lap to sleep for the journey back to Oxfordshire. I wouldn't think any more about it today; like my favourite heroine, Scarlett O'Hara, I would think about it tomorrow. Of course the truth had to come out the next day. Jeremy, thinking realistically about all the things that would have to fall into place, was adamant it couldn't be done without a lot of risk. But luckily Rory was more sanguine: he and Miranda could muck in and help in any way they could, bless them. Even Miranda's boyfriend offered to help at weekends. Of course Jeremy said he was right behind me too … even if he was tugging me in the opposite direction.

Then we realised we had a significant hurdle to overcome: we had to pay for everything in advance, including the printing. I had been with the same bank since I was fifteen, when my father opened my first account for me. Simple enough, I thought; you couldn't turn on a television or radio at that time without hearing how banks were so very keen to help small businesses. I made an appointment to see the manager of the nearest branch in Witney, fondly imagining I would have the same reception I had enjoyed when I lived in Cyprus and opened an account with my bank's International branch in Limassol.

Before Jeremy and I were married in 1980, I had been earning quite a lot of Cyprus pounds from fashion modelling, show production and television commercials. The manager was a charming, middle aged Cypriot family man who greeted me in perfect English as I was ushered into his luxurious air-conditioned office, where his assistant brought in coffee and dainty pastries on a tray. An account was quickly opened in my name and as we were shaking hands to say goodbye, he asked me if he could take me to dinner later in the week to celebrate what he imagined would be a very lucrative account. He picked me up in his smart black Mercedes and we enjoyed a wonderful seven-course mezze at a taverna on the beach near Amathus, (now sadly buried beside cliffs of concrete and glass). He was very good company in his avuncular way, giving a detailed history of the area and explaining the best recipes for the dishes of the feast before us as I sipped the delicious ice-cold Bellapais. Later he dropped me back at the house I was renting and said he would look forward to seeing me again, insisting I should call him at the bank if I ever needed advice on anything at all.

So I was looking forward to the meeting in Witney, confident that it would be a similarly pleasant experience. I dressed carefully for a meeting with a bank manager in my smart black pencil skirt, crisp white shirt, Chanel-style red leather jacket I had bought a few years before in Corfu Town and teamed the outfit with a few strings of 'costume' pearls and smart black patent high heeled shoes. I felt this ensemble would blend an air of professionalism with femininity. Jeremy, fashion guru to the rich and famous, would have suggested jeans, a jersey and a good pair of deck shoes, but that's what he always preferred me to wear. For once he might have been right – I certainly hadn't reckoned on climbing two flights of very steep, scruffy stairs to the Business Manager's even scruffier office with my unreliably dodgy knee. I held tightly to the metal bannisters and prayed my clicking knee would not give way or lock up completely, as it had often been inclined to do. I was shown into the manager's office where I sat waiting for a full twenty minutes, so I had more than enough time to extract the various papers from my briefcase and lay them neatly on his desk.

Eventually a youngish chap in a green sweatshirt ambled in. He grunted a casual 'Ur,' which I took as a greeting, but as he offered no apology for keeping me waiting or even a handshake, I had assumed he must be a cleaner until he sat down behind the desk. I informed him I had recently opened a business account and now needed a loan to buy stock for this large order from the RNLI, explaining further that credit would only be required until I was paid with a substantial profit. I waved the official RNLI order in his direction but he ignored it.

"First we'll need to run a credit check on the RNLI," he announced. "They're an animal charity aren't they?"

I should have walked out at that point, but I needed the loan.

"Um, actually I think you'll find they're the largest and probably the wealthiest charity in Britain. They save lives at sea," I explained, hardly believing what I had just heard from Mr. Slovenly Schoolboy sitting opposite me. He might as well have asked for a credit check on Bill Gates, but I ignored him and carried on with the speech I had rehearsed earlier.

"I just need a small loan for three months, the RNLI will be paying me in full upon delivery of the order, as you can see from this contract".

"What collateral can you offer?"

"Well, I didn't think I would need that, as I only need to borrow £12,000 for three months and this is a cast iron contract," I replied as he shuffled some papers on his desk and got up.

"We won't be able to give you a loan without collateral," he repeated, opening the door to go out before me as I rapidly gathered my papers and stuffed them in my briefcase.

Tripping down the stairs with eyes full of tears, the pain nearly forced me to take off my high heels and walk back to the car in bare feet. This really was a low point. Without a loan my lucrative order was dead in the water; I didn't have a single pound to spare at the time. Jeremy was livid of course, fuming that it confirmed what he had always thought of all banks. Back in our bedroom, as I peeled off the outfit I was sure would have helped to secure the loan, and most probably an invitation to lunch or dinner to discuss my future plans for expansion, I wondered what to do next. Then out of the blue David Cameron's name popped into my head – well he was our local MP as well as Prime Minister, so if he couldn't intervene, nobody could.

He had already been kind enough to help Miranda after she had been involved in an accident at work a few weeks earlier. As PA to a wealthy Cotswold family, Miranda had been returning from the school run in one of their many cars, when she was hit from behind at speed as she queued in stationary traffic. Both cars were beyond repair, but more importantly she had suffered a horrible whiplash injury and some heavy bruising. Sure enough, and despite specialist diagnosis of the injury, Miranda was referred to the government assessment unit who would decide whether or not she could obtain any benefits until she could resume work. After some frightful old Trunchbull of an assessor had finished her interrogation, (could Miranda make a cup of tea by herself and walk five paces unassisted in her neck brace and sling), she was deemed fit for work and therefore ineligible for any sickness benefit. To add insult to her painful injuries her shameless employer had sacked Miranda the day after the accident; however the private assessment company eventually lost its government contract some months later amidst a great scandal.

I had been incensed by such callous treatment and posted an express letter to David Cameron, without holding out much hope of a reply. However, early the following morning I took a call from one of the Prime Minister's personal assistants: she was absolutely sweet, enquiring after Miranda and telling me David was most concerned about her.

"We're on the train on the way back to London," she explained above the background noise, "but David has just read your letter and asked me to phone you. He is at Westminster all day today but will look into this case as a matter of urgency."

Within two days Miranda received a letter from social services confirming she was, after all, eligible for benefits for the duration of the time she was unable to work. David instantly became my hero and I sent him an effusive letter of thanks; months afterwards I was able to send him some of the first copies of *The Manor House Stories* for his younger children to show my gratitude more properly. Days later I received a personal letter from him saying he hoped Miranda was fully recovered and thanking me for the little books. He added he was particularly glad to have some new books to read to his children as he was, in his own handwriting, 'Maisie'd out!'† I have kept his letter.

Whatever one's politics it was certainly worth another quick letter to our Prime Minister, in which I explained everything about the RNLI commission and the bank's reaction. At the time David

---

† A popular children's book series by Lucy Cousins.

was keen to promote his government's support for small businesses, and you certainly couldn't get much smaller than mine. Two days later I received a copy of a personal letter from David to the top man at the bank's head office, asking why I had been denied a very modest loan. Within the week I received a letter from my repentant bank enclosing a shiny gold Business Credit Card. I hadn't known there was such a thing and it certainly wasn't mentioned when I opened the business account. Then I read the credit limit and realised this was yet another slap in the face. Trembling with rage I called the number on the letter and asked the unfortunate lady who answered how £1,000 could be of any use whatsoever when I needed £12,000.

"Look again Mrs Chaplin," she said, "Your credit limit is £10,000!".

I had misread the figure, as I often did, having diagnosed myself as 'numerically dyslexic,' if not completely innumerate. (This was entirely the fault of a very sadistic and spiteful headmistress at my first school when I was only six. Mrs. Butland had called me into her office one morning because I had been struggling with long division. She pointed a sharp pencil just two inches away between my eyes, making me go cross-eyed as she shouted 'Jane, you WILL do long division!' Immediately I ran in tears to my former teacher of the reception class, who I adored. Dear, kind Mrs. Tarry, who never called me Jane, explained arithmetic so patiently that I had always done well; it was only when I moved up a year to Mrs. Butland's class that I began to fail. I am still very friendly with a few girls from that school and, although now in their seventies, they are all useless at figures because of that wretched woman. I was equally unfortunate with my maths teacher at boarding school, where a fierce old gorgon with red-dyed hair regularly threw the wooden blackboard rubber at any girl she thought was not paying attention).

Now I only had an extra £2,000 to find and this came from a very kind girlfriend, (yes, you! xx). Analysing the bank's refusal, Jeremy surmised that a loan for three months wouldn't generate any serious interest payments for them – even at their usurious rates. In my innocence I had thought the brief loan period would be a positive for them, but obviously I should have applied for a loan for five years or more; of course they won in the end by charging even more interest on the credit card. So much for banks advertising their aim to help small businesses. How did they have the nerve to do this? Certainly Jeremy and I were no longer 'good' for the six-figure loans our banks had frequently begged us to take in days gone by; but yes, I was the same person with a firm contract to deliver. Mr. Schoolboy was incapable of exercising any discretion, even if he knew the meaning of the word, because he followed a box-ticking process that could not be overruled by the old fashioned bank manager of yore, who had probably known most of his customers since they opened their pocket money accounts when they were seven. No wonder, fumed Jeremy, Britain was fast becoming a third world country.

Then the RNLI sent a ream of conditions and specifications that made us wilt. One of the most frightening terms was printed in bold type: if we did not deliver the complete order by the required date, the RNLI would cancel the order without us having any right to compensation. Printers and suppliers demanded payment up front from new customers such as myself: apart from the cards themselves, we required two different varieties of sticky labels, 150,000 bespoke envelopes and cellophane wraps – all of which had to be ordered and paid for. This meant we would lose a great deal of money if we couldn't deliver bang on time; we would also be left with a vast pile of stock we would never be allowed to sell. Terrifying. But the rewards would be substantial if we could pull it off, providing enough to pay the rent and most of our living expenses for another whole year.

So we looked for a printer who could fit us into their schedule and soon alighted on a firm without too much trouble. Or so we thought. Jeremy and I had been introduced to our chosen printers via a rather shady middle man; his sole purpose in life appeared to be to hand out lucrative contracts on behalf of the local council for whom, technically, he worked. When he asked us for 'three bags of sand up front,' to guarantee the price, he had to sit us innocents down and gently explain he wanted three grand – three thousand pounds in cash. We eventually agreed to hand over the money as soon as we had seen the sheets of cards coming off the press.

I set up my architect's easel in a corner of the big sitting room and searched through our belongings for my art materials. As I worked at the painting Jeremy took charge of procuring everything and set up the long dining table as a workstation, complete with his own home-made dispensers for the countless reels of sticky labels, which we had to design from scratch. Bearing in mind that Jeremy is no more a graphic designer than he is a quantum physicist, a great deal of cursing and shouting at the computer filled the air for the following weeks.

The most difficult part of the painting was going to be the Christmas star. I was using an airbrush for the night sky and the sea, which meant masking a perfect star on the paper before spraying on the paint. It was rather tricky cutting a four-point star out of clear adhesive film and placing it in position on the blank paper with tweezers. It took all my courage to spray the ultramarine wash over the watercolour paper, all the time praying the paint didn't bleed under the film.

The fabulous thing about using an airbrush is the ability to graduate the colour from the palest tint through to a deep saturation with no visible dividing lines. For years I had tried to achieve this with brushes but I found it impossible to get an even graduation. After Miranda qualified as a beauty therapist at Champneys, she took a specialist course at the London School of Make-up, where she was required to buy an airbrush for applying liquid foundation smoothly and evenly – as was essential for television and film work. I experimented with this airbrush using a thin mixture of gouache paint and water. It worked like a dream and was so satisfying to use that Miranda never got it back. With my heart in my mouth I carefully removed the film with a needle to reveal a perfect white star in the dark blue sky. Phew! The rest of the painting went smoothly although I did have to work on it for fifteen hours a day, only breaking each evening for supper cooked by Miranda and eaten on trays in front of the television – the tables having been completely taken over by the evolving production line.

As soon as the printed cards arrived the entire house was ordered to action stations. Although 150,000 cards and envelopes will just about fit into a medium sized lorry, we quickly discovered they won't easily fit into a Cotswold cottage; soon every downstairs room turned into a maze of narrow corridors formed between six-foot high walls of cardboard boxes.

Then one hot morning in the midst of all this, as I was making the bed, I heard a tremendous explosion outside. I ran onto the balcony and found the electricity pole that stood a couple of yards from the cottage was on fire. I grabbed my phone and called the fire brigade. They took my address and told me to leave the house immediately, to which I replied I was not going anywhere when so much uninsured stock for the RNLI was yards away from the fire. Besides, the prospect of a deranged woman refusing to leave her blazing cottage might persuade the fire engine driver to go a little faster.

Jeremy and Rory were already on the scene with buckets of water, dousing our high conifer hedge in the hope it wouldn't catch alight. There was a strong breeze that morning which blew smoke and sparks straight towards the cottage, so I shut all the windows and doors and prayed the fire brigade would arrive quickly. Jeremy, having had more than his fair share of experience with fires, quickly deployed the garden hose to soak the timber cladding of the next door cottage; but the fire at the top of the pole, which had already spread to the higher branches of the nearby trees, was beyond the reach of our feeble water pressure. Ten minutes later the firemen arrived and took over with calm efficiency, putting out the fire and waiting for several hours to make sure it didn't rekindle. I gave them all chilled orange squash and we were soon chatting amiably about the various fires we had experienced. They commended Jeremy and Rory for their quick thinking, which had definitely saved the cottage next door, the owners being away on holiday; had we also been away, our cottage as well as our neighbour's – and probably the entire copse– would have been lost. It turned out that an electricity transformer on the pole had decided to explode and catch fire. It had been a very lucky escape; but of all the poles in all of Oxfordshire it had to be the one that was six feet away from our cottage.

Rory and Miranda spent all their free time helping us to collate the cards and envelopes into their packets; I added the labels myself to ensure they were perfectly straight. The printers had been late delivering to us, but eventually the last box was packed and we were able to deliver them to Poole a week before the deadline. It was a beautiful sunny morning as we pulled into the forecourt of the RNLI warehouse to be met by a couple of warehousemen who looked astonished as they read the branding on Rory's van and trailer. One of the men read the strap line out loud.

"RJCC Events – 100% on every event. Crikey! Are we having a party?" one man quipped to the other, as Jeremy explained we had borrowed our son's van to deliver the three tons of Christmas cards.

"Well yours is the first delivery of Christmas cards we've had this year," he replied, somewhat startled. "None of the bigger companies have managed to deliver anything yet!"

I hoped this would impress the Sales & Marketing Department and stand us in good stead for future years. Looking back at photographs of the boxes as they were unloaded by forklift trucks and taken into the vast warehouse, I can't imagine how we ever managed it. Before the drive home we congratulated each other heartily and celebrated with a flask of tea and some chocolate biscuits. The task had been accomplished and we felt inordinately pleased with ourselves.

"Thank God that's over and done with!" Jeremy said as we drove away from Poole with an empty van and trailer.

Then at the end of September, having caught up with some well deserved sleep, I received an email from the RNLI Sales Manager. They had sold out of my Puffin cards and were placing their order for another 50,000 to be delivered within five weeks. If not exactly flush, we could at least survive for a while on the proceeds.

As for the printers … Well, it could only happen to us. A week after we had delivered the final consignment of cards to the RNLI, Jeremy took a phone call from a very anxious lady in the local council's finance department: vast sums of money had gone missing from the council, the middle man had disappeared and so had the printers – literally! Their premises had been cleared out one night and every piece of equipment removed; that was no mean feat considering a four-colour press weighs in at fifty tons. Three bags of sand to the worse, it was exactly the sort of scenario Jeremy had feared; fortunately a clandestine recording of the scoundrel's original demand for the cash was enough to let us off the hook – Jeremy and I liked to trust people, but we had already learnt a hard lesson with The Lion House. I imagine the middle man is now collecting bags of sand on the Costa del Sol, that is if he's not actually sewing the bags in H M Prison Wandsworth.

Chapter Two

Being Brave

Big results require big ambitions

Heraclitus of Ephesus, 6thc. BC

At the end of November I made an appointment to meet the retail manager of the gift shop at Blenheim Palace, thinking he might like a bespoke card designed and produced for them. I took along samples of the cards I had previously designed for Glamis Castle, Scone Palace and Cawdor Castle; as the manager was Scottish, the subjects couldn't have been better chosen. All my Scottish Castle commissions had been painted several years before our adventures began in Corfu. That really did seem a lifetime ago …

Way back in 1992 I had been so excited at the thought of visiting Scotland for the first time. I had been regaled with so many happy stories about the country by my parents, who were stationed there for a time during the war. Jeremy and I would be visiting Glamis Castle first, spending the night at a B&B before driving on to Cawdor Castle near Inverness the following morning and journeying home that evening – a round trip of fifteen hundred miles. As I would be in the Highlands, I knew exactly what to pack. It was May, but it would surely be very much cooler in Scotland than South Devon, so out of the cupboards came my red cashmere sweater and smartest jeans for the B&B and pub supper. For my meetings at Glamis and Cawdor – undoubtedly even colder within – I chose my favourite Geiger outfit, a moss green wool jacket, a paisley pleated skirt in golds and greens, a dark green silk blouse and soft green semi-opaque tights; to this I added a beautiful outsize scarf printed with pheasants and autumn leaves, to be folded and worn over one shoulder, attached to the jacket by a Celtic brooch from The Scotch House. Jeremy, in his capacity as roving fashion spotter for Vogue magazine, could never understand this trend for draped scarves, which looked to him as if a random length of material from a curtain shop had snagged on the shoulder by mistake. I am delighted to say those incomparable Dames of the British Empire, Judi Dench and Joanna Lumley frequently adopt this attractive fashion.

It took more than ten hours to drive from South Devon to Glamis, but eventually we arrived at the nearby B&B recommended to us by the castle's Factor and run by a friendly Scottish landlady most aptly called Mrs. Oats. Our room was a bit more crocheted loo roll cover and lilac nylon sheets than we had hoped, but the pub she recommended for supper was splendid. A log fire burned and crackled merrily in an inglenook fireplace, its flames setting shadows dancing amongst the antlers, antique swords and rifles on the rust-red walls. Pride of place was given, predictably enough to a print of the stunning *Monarch of the Glen.* At the bar Jeremy asked me what I would like to drink before dinner; my usual tipple would be either Tio Pepe or Dry Martini, but here I was in Scotland and I felt obliged to ask for whisky.

"But you loathe Scotch!" Jeremy reminded me. "You always complain it smells of burnt tyres."

The barman, a sturdy fellow with a magnificent beard, glowered at us for an instant before very politely suggesting I try a dram of his favourite Speyside single malt with a little water. With my first sip I realised this tasted nothing like the whiskies I had so readily spurned. It was smooth and mellow, warming me even more at every taste. I mentioned this to the barman and he explained it was all down to the water; theirs came from the local burn, flowing dark and clear beyond the terrace; I believed him as there could be no other explanation. The locally caught salmon was delicious, but sadly left no room for the traditional raspberry and cream Cranachan I had spotted on the menu.

Before retiring to bed, Mrs. Oats asked us if we would like porridge for breakfast; we felt obliged to say yes, as she proudly explained the oats had to be prepared the night before. Next morning our porridge arrived, our hostess insisting we should add no sugar as it was already flavoured in the Scottish tradition. I had never before realised that a knife and fork were needed to eat traditional porridge – preferably a steak knife at that. Jeremy did eventually manage to pierce the surface with his spoon, only to find it stuck fast like a boot in quicksand. We tried valiantly to chew a little of the highly salted adhesive, not wanting to offend Mrs. Oats, but we were not up to the struggle. Seeing our bowls still full as she returned with some toast, she looked disappointed – probably at the prospect of having to chisel the fully set cement from her china. Jeremy and I bravely confessed that feeble Sassenachs such as ourselves were thoroughly unworthy of her generous portions. Nowadays we enjoy the trend of adding salt to chocolate, caramel ice cream and so on, but we stick to milky porridge untouched by salt.

Glamis was extraordinary, a true fairytale castle with its graceful slate covered conical turrets gleaming in the morning sun. The Factor met me and gave me a tour inside, culminating in a visit to the very highest part of the roof. He led me up endless narrow twisting stone stairs, until we ducked through a tiny door and came out on the roof. The views from such a height were spectacular, but the Factor explained the general public were prohibited – health and safety regulations having to pander to silly people – adding that if ever I wanted to bring my family he would personally escort us all. Outside again I made sketches and took photographs before we left to drive to our next B&B, this time a splendid early Georgian Wolsey Lodge* outside Nairn, to the east of Inverness. After a kitchen supper with our delightful hosts, we retired for coffee in the principal drawing room where we marvelled at the most beautiful curtains that were drawn over the wide expanse of floor to ceiling windows. Now threadbare, peeling away like the bark of a maple tree and disintegrating before our eyes, the two hundred year-old hand painted silk still radiated the perfect colours of butterflies, exotic birds and delicate greenery wherever a few square inches remained intact. The owners quite rightly could not bear to discard them. Here was genuine genteel dilapidation at its very best.

The following morning we set off for Cawdor as the temperature rose. By the time we reached Cawdor Castle for my appointment with Angelika, the glamorous blonde Countess of Cawdor, the temperature had soared into the high seventies. The sun blazed out of a clear blue sky and as we sat outside in her garden for coffee and shortbread my silk shirt was sticking to me, which made it impossible to remove my jacket. Beads of sweat must have been noticeable on my face, but Angelika seemed not to feel the heat as I did; she was polite enough not to ask why I was dressed for winter in a Highland heatwave. We discussed ideas for the design of her card, for which I would send a detailed pencil drawing for her approval. When she asked if I had come alone, I explained Jeremy was waiting in the car.

"Oh for goodness sake!" she exclaimed, "I'll ask my assistant to go and get him right away, poor man!"

---

* Wolsey Lodges are named after Cardinal Wolsey, Henry V111's Lord Chancellor who toured the realm in the 16th Century. He received sumptuous free hospitality at numerous country houses along his way.

So Jeremy was summoned for coffee, which was brought to us at a table in the full sun; after an hour I really thought I was going to expire. Not a moment too soon we went inside the chilly castle to marvel at the famous Campbell 'blue modern' tartan rugs that ran across the hall and up the wide stairs.

"I had those put in," Angelika said when I admired them, making a mental note that I could replicate the idea in our own home using my Tully family tartan, Dress Barclay, which is woven in a very attractive emerald green and navy blue; to my mind it was a more interesting colour scheme than Hunting Barclay, which was yellow and black and resembled the bumble bee colours of the Cornish tartan. As we said our goodbyes the Countess told me she had also invented their slogan: *Three out of four ghosts prefer Cawdor*, because it was said to be haunted by three spectres.

"That's so clever," I remarked. "I must include it in the design of the card."

"You're a commercial animal, Jani, just like me!" she laughed.

After completing some pencil sketches and taking detailed reference photographs I collapsed into the car and Jeremy drove away from the castle. Unfortunately there was no air conditioning – school fees having ruled out the deluxe model – so we headed south with all the windows open as the sun blazed relentlessly through the windscreen. I kept complaining bitterly about the sun always being on me wherever we drove, until Jeremy became so exasperated that he asked if I would like him to reverse all the way back to Devon to keep me in the shade. (When an elderly friend of the family had come to stay with us on board Aries in Cyprus, she had sought Jeremy's advice on the best way to take a photograph of a particularly radiant sunset over the ruins of ancient Curium; she was concerned that the sun's brightness would cause too much contrast and turn the detail of the ruins into a dark silhouette.

Perhaps, she had most perplexingly suggested, she might avoid the problem if she pointed the camera in the opposite direction, away from the sun and the ruins.)

In the car I stripped off everything I could and by the time we reached the motorway I was down to my underwear. Jeremy was horrified at the idea of creating such a spectacle, but I replied that only lorry drivers would see me and I couldn't care less what they thought and would take my chances. I promptly fell asleep and by the time we had reached the Lake District the sun had disappeared and the car had at last cooled down. We were both very tired, so Jeremy suggested we find a hotel for the night. We stopped at several that were recommended in the guide book – the only reference available in those pre-internet days – but they were all fully booked. After the fifth disappointment we were getting desperately hungry; it was time to ramp up our budget. The four-star hotel on the banks of the famous lake would be fiendishly expensive, but we were exhausted and couldn't face driving all the way home that night. The receptionist informed me they did indeed have one superior double room with ensuite available, overlooking the lake. Surprise, surprise: it's never the perfectly adequate room in the annexe at half price.

"Oh thank goodness, I'll get my husband and our luggage and we can have a quick bath before dinner. Can you keep a table for us?"

"Sorry Madam, our chef's just gone home and the restaurant is closed."

"But it's only a few minutes after eight!" I gasped.

"We can do you a sandwich. Ham or cheese?"

"You mean that's all you can offer us for three hundred pounds a night? That's more than a weekend in Florence! Forget it!" I ranted, storming out.

We drove into Windermere in the vanishing hope of finding any restaurant that paid its chef until nine in the evening. To our amazement and delight we spotted a Greek Taverna in the main street. The familiar uncontained sound of cheerful Greek voices and the aromas of Greek cookery were balm to our bruised souls as we walked in that night; the effusive welcome from the Greek Cypriot family who owned the restaurant was as warm as we remembered from our blissful days living in Cyprus on our first catamaran. I had really set my heart on some proper taramas and tzatziki, but the kitchen had run out after a busy evening. Without a second thought, the owner telephoned his mother and minutes later copious servings of the delicious home made accompaniments arrived at our table. Inevitably it turned into a long and very enjoyable evening, even if Jeremy would have to drive through the rest of the night to get home. It didn't matter could reminisce about Cyprus for hours on the long journey. In fact we did just that, and Jeremy even stayed awake despite having driven over six-hundred miles since lunchtime the day before.

During the two carefree years Jeremy and I lived aboard Aries at Larnaca in the early 1980's I was asked to organise a fashion show for a boutique in the town, owned by the effervescent and beautiful Angela. Her sister-in-law had recommended me after I had directed and modelled in a show for her Limassol boutique at the luxurious Curium Palace Hotel. Money was no object so I had arranged for a catwalk to span the large swimming pool, which was surrounded by tables for diners to eat under the stars. This had been a very novel idea for Cyprus and involved scaffolding being lowered into the pool by several burly Cypriot builders wearing only swimming trunks. By the time the florists had decorated the carpeted catwalk with festoons of white ribbons and flowers, the effect was stunning, especially when the pool was illuminated at night. I was thrilled with it until my models arrived for the rehearsal on the afternoon of the show. One of them was holding back and refusing to leave the changing room, explaining she was terrified of heights. The catwalk was only two feet above the water, but she was sure her vertigo would unbalance her and she would fall in; it seemed very odd for a girl who was as an air hostess with Cyprus Airways. Unbeknown to me, the other models plied her with Greek brandy until the show began. I thought she was wobbling a bit as she sashayed over the pool, but put it down to her vertigo.

I had wanted the finalé to be accompanied by a display of fireworks synchronised to Tchaikovsky's 1812 Overture. I needed all the models to run onto the catwalk wearing swimwear and dive into the pool as the music reached its explosive crescendo. Unfortunately, despite a compulsory meeting with the Chief of Police, I was refused permission for the fireworks as he felt the rest of the island would suspect another attack by the Turks – still a very raw nerve at the time, being only four years after the invasion that divided the island in two. In the end the other models flatly refused to ruin their hair and make up by diving in the pool, so I had to do it myself with just the two male models. As the Overture blared from the speakers, I thought my dive from the catwalk went very well. I was surging towards the end of the pool in my best crawl when I suddenly got cramp in my leg. I had to revert to a lame breast stroke, using only one leg, until I reached the steps, whereupon I half limped, half hopped back to the changing room. Luckily all the lights around the pool had been turned off for the show, so I don't think the audience noticed my very embarrassing exit.

Angela was an irresistible, delicious combination of the goddess Aphrodite and Eliza Doolittle before her transformation; we instantly became best friends. She was a pretty, bubbly blonde with fair skin and, for a Greek, an uncharacteristically retroussé nose. We were often mistaken for sisters. The only woman I ever knew who used felt tip pen as a lip liner because it stayed put all day, she had an infectiously exuberant personality and a sense of humour that often left us giggling like schoolgirls. Angela's delightful cockney accent had been picked up during the years she and her husband Chris had owned a fish and chip shop in London, where they lived above the business until they had saved enough to buy their home and Angela's boutique in Larnaca. But Angela was pure Greek in her forthright attitude, always speaking her mind and leaving you no doubt where she stood; heaven help anyone who tried to cross her; she definitely had Spartan blood coursing through her veins. She often mixed her languages when she was complaining about something to me; if she couldn't find a bad enough word in English, she would find a more outrageous one in Greek. As a result my earliest attempts to speak Greek were peppered with some choice insults and expletives, which she found hilarious coming from me.

"You can't say *that*, Jani!" she would exclaim.

"Why not?" I would answer. "You do!"

"Because you're a bleedin' English lady, int yer!" She had always described Jeremy as *poli aristocratico.*

On our first wedding anniversary Angela invited us to her home for dinner with the family. Afterwards she suggested we could all watch an English video she had hired for the occasion, videos being quite a novelty in the early 1980's.

"You and Jeremy will love it," she promised. "It's a comedy called *Far from the Maddenin' Crowd*."

To this day we haven't had the heart to tell her.

To fund Angela's elaborate fashion show we decided she needed some sponsors. Fortunately it was easy to extract money from the newly wealthy Cypriot businessmen in those days; they were doing very well in the growing Middle Eastern markets and most were keen for any promotion and advertising, especially the big cigarette or drinks manufacturers with factories in Cyprus. One morning Angela and I drove to an industrial estate outside Larnaca, where the business she had chosen made shoes; she thought this would be a perfect fit for sponsorship of her fashion show and had assumed the company would also provide footwear for the models. Ushered by the receptionist into a large office, we were welcomed by the two brothers who owned the business. We were offered coffee and pastries as we explained, in English, how they could benefit from their participation in the show. The men smiled and nodded politely and I thought we were home and dry. Then the pair started speaking furtively to each other in Greek.

Suddenly Angela leapt to her feet, grabbing my arm and pulling me out of my chair before I could finish snaffling my first sticky baklava. Letting rip at the men with a hail of Greek insults delivered quicker than machine-gun fire, shrieking profanities I could only guess at, Angela propelled me out of the door as the men sat there dumbstruck and open mouthed. Still feeling miffed about my uneaten baklava as we reached the car, I asked Angela what had just happened.

"They thought we were both English and couldn't understand Greek; they were planning to string us along and trick us into going home with them one night. The bleedin' *malákas* called us *poutánes*! You know, hookers!"

Although Angela wore the trousers in their marriage – a legacy of living in England for too long – there were definite concessions she reluctantly made to her Cypriot husband Chris. One of these was smoking, or rather *not* smoking. Angela's boutique provided the perfect opportunity for her to enjoy her secret stash of fags.

I was with her most mornings in the run up to the show, and at other times when Jeremy was busy with boat maintenance. I would cycle into the town and spend a couple of hours in the shop with Angela; Greek coffee and water would be brought from a nearby kafenion on a metal tray swinging from three chains. Between customers we would chat away happily, smoking our cigarettes, until the morning Chris unexpectedly came into the shop, whereupon Angela deftly shoved her cigarette between my fingers. Chris glared suspiciously through the haze of cigarette smoke, first at Angela, then at me.

"Jani, why you smoking two fags at same time?"

Angela imported all the stock for her shop from the UK or Italy, being disdainful of clothes and shoes made in Greece – most of which I loved. Twice each year she would fly back to London to buy for her boutique, taking Greek specialities for her friends and relations still living there. On the return journey she would bring English delicacies for her Cypriot family and friends, including a cousin who worked at Larnaca Airport.

When we eventually left Cyprus late in 1981 to return to Devon for the birth of our son Rory, we had a mountain of luggage to repatriate; everything we owned, including our wedding presents had been with us on our catamaran. I was seven months pregnant with Rory at the time, beyond which British Airways would not allow an expectant mother to fly with them; we had prolonged our departure for as long as possible, not wanting to leave Aries or Cyprus. Jeremy was terrified of the extra baggage fees he would have to pay, but when I told Angela about our concerns she had assured us there would be no charge. Nevertheless Jeremy remained sceptical about such a claim. At the airport a smartly uniformed customs officer approached us as we struggled towards the check-in desk with our four trolleys heavily laden with suitcases and boxes.

"Now we're well and truly for it!" groaned Jeremy as the official asked us to leave the queue and follow him.

At this point Jeremy resigned himself to abandoning all our possessions, rather than pay a colossal bill for excess baggage. Being heavily pregnant, I trailed forlornly behind the two men and our mounds of luggage. Then, instructing Jeremy to leave the laden trolleys by his office, it suddenly dawned on me that the officer was leading us straight into the departure lounge, thus avoiding all the check-in and weighing formalities.

"I am Kosti," he informed us with a broad smile. "My cousin Angela has asked me to look after you. I will deal with all your luggage and you will board first, before other passengers."

We couldn't believe our luck and I telephoned Angela the moment we arrived at Heathrow.

"I was hoping to come to see you off myself," she explained. "But my bleedin' car wouldn't start this morning!"

I thanked her for arranging our smooth passage through the airport and asked how on earth she managed it.

"Easy," she answered. "I promised Kosti a bleedin' great crab next time I come back from England!"

Oh, for Greek indifference to rules and red tape!

The traffic lights were all green for us that day. Snowstorms had settled over London and our flight was diverted to Amsterdam, where the temperature had dropped well below freezing as night fell. From the portholes we watched men walking all over the wings of our aircraft, scraping off layers of snow and spraying de-icer liberally. Eventually we took off again into the black night, but all too soon we heard the undercarriage being lowered for landing and assumed we had been forced to return to Schiphol airport. Not a single glimmer of light was visible through the portholes, even when we felt the aircraft twitching and yawing on its final approach through the buffeting winds. Anticipating the landing we felt as if we had been ordered to jump off a wall of unknown height in the dark. It was a most unnerving feeling that brought on a fit of kicking from my unborn baby.

(At the time I suddenly remembered a party game from my childhood, involving a blindfolded victim standing on a short plank of wood on the floor. The plank, it was explained to the child, was to be lifted up by an adult at either end until the child's head touched the ceiling; for stability the victim was asked to place a hand on the kneeling adult's heads. The adults would wobble the plank slightly to give the illusion they were rising to their feet as they lifted the child, all the while exclaiming how high the victim was being raised above the floor; a heavy book placed on the child's head finally confirmed that he or she had reached the ceiling. At that point the victim would be told to jump off the plank, only to discover – knees already braced as they leapt in terror – there was no drop whatsoever.)

Only after our aircraft's wheels had hit the tarmac could we make out a vague loom of runway markers flashing past in the dense flurries of snow. As the plane came to a halt the captain spoke to his passengers.

"Ladies and gentlemen, you have just witnessed the extraordinary capabilities of this Lockheed Tristar, which has just landed itself without any human assistance. This is the only flight that has been able to land tonight in such atrocious conditions. Welcome to Heathrow!"

Cue spontaneous applause and cheers – and more violent kicks inside my tummy.

* * *

Following our exciting visit to Scotland, the card I produced for Cawdor a couple of months later was painted in the style of a medieval triptych, on a background of dark green Campbell of Cawdor tartan. Each panel was framed by a stone Gothic arch, the central one was larger than the two at the sides and bore the Campbell family crest at the top. I illustrated the history and legends of the castle; the central panel depicted Henry the Grouse, the Cawdor family's favourite bird, standing before the castle drawbridge, wearing a Campbell tartan flying plaid (obviously the forerunner to Jeremy's favourite over the shoulder scarves!) The right hand panel depicts the moment in the late 14th century when the site of the castle was chosen by the Thane of Cawdor's donkey, laden with a coffer of gold. After due rumination the animal rested beneath a holly tree which, as visitors will see, stands to this day rooted and alive after 500 years growing inside the dimly lit central tower house. The left panel illustrates the opening scene from the production of Shakespeare's *Macbeth*, performed by three members of Cawdor's prolific Jackdaw colony. The spectre above, three ghostly white Jackdaws, affirms the castle's claim that three out of four ghosts prefer Cawdor. Countess Angelika was delighted with the cards and they sold well in the gift shop.

The Glamis Castle card design replicated the oak door of the dining room, on which hangs a small wooden shield painted with the crest of the Bowes-Lyon family – a blue lion rampant with three red archers' bows. On the reproduced shield I painted a pheasant draped in a flying plaid of Hunting Stewart, worn in deference to the first Stewart King of Scotland, Robert the Second, who in 1372 bestowed the thaneage of Glamis on Sir John Lyon. The castle is in the background, with the thistle of Scotland and a sprig of heather in the foreground. Under the pheasant is the 'gold' cypher of the Earl of Strathmore and Kinghorn. Glamis Castle has been a royal residence since 1372; it was the childhood home of HM Queen Elizabeth The Queen Mother and was the birthplace of HRH The Princess Margaret. Glamis was also the legendary setting for Shakespeare's *Macbeth*; both Glamis and Cawdor cannily claim their connections to Mr. Shakespeare.

I travelled alone for my next visit to Scotland, Jeremy dropping me at Bristol Airport, from where I flew in a smart, leather seated Dash 500 to Edinburgh. The Countess of Mansfield had seen my Glamis card at a friend's house and decided that she would like a similar one of her home, Scone Palace. In her letter asking if she could commission bespoke cards for Scone, Lady Mansfield said I would find plenty of inspiration for the design as Scone was ' full of beautiful trees and flowers, Highland cattle and hairy men in kilts!' I knew from that moment we would hit it off. It was early March and as the cards were wanted in time for Easter, Lady Mansfield had suggested I flew to Scotland, all expenses paid; a train journey from South Devon and back would waste two exhausting days of precious time. Unbelievably a flight would be less expensive, a situation that says everything about our railway companies.

Waiting for me at Edinburgh airport arrivals gate I spotted a very tall, slim, red-headed man in a smart black chauffeur's livery, holding aloft an enormously long sign with MRS JANI TULLY CHAPLIN printed in large capital letters; obviously Angus, the Mansfield's chauffeur, had been expecting a shortsighted little old lady. The rest of my thirty fellow passengers gawped as they walked past him, turning their heads to see who this illustrious person could be. Angus gallantly produced a huge umbrella as we left the building, holding it over my head to shield me from the torrential rain. From the back seat of the limousine I started a conversation and discovered he had been in the special forces until he was employed by the Mansfields as chauffeur and sometime bodyguard. In his attractively lilting Scottish accent Angus told me a little of his former career, which included several years spent in the tropical wet heat of the jungles of South America, hunting down drugs barons. He much preferred his job in the familiar climate of the Scottish Highlands.

Angus shielded me from the downpour between car and imposing front door of the Palace, whence I was escorted by the butler to meet the elegant Countess of Mansfield, who was waiting for me in the private quarters. The oak panelled breakfast room was warm, welcoming and glowing cosily with a large log fire blazing.

"Please help yourself to breakfast," said Lady Mansfield, "We've kept everything hot for you."

As she spoke I noticed an involuntary flicker of feminine interest as her eyes took in my Austrian outfit, especially the skirt featuring my 'Highland Birds' design. Of course she was far too well mannered to comment, but I was amused that she obviously appreciated it. I thanked her but explained that I had enjoyed an excellent Scottish breakfast on the plane. She led me into the adjoining study to meet her husband William, the Twice Belted 8th Earl of Mansfield. He was charmingly informal, casually but warmly dressed in thick woollen sweater under a quilted gilet with well worn elephant cords, just like Jeremy's winter clothes – although Jeremy didn't yet need two belts. I was a little disappointed that he wasn't sporting a kilt, but Palaces can be extremely draughty. We had coffee together in front of the fire and Lord Mansfield asked me if I had brought a raincoat to explore the grounds. It was at that moment I realised to my horror that I hadn't got my 'Drizabone' Australian full length stockman's coat, bought in the Snowy Mountains for such a day as this. I knew I had put it in the car with my overnight case, but then I remembered seeing it, still over Jeremy's arm, as he waved me goodbye at Bristol Airport.

"Don't worry," said Lady Mansfield. "You can borrow one of mine. And please call me Pamela."

She led me out into the long corridor and waved an arm at the longest line of outdoor clothing I had ever seen, even at Burberrys. Brass hooks held coats, jackets and mackintoshes of every possible design; a shelf above held dozens of hats of every description, from riding hats to deerstalkers to sou'westers. The lower shelves housed a plethora of footwear, outdoor shoes and boots in a huge variety of shapes and sizes.

"Help yourself to whichever one you like; boots too if you need them," said Pamela.

I changed out of my court shoes into my waterproof 'Muckers' stable boots from my wheelie case, just as the Mansfield's teenage son came around the corner, almost bumping into me. Handsome Jamie was home from university for the weekend. Lady Mansfield introduced us and we shook hands;

"Cool boots!" he remarked laughingly as he noticed my odd footwear.

I chose a wonderful waterproof moss green cape with a generous hood and a warm plaid lining, which smelt of expensive scent as I gratefully wrapped it around me and headed out into the Scottish monsoon.

The rest of the dim daylight hours were needed to complete some sketches of the Palace, including the small architectural details that are always so tricky to replicate from photographs. On the great lawns in front of the Palace was a pride of pure white peacocks, looking like ghosts made of white lace gliding above the grass, their legs obscured by a low hanging mist. The Head Gardener escorted me around the grounds and pointed out various features of interest: where the blue poppies grew in summer and, in the giant tree arboretum, the very first Douglas Fir to grow in Britain. We visited the Jacob Sheep and some Highland cattle with their shaggy coats and amazingly long horns. I was shown the Hill of Coronation, or Moot Hill, crowned by a replica of the Stone of Scone, Scotland's Stone of Destiny, where forty-eight of Scotland's Kings had been crowned.

There was just enough time to have a quick look around the Palace state rooms before Angus drove me to my lodgings for the night. In a ground floor corridor I noticed a stuffed peacock; I crouched down and rapidly sketched the bird's feet, which had been invisible as the birds walked on the lawns. A lady guide started chatting to me, obviously wondering why on earth this dripping apparition was intent on drawing the stuffed bird. She told me the peacock's name was Alexander, who had lived his many years at Scone but eventually became somewhat temperamental. He had a penchant for attacking visitors without the slightest provocation and had violently attacked a visiting dignitary's Rolls Royce one day, causing so much damage that the car had to be resprayed. This skirmish proved to be Alexander's swansong, or peacock-song, and he was dispatched and stuffed forthwith; perhaps his ghost was one of the ethereal white spectres I had seen on the lawn earlier.

Not a moment too soon I was sitting by the fireside in the drawing room of a small country house, now successfully run as a boutique B&B. My hosts sat with me as I thawed out after my wet day outdoors, serving tea and gingerbread as we chatted. When my hostess admired my skirt I recounted the story of how my designs of highland birds for The Scotch House cards had been illegally copied; I explained how I had very successfully sued the famous Austrian fashion house, but had always wondered how my Scotch House designs had ever come to the attention of of such a faraway company. The lady turned to her husband and mentioned a lady's name.

"It must be her!" he exclaimed to his wife, much to my puzzlement. "Too much of a coincidence."

"Jani, this is quite extraordinary!" my hostess exclaimed. "We had a good friend who worked for The Scotch House for many years, until she left rather suddenly and went to work in Austria for Geiger."

The riddle had finally been solved. What were the chances of such a revelation?

Over a kitchen supper my hosts asked me if I had enjoyed my visit to Scotland. I said it had been wonderful, although I was disappointed not to have seen any red squirrels, especially as I would be incorporating one into my Scone Palace card design.

"Come down for breakfast at 8.15," said my host intriguingly.

I assumed such precise timing would ensure I could enjoy a cooked breakfast before Angus arrived to take me to the airport. My exquisitely furnished bedroom had stunning views of distant heather covered hills; on the antique dressing table was a vase full of Pheasant's Eye narcissus, their scent filling the room. Before going to bed I drew the flowers in my sketch book, having seen dozens of them at Scone and requiring some for my design. Next morning breakfast was served in the large farmhouse kitchen, where my place had been laid on a table next to the bay window, beyond which a couple of bird feeders hung outside. I sat down and within seconds a red squirrel jumped onto one of the feeders and began nibbling at the peanuts. I squealed with delight! Then another squirrel appeared, and another until there were five, their chestnut coats gleaming in the low sun and their impossibly long ear tufts waving delicately in the early morning Scottish breeze. It was a perfect memory to take home with me to Devon.

* * *

The meeting at Blenheim Palace was particularly important; it could open up many avenues that could earn me some much needed funds. Once again I needed to dress for the occasion and hoped it would make more of an impression than the outfit I had worn to the bank.

It was strange to search through the suitcases for something suitable to wear to such a meeting; clothes that had never been needed during all those years we were living in Corfu. Suits, skirts, smart coats and jackets, court shoes and gloves that had been safely packed away in storage were pulled out and laid on the bed for consideration. Eventually I chose a powder pink suit, with matching shoes and bag, all bought in Sydney for an unexpected meeting with the owner of one of Australia's leading card and calendar companies who was interested in my designs.

We had been on holiday in Australia to visit my cousins who emigrated there in the 1960s. I had bought some beautiful, outsize postcards at Darling Harbour and immediately thought the company that made them might like my Australian Bird Characters, originally designed for Hallmark Australia a couple of years before. (The designs were never used; Hallmark eventually decided on Andrew Brownsword's *Forever Friends* teddy bears instead of my birds – for me this was a near miss at fame, fortune and world domination). Luckily my favourite aunt and godmother, who had lived in Sydney for 35 years, had kept all my card designs I had sent her over the years and was able to lend them to me for my meeting. I had called the telephone number on the back of the postcards, not expecting to speak to anyone in authority. I explained briefly to the receptionist that I was visiting from England for a couple of weeks and had some designs they might like to see. With that she put me straight through to the Managing Director. I was staggered; this had never happened in Britain. Usually the telephonist would take it upon herself to advise me the company wasn't interested; if I was lucky she would offer me a meeting with the janitor or the boy in charge of the stationery cupboard.

A man's voice with a delightful Australian accent answered with a cheerful 'G'day Ma'am,' introduced himself as Kevin and asked how he could help. I told him my idea and he offered me an appointment at the company headquarters in downtown Sydney the following morning. My dear lady readers will imagine the ensuing panic: here I was in Australia, not so fresh from a week in Thailand, with a suitcase full of holiday clothes, flip-flops and beachwear. As Marilyn Monroe wisely said; 'Give a girl the right shoes and she can conquer the world.' Luckily I was born to shop and here I was in one of the most sophisticated cities in the world with a plethora of smart boutiques and a couple of department stores that rivalled Harrods.

We were staying in an apartment on the thirteenth floor of a modern apartment block at McMahon's Point on the banks of Sydney Harbour. If you remember the Sydney hotel suite in *Crocodile Dundee,* where the heroine stays when she first arrives in Australia, it was just like that. The views from our floor to ceiling windows were spectacular; to the left Sydney Harbour Bridge framed the iconic Opera House; in front of us the skyline of the city rose dramatically above the bustling harbour. There was a handy jetty in front of the building from where we often took an early ferry for delicious breakfasts at Darling Harbour. But the most amazing sights for us Pommies were the flocks of multi-coloured parrots, parakeets and snowy white cockatoos regularly flying past the windows, often just below our eye level so we could fully appreciate the plumage; it was like being in the middle of *Wildlife On One.*

I didn't tell the family my exciting news, preferring to wait for the outcome. I suggested we went into the city for some sightseeing and lunch. While the children and Jeremy were happily looking at boats in the marina, I told them I would meet them for lunch an hour later and sped off towards the shops. I headed for Grace Brothers, slightly less expensive than David Jones which was full of European designer clothes. I took an escalator to the first floor with the familiar lift operator's voice from the amusingly camp 1970's television series, *Are You Being Served*, jingling in my head. As I reached the top, a display mannequin beside the escalator was dressed in a beautiful pale pink bouclé skirt suit with a short Chanel-style jacket; it was exactly what I wanted – just perfect for a spring business meeting Down Under! In seconds I had grabbed an assistant who asked my size and led me to the changing rooms. Instead of the usual cramped English version smelling of old socks, each spacious room had a sturdy, locking door, a comfortable armchair and a coffee table on which to put your handbag. How very civilised. The helpful assistant had brought the suit in two sizes so I would have a choice.

The size 10 fitted like a glove, as did the pure silk short-sleeved blouse that went with it. I took my purchase up to the next floor and chose a pair of plain leather court shoes and matching bag. I would also need some tights, so I looked on the board by the escalator to find the floor where they would be sold. I searched the products on every floor, but none mentioned underwear. I must have stood there for ages looking puzzled, because a young man in a smart Grace Brothers livery approached:

"Can I help you Ma'am? I am the store guide." (Could his name be Mr. Peacock, the floorwalker?).

"I'm looking for ladies underwear," I said.

"Ah! I see, it's on the fourth floor Ma'am," he replied courteously. "But we call it something different here in Australia."

He pointed to the fourth floor listings by the escalator where the more genteel description *Intimate Apparel* was plain for all to see. While I was on this floor I also discovered that 'thongs' Down Under (well that is where they are worn) are what we call flip-flops.

I had to get a move on to meet the family at our chosen restaurant, The Gum Nut Café, a stone's throw from Circular Quay. My cousins had taken us there a couple of days before and we had been grateful for its charming terrace in the cool shade of whispering eucalyptus trees. My sense of direction was never good, but after walking briskly along the quay for about twenty minutes I eventually stumbled upon it. Hiding my carrier bags under the table, I sank gratefully onto a chair and told the family about the meeting arranged for the next morning, omitting any details about the new outfit. I knew Jeremy would think it an unnecessary extravagance, but I needed to look the part for my meeting, I could hardly turn up in shorts and tee shirt or a sarong, although Jeremy would disagree.

Feeling very confident in my new outfit, I took a taxi to my meeting the following morning, was welcomed warmly by Kevin's secretary and ushered into the boardroom where Kevin was waiting. I laid my cards on the table, literally, and Kevin's twinkly blue eyes lit up. I immediately thought he looked just like a koala with his silvering hair and short beard – this of course became his nickname, 'Kevin Koala'. (I often envisage people as birds or animals; I saw my father-in-law as the personification of a careworn old heron and Jeremy's mother as a dainty wren.)

Most enthusiastically he said his company had been looking for something like them for years. He would need a set of thirteen pictures of Australian bird characters in their native backgrounds, explaining he wanted to make calendars of them, one picture for each month of the year and an extra one for the cover.

… So the new pink outfit had earned its keep all those years ago and I hoped it would do its duty again at Blenheim; at the very least it would provide me with a shot of confidence.

I had never visited Blenheim Palace before and was suitably taken aback by the sheer scale and grandeur of the place, as I swept through the giant wrought iron gates in Woodstock and bowled down the long drive stretching ahead through most beautifully manicured parkland. I was so glad I had dressed smartly for the occasion. The meeting went well and the retail manager asked me to prepare a detailed drawing of the design I intended for a bespoke card. He gave me a brochure of Blenheim Palace to help with my research and invited me to tour the Palace to get further ideas. I made some pencil sketches as I walked around the staterooms, in which there was more than enough fascinating material to include in my design; however there was nothing of note in Winston Churchill's tiny, sparsely furnished and rather spartan bedroom. Once back at the cottage I researched the history of Blenheim and a design began to form in my mind. I imagined John Churchill, 1st Duke of Marlborough as a Peregrine Falcon, sporting the striking uniform he wears in his most famous portrait. In the background would be the Palace and in the foreground I could paint the delicate pink *Rosa Blenheim*. At each side of the card would be a Blenheim King Charles Cavalier Spaniel, for which Dash could be the model. Blenheim is the name for the chestnut and white colouring of Cavaliers, the original dog with this colouring having been bred at the Palace by the first Duchess of Marlborough. On the heads of each dog would be the Ducal coronet, which I had drawn from life in one of the staterooms in the Palace where the Coronation Robes were on display; I had to sit on the floor with my sketchbook, as close to the display as the red rope barrier would allow.

At home, Dash took to posing like a duck to water, sitting patiently while I drew him. Occasionally his eyes would close, his head would gently sink and I would have to reach for a treat to encourage him to sit up again. I swear Dash would have jumped through a hoop of fire for a gravy bone biscuit. When the mock-up card was completed in colour, I took it to the manager at Blenheim who seemed to like it enough to show the Duke and the directors at their next meeting in a week's time. I met the elderly Duke of Marlborough a few years later and he confessed to never having seen my design. Oh well, you can't win them all.

Exploring other means of raising funds, I suddenly recalled a licensing agreement I had signed with a company of Belgian weavers some fifteen years earlier; they had manufactured tapestry cushions using two of my bird character designs, *Kenneth Kingfisher the Fisherman* and *Bertie Bluetit the Golfer*. Modest royalties had trickled in over the years, all of them paid to me by cheque in euros; it was hardly worth cashing them as the transfer fee was almost as much as the payment. I searched the internet for other tapestry companies and amazingly the first to come up on the screen was based in Oxford. This had to be a sign. I am a great believer in the power of The Universe, having read and followed some of the advice in Rhonda Byrne's extraordinary book, *The Secret*. Unlike most 'self-help' books, it is simply written and has short chapters about different aspects of everyday life. I skipped the chapter on '*Health*' because, thank heavens, I had it, and '*Romance*,' because I didn't. I just went straight to '*Money*,' because I no longer had that either. You can imagine what Jeremy thinks about Ms Byrne and her books.

A few days later I showed the two existing cushions to the directors, a charming father and son, who were very enthusiastic and were keen to look through the rest of my portfolio. Within the week a contract was signed and they became my licensees for tapestries woven in Belgium and assembled in Oxford. The royalties from the tapestries would certainly come in useful, but again they would take time to trickle through. Each tapestry had to be hand woven in Belgium before the sample could be reproduced mechanically on the looms; finally the company in Oxford would have to work the panels into cushions and other luxury homeware items.

My new licensees in Oxford also chose another of my bird characters, *Phillip Pheasant the Gamekeeper*, the first of the series originally painted in 1982 when Rory was a tiny baby. I had been somewhat at a loss after Rory was born, living deep in the countryside of the South Hams and, like Jeremy, totally unprepared for our new life together as parents. After two carefree years aboard our first catamaran based in Cyprus, sailing wherever the whim took us, I found it all very restricting. Rory had been born by emergency Caesarean section on the day the Falklands were invaded by Argentina. My private gynaecologist and his team, and Jeremy, were so engrossed with the running commentary on the radio that it was a wonder I ever gave birth at all. We toyed with the idea of including Stanley as one of our newborn's Christian names, but at the time nobody knew if Port Stanley would be successfully recaptured and we certainly didn't want to name him after a military disaster. Stanley was also a family name, but as with Jenner there were other unwanted connotations. My mother-in-law's family were related to Dr Edward Jenner of smallpox vaccine fame; his surname had been passed down the generations although it had skipped Jeremy. But in the 1980's a cult television series *Dallas* featured a character called Jenna Wade, played by Priscilla Presley. Jenner as a second name for Rory had suddenly become highly unsuitable, all thanks to a soap opera.

(Naming a child can be a minefield; yesterday's trends can so easily turn into tomorrow's unwanted labels. I am constantly surprised by some of the children's names I am asked to inscribe in *The*

Manor House Stories; more often than not the grandparents who are buying the books are rather embarrassed and even apologetic when they tell me the names of their treasured little darlings. Here are just a select few that have stuck in my memory like treacle toffee: Tallulah-Kiwi and her sister Autumn-Rayne, Brooklyn Balthazar, Taya Moon, Arizona Sky, Aurora Cosette, Indiana Phoenix, Beauregard Trey and Tigerlily Casbah. It must be torture for those young children struggling to learn how to spell their names at nursery school. The first time I was asked to write 'Jensen' in a book I assumed it would be spelt like the car, an old flame having driven me around in a Jensen Interceptor, but was told by the puzzled parents it was after the racing driver, Jenson Button. I have had a few Portias too and always have to resist saying, 'ah yes, after the car'. Some of today's popular names, such as Meadow, Sienna, Willow, India, Savanna and Scarlett are those I wish my mother had chosen instead of plain Jane. When I frequently complained about my very boring name, Mummy called the more exotic names I longed for 'far too bookish'; she knew Jane could never be abbreviated, but never imagined it would be embellished with an extra syllable. Thank the Lord for the lady who looked into my pram and asked Mummy my name; when she was told she exclaimed 'Oh, she's a little Janie,' which stuck. Bless her, whoever she was. I dropped the 'e' in the 'sixties when it first became fashionable to end one's name with an 'i' instead – hence Judi Dench, Suzi Quatro, Jimi Hendrix and so on.)

I had loved our remote home in the country, but as Rory slept for four hours at a time during the day, I felt the need to do something creative with my free time. March, April and May of 1982 had been gloriously warm and sunny, helping the hedgerows on our land sparkle with an abundance of sweetly scented wild primroses and Devon violets – more than I had ever seen anywhere before. I took my afternoon nap each day on a sunbed in the garden with Rory in his pram beside me, lulled to sleep by the distant sounds of curlews and oystercatchers from the estuary. I had been watching one of the resident pheasants who took his constitutional through our field in front of the house every day at the same time; he would pause to drink from the spring then turn on his heel and walk sedately back again towards the foreshore. I told Jeremy he reminded me of a gamekeeper, imagining him dressed in plus fours with a deerstalker on his head. Jeremy suggested I paint him just as I had described and find three more characters to make a set of four whimsical, but ornithologically correct pictures.

We also had a pair of beautiful hares that hopped, skipped and 'boxed' just feet in front of our bedroom window, as well as a family of badgers living in a vast sett at the bottom of the valley. Although one of my father-in-law's horses had come to grief, stumbling into one of the many badger holes, we found the bristly cubs quite enchanting. Friends with a young family owned a holiday cottage on the other side of the estuary; they had never seen a badger in the wild, so we invited them to have a kitchen supper with us one evening. We had regularly seen several badgers trotting up the field at dusk each night to drink from the stream and hoped that night would not be the exception. A full moon was rising in the dimming sky as we stared across the garden; sure enough the first badger loped his way towards the stream, less than fifty yards distant. Our friends were thrilled and within seconds a younger badger followed the first, then another, then another. Our pudding sat untouched on the table as we watched this cavalcade of nocturnal visitors. By the time we counted the thirteenth badger we thought it high time to turn on the lights and return to the table. Jeremy insisted he had spent the previous year training three badgers to go round in never ending circuits of the field.

When our home was destroyed by fire a year later, all four framed paintings in this series should have been hanging in our sitting room. Instead, and most fortunately, they had been at the National Trust headquarters in Wiltshire, where a committee of myopic elders were desperately searching for any reason to reject them as greeting cards. In fact Jeremy and I had entirely forgotten where they were for several months after the fire and had assumed the pictures had been burnt. Six years later, after I had added another eight designs to the collection, we eventually printed them as greeting cards ourselves and they sold very well.

So it was not until 1990 that I sent a card of *Philip Pheasant the Gamekeeper* to the Chairman of Burberry in London, (actually a Mr. Peacock!) asking if they would like to sell the cards in their stores. In my innocence I had not realised that my pheasant sporting a Burberry check deerstalker and matching scarf – the check copied directly from my own silk scarf – was a blatant infringement of their iconic copyright design. But once again The Universe was working in my favour and my letter and card were passed on to Burberry Managing Director, David Quelch.

David wrote me a charming letter saying how much my card had been admired by his sales team, asking if I would be willing to design and produce a bespoke corporate Christmas card for Burberry. He invited me to London to show him the sketch of the design and took me to lunch at a chic seafood restaurant just yards from the flagship store in Haymarket. The card design portrayed a lady and gentleman pheasant, wearing Burberry check Victorian winter clothes, holding a lantern and singing carols in the snow in front of a beautiful oak door, decorated with Christmas greenery. The door I painted was actually the front door of The Manor House Hotel, Moretonhampstead, which was later bought by Peter de Savary and renamed Bovey Castle.†

Had David Quelch been a different character, he could have stirred up a hornets' nest of trouble for me. Instead the kind and imaginative soul I quickly found him to be turned everything around; he realised I had been innocently naïve and decided he would use my artwork to Burberry's benefit. Nevertheless Jeremy and I were summoned to their lawyers in Gray's Inn, where we were politely but firmly reminded about the perils of breaking copyright law. The following January I received a charming letter from David telling me the worldwide response to the Christmas card had been so enthusiastic that he would like me to design and produce a series of eight cards for The Scotch House, then owned by Burberry. I was to paint eight different birds native to Scotland, wearing the appropriate tartan for their background locations – in most cases a famous castle, ruined or intact. On the back of each card there would be a description of the bird and background, some history of the tartan and The Scotch House crest; the set of cards were to be presented in a luxury gift box of my design. It was an enormous order that would be required in time for Easter, only four months away, when The Scotch House opened a new outlet at Heathrow airport. Why did I always find myself up against such tight deadlines? It would be so refreshing to be asked to produce something whenever I could find the time, provided it was before my appointment with the old folks' home.

I was immediately invited to London to visit The Scotch House, at the time situated at Scotch Corner in Knightsbridge. I took a girlfriend for company and we stayed overnight at the Royal

---

† Some readers may recall from *The Swallows Fly Back* how Jeremy and I had met PdS in Corfu and were invited for drinks on his beautiful schooner, *Gloria*, shortly before he sold it to Pete Townshend of *The Who*. RIP PdS 1944–2022

Thames Yacht Club, with whom our own Royal Dart Yacht Club had reciprocal membership. It was the most reasonably priced and delightful place to stay in town and most handily was only yards from The Scotch House, although my legs invariably took me first on an automatic diversion to Harvey Nics, directly opposite the club. The dining room overlooked the rides in Hyde Park and, both being horse mad, my girlfriend and I were enthralled to watch the Lifeguards exercising their horses as we took breakfast.

I was like a little girl let loose in a sweet shop when I visited the large Scotch House store. The general manager introduced me to a young lady assistant to guide me around the shop as I collected items for use in my designs; these would be on loan for as long as I wanted them, but naturally I bought a few things I couldn't bear to return. For reference to the required tartans I chose scarves and serapes that would be more convenient than lengths of wool fabric from the tartan library, a circular oak panelled room where floor to ceiling mahogany shelves were filled with bolts of every imaginable tartan. Within half an hour my assistant's arms were overflowing with goodies, she took them to a counter and returned with a large box for the smaller items. Silver Celtic brooches (two of those, please) and Tam o' Shanters were added. In a locked glass cabinet I spotted examples of the ornate but deadly looking Skean dhu, the Scottish ceremonial stabbing knife typically worn with full traditional Highland dress, tucked into the top of the long sock. I just had to have one of those too. Soon I had enough for my research, filling two very large Scotch House branded boxes that I couldn't possibly take back on the 6.30 train from Paddington to Newton Abbot – especially the lethal dagger for which I could be arrested. Realising not for the first time that I had chosen more than I could carry, I expressed my concern to the manager.

"Don't worry, we'll deliver it all to your home in Devon tomorrow morning," he said soothingly. How the other half live! Sure enough a private courier's van pulled into our drive before noon next day.

I worked tirelessly at my easel for the next six weeks, only stopping for snatched meals or to read bedtime stories to the children, while Jeremy spent hours researching relevant history and writing interesting texts for the back of each design. Rory was at prep school during the day and we had employed a wonderful young nanny for 3 year-old Miranda. Lisa was the most tremendous help during this time, not only keeping Miranda occupied during the day when I was working, but also teaching her with a natural ability and flair, making learning numbers and the alphabet fun. Lisa was also very artistic and helped me when I was struggling to paint the nine tartans, (one card featured two) cleverly working out the particular order in which I had to paint the different weaves of colour in the fabric – the finest white lines being the last. One of the designs featured a Peregrine Falcon as Bonnie Prince Charlie bowing to Flora Macdonald, with a small sailing boat in the background. In the misty distance was the Isle of Skye, where she accompanied the fleeing Prince to safety following the rout of the Jacobite army at Culloden. A problem arose when I wanted to paint the Prince wearing a kilt and flying plaid (a men's cape) of Royal Stewart tartan. I knew this particular tartan was owned by Her Majesty Queen Elizabeth II and thought I may need permission to reproduce it on my card. Time being of the essence, I sent a letter to Buckingham Palace. A couple of days later I received this disturbing fax:

The Royal Stewart Tartan is the sole property of Her Majesty Queen Elizabeth The Second. Her Majesty has made it available for public use. However, to claim the tartan as your own is considered an Act of Treason and is punishable by Death.

As soon as the cards were printed, we enlisted the help of local friends to sort the cards and envelopes into the gift boxes I had designed – a dark green box with The Scotch House logo in red on the folding lid, the inside of which was printed with postage stamp sized images of each of the eight designs. Exhausted after such a frantic rush, Jeremy hired a lorry and together we delivered the cards to the Scotch House five days before Easter. (All too aware of my penchant for shopping, as well as the proximity of some of the most expensive shops in the country, he wouldn't let me out of the cab!). No wonder we were so tired. The thousands of cards, envelopes and boxes had arrived by lorry the very day before we moved into our manor house. Our removal firm were not best pleased either.

Chapter 3
The Jolly Good Fellowes

A wise girl knows her limits, a smart girl knows she has none.

Marilyn Monroe

During our final months in Corfu I had made contact with a gentleman who published several small guidebooks, including one that touched on the island. I was seeking advice about publishing a gift book featuring the dozens of watercolours I had painted during and after our years on Sarava; the studies of wild plants, flowers, birds, animals and fascinating natural objects I had observed or collected in the Ionian would, I thought, make an interesting illustrated journal. The man seemed keen to help and I was encouraged by his positive reaction to my idea.

Back in Oxfordshire I called this prospective publisher's London number and suggested he came to lunch at our cottage, where he would be able to look through my portfolios of work at his leisure. A week later, smartly dressed in navy blazer, open necked white shirt with fashionable dark denim jeans, he was affable enough; I liked this contemporary mixture of styles, which according to Jeremy, fashionista extraordinary, was the pretentious sort of London look he had no time for at all. Exactly why I should have judged the potential of a new business partner by his outfit was not entirely logical, but I suppose my mantra, 'handsome is as handsome does,' would be a starting point. (Jeremy would of course have countered that with 'appearances can be deceptive'.) Besides, the blazer reminded me of the day I should have been introduced to Pierce Brosnan, when he was at the height of his fame as James Bond.

We had been at Millfield for Speech Day, along with a thousand other parents milling around on the lawns. With cups of tea and plates of scones in hand, the crowd was slowly edging towards the marquee, where a pep talk designed to justify the colossal school fees awaited us. I was deep in conversation with the mother of a friend of Rory's from Singapore, who had very generously shown us around and treated us to Singapore Slings at Raffles during our stopover from Australia the previous year. Suddenly I felt an arm around me.

"Mummy, do you want to meet Pierce Brosnan?" asked Rory casually.

All too aware of Rory's penchant for practical jokes, and remembering how many times I had been bamboozled, I just laughed at him and carried on talking with my friend. Out of the corner of my eye I watched Rory saunter a few yards from us and shake hands with a tall man who had his back to us. They chatted for a while and as the man turned around – you've guessed it – it *was* the famous actor. Pierce's adopted son was a form below Rory but they had made friends through a shared interest in the school's excellent Meyer Theatre. I could have kicked myself, but it would have been too rude for words to break away from my friend to chase after Rory. However I did notice that Pierce was wearing a navy blazer, dark denim designer jeans, a deep Prussian blue shirt and tan loafers, very obviously Italian. It was an unusual combination at the time but it looked stunning on such a handsome man.

As we left Millfield for the airport that afternoon, bound for another glorious summer in Corfu, Rory related how he had asked Pierce if he would be willing to make a surprise entrance at a sixth form hop he was organising in the theatre the following term; the theme was 007, so naturally Rory thought it would be a pretty cool way to begin the evening. Pierce told Rory very gently that under the terms of his contract he was forbidden to make guest appearances as James Bond, but that if he was in England at the time he would definitely try to pop in as himself. (Not to be outdone, Miranda announced halfway through the following year's Speech Day that she would be joining us earthlings separately at Heathrow, having been offered a lift in Mark Knopfler's helicopter).

On my next shopping trip in Corfu Town that summer I had bought Jeremy some smart jeans to wear with his summer blazer, as well as a shirt in the identical shade to Pierce's – taking care not to tell Jeremy the reason until after he had worn the outfit for the first (and last) time. Jeremy remained distinctly unimpressed, insisting he was never going to resemble any screen idol unless Worzel Gummidge counted as one. Besides, according to Jeremy's encyclopaedic knowledge of fashion and style, blazers were the preserve of yacht clubs, and jeans were for wiping your hands on.

Unfortunately my would-be publisher reminded me less and less of Mr. Brosnan as he pored over the mock-up book, which I had provisionally titled *A Greek Island Nature Diary*. Making complimentary remarks about my artwork, he asked what other work I had done in the art world; when I had finished showing him the originals of my Burberry, Scottish castles and all the other commissions I had completed over the years, he was positively salivating. Then, tucked inside a portmanteau, he spotted a tiny mock-up book I had made twenty-five years ago for my children; it ran to ten pages, a couple of hand drawn illustrations and a cover with an original painting of two willow tits dressed in woolly pom-pom hats and sleeveless Fairisle knitted vests, playing with autumn leaves. The handwritten title was *The Manor House Stories*.

Taking it carefully out of its folder he asked if I had any more illustrations for the story. I explained it was just something I had put together for Rory and Miranda donkeys' years ago when they were small, adding that I had typed up more stories to read at bedtime. He was quiet for a moment, leafing through the pages again before offering to publish the stories forthwith, adding that they would make my name. Before leaving us that day he asked me to complete a fully edited and illustrated version of the original story as soon as possible. You could have knocked me over with a feather!

Jeremy insisted this was a complete red herring and remained firmly against the idea of publishing my children's stories, unless a major publishing house took them on and did them full justice. Knowing how so many authors had been rejected by publishers, he was quite rightly pessimistic it would ever happen. He reminded me that the Brontë sisters initially suffered this fate – each one of them forced to write under a male nom-de-plume. Unbelievably, Rudyard Kipling was told by one publisher that he couldn't even compose a sentence correctly. D. H. Lawrence, Kenneth Grahame, John le Carré and others too numerous to mention were also rejected out of hand; Louisa May Alcott was told to stick to teaching when she submitted *Little Women*; Agatha Christie had to wait four years to get her first book published; Marcel Proust had so many rejections that he decided to self-publish. More recently it is common knowledge that JK Rowling was rejected by countless publishers before the first *Harry Potter* book was eventually published as a small print run by a little known independent publisher – a friend of a friend of mine who must have done rather well out of it!

Each time we had returned to England from Corfu over the years to collect something from my father-in-law's attic, I had noticed the little silver suitcase in which all my sketches, original manuscripts, notes and ideas for *The Manor House Stories* had been stored. How often had I wistfully said to Jeremy that we should really try to get them published. Tired of my pestering, he explained in more detail one day.

"You would never get a serious publisher interested, just look at Beatrix Potter; for ten years she tried every publisher in London. *Peter Rabbit* was rejected by them all until she gave up. It was only because Hardie was so determined her stories should be shown to the world that it was published at all."

I had never heard about 'Hardie' before, so I asked Jeremy to elaborate. Canon Hardwicke Rawnsley was closely related to the family by marriage – his twin sister, two cousins and other family members having all married Chaplins. Evidently there was an irresistible attraction between Chaplins and Rawnsleys in the late 19th century, or perhaps they all met at the same wedding reception – an early inspiration for *Four Weddings and a Funeral*. Hardie was also a great friend of the Potter family and in 1882, as Vicar of Wray in Cumbria, he began a close, lifelong friendship with Beatrix Potter; she was just 12 years old when her family took Wray Castle, then owned by Hardie's cousin Preston Rawnsley, for a summer holiday. Hardie offered constant encouragement to the young Beatrix and recognised her incredible artistic talent; but seeing her dejection at first hand, he took the manuscript and some illustrations for *Peter Rabbit* and battered at the door of Frederick Warne & Co. He persuaded them to publish *The Tale of Peter Rabbit* in colour and the rest, as they say, is history.

Unforgivably no mention was made of Hardie in the delightful film, *Miss Potter*, which starred Renée Zellweger as Beatrix and Ewan McGregor as Norman Warne, (a stranger than fiction link to Mr McGregor, the angry gardener in *Peter Rabbit*). Ewan McGregor looked uncannily like Norman Warne, who he played to perfection; no wonder Beatrix fell madly in love with the handsome Norman, who was put in charge of publishing her 'Little Bunny Books,' as his older brothers disparagingly described them. Beatrix and Norman were secretly engaged before his untimely and very sudden death broke her heart. Beatrix Potter's books became the best selling children's books of all time and were translated into numerous languages, for many years the only books allowed into Communist China to help teach English to children.

Hardwicke Rawnsley, with Sir Robert Hunter and Octavia Hill, were the three founders of The National Trust. A mercurial and energetic man, he was arguably the catalyst for the Trust's initial success, using his friendships with Browning, Ruskin and Alfred Lord Tennyson (his godfather, who was married to yet another Rawnsley cousin) to garner support and funds for the Trust. Beatrix and Hardie were utterly devoted to the preservation of the Lake District in particular. She was 'the love of his life' and some have suggested that, in more convenient circumstances of timing, Beatrix would have married Hardie instead of William Heelis.

I have loved Beatrix Potter's books all my life, as I still do; I read my copies to Rory every night in his cot from the age of nine months. By the time he was eighteen months old he would tell me if I had skipped a page. By the time he was two he would say, 'Mummy, don't read the bit about the rat showing his yellow teeth at me and whisking down the hole!' referring to *The Tale of Samuel Whiskers*. Miranda's favourite story was *The Tale of Mrs. Tiggywinkle* with her laundry baskets and flat iron, because she loved hedgehogs and the domesticity of Mrs. Tiggywinkle; Miranda has grown up to be extremely tidy and practical, totally unlike her mother, and Rory still loathes rats. Naturally I have felt this serendipitous connection to Beatrix Potter very keenly and I liked to imagine Beatrix guiding my less accomplished hand as I wrote and illustrated my own children's stories.

We quickly realised we would need someone to write a foreword to the books, but who would be the perfect fit? The family put their heads together; Rory suggested Sir David Attenborough, but Jeremy thought the great man may not approve of anthropomorphised animals and birds. I telephoned a few friends to ask for their suggestions and Lynda, a dear friend we first met during our year's sabbatical in Spain when the children were small, had a brainwave.

"Why not ask Julian Fellowes?"

"Golly, yes! Do you think he'd consider it?" I replied. " We do have some friends in common, I think."

"Well if you don't ask you don't get, it's only the cost of a stamp you stand to lose," she answered. "And you couldn't have anyone better as he knows everything there is to know about grand country houses!"

For anyone who may have spent the past two decades meditating on a remote atoll in the Pacific, Julian Fellowes wrote the screenplay for *Gosford Park, Young Victoria, The English Game* and is best known as the creator and writer of *Downton Abbey,* the fabulous and extraordinarily popular television series first aired in September 2010, telling the upstairs downstairs story of the aristocratic Crawley family and their domestic servants. Besides which Julian Fellowes just happened to have played my favourite character in the original television series *Monarch of the Glen*, with Richard Briers and Susan Hampshire, in which he played Lord Kilwillie so superbly.

At the time *Downton Abbey*, which I watched religiously every Sunday night along with 12 million other viewers in Britain, had already won numerous accolades including a *Golden Globe Award*. Fortunately I had written the first of my children's stories many years earlier, so I could truthfully say I hadn't got the whole upstairs downstairs theme from Julian. But would such an acclaimed writer be prepared to write a foreword to my little books?

Jeremy helped me compose a suitable letter which combined

his sensible brevity with a little of my more flowery exuberance. Enclosing the dummy copy of *Sarah Sparrow the Scullery Maid* with the letter, I pushed the package into the little red post box in our wall. Then, as usually happens with me, I promptly forgot about it; once something is done it's done and I move straight on to the next thing. It must be an Arian trait. My mobile phone rang a couple of days later on a fine Saturday morning as I was upstairs making our four-poster bed.

"Hello, is that Jani?" asked a very cultured lady's voice. I wasn't expecting any business calls on a Saturday and couldn't think who this caller could be.

"This is Emma Fellowes," my heart almost stopped. Here comes the gentle let down, I immediately thought: Julian has asked his wife to tell me he won't write the foreword to my books.

"I'm just about to take Julian to Heathrow as he's flying to LA today, but he asked me to ring you in reply to your letter." I prepared myself, waiting for the inevitable.

"Since the success of Downton," Emma continued, "Julian has been inundated with requests to write forewords and endorsements and he has to refuse as there are so many…"

"Oh yes, I quite understand." I interrupted, keen to spare Emma the burden of further explanation.

"No! Wait, Jani! You don't know what I'm going to say! We both thought the mock-up book of *Sarah Sparrow* was so enchanting that in your case Julian will make an exception and would be delighted to write a foreword."

I could hardly believe my ears!

"He will email it to you from LA in a few days."

I jumped up and down on the spot in the bedroom like Zebedee, squealing to myself with glee, then raced downstairs to tell Jeremy.

"Julian Fellowes must be an incredibly busy man right now, so

I'll believe that when I see it," he said, adding his usual dose of realism. But he had to eat his words two days later when an email came through from Julian with the following foreword:

> *The Manor House Stories create a wonderful and detailed world in miniature full of truth and consequence, like all good stories should, giving us lessons about life but in the most charming way imaginable.*
>
> *No one can accuse the book of soft-soaping the realities of work in a great house; there is plenty of elbow grease required from all the animals and birds employed there, as I should know, but you will find kindness in these pages too, and I suppose I believe that while fate may be challenging for everyone, there is often some kindness in the mix. In my experience anyway.*
>
> *These lovely little tales contain comments and observations that will be very useful to young readers in the years to come, and they will be useful to older readers, too, if I am anything to go by.*

I simply couldn't believe my luck, nor could my family; my publisher was utterly stunned. I immediately called Lynda to tell her the good news and thank her for her marvellous suggestion. A few weeks later I received an invitation from Emma to meet her and Julian at the Althorpe Literary Festival, where Julian was one of the guest speakers. I had always wanted to visit the ancestral home of the Spencer family in Northamptonshire, where Princess Diana is buried on an island in the lake.

"Althorpe's virtually next door to me," said Lynda when I told her. "I'll buy the tickets and we can meet there."

Julian's talk was completely sold out, so Jeremy and I opted to hear Sandi Toksvig instead. When we arrived, Lynda met us in front of the house and we went into the stable block café for coffee and cake. After Sandi's talk we left the marquee, whereupon Jeremy returned to the car complaining of feeling ill and cursing the cake he had just eaten. Lynda and I made our way to another marquee where neat piles of Julian's various books were displayed on long trestle tables, behind which a regiment of uniformed Waterstones' staff eagerly awaited; they were obviously anticipating a substantial volume of sales.

My friend and I waited discreetly at the side of the tent as a queue of several hundred people had their books personally signed by Julian. Most of them wanted to chat to the famous man and an hour passed before the last person had left the tent and we were finally able to approach the table.

"Hello, I'm Jani," I said to a rather puzzled looking Julian. Emma leapt to her feet and hugged me warmly.

"This is Jani Tully Chaplin who wrote Sarah Sparrow and the other Manor House Stories!" she explained to Julian, who promptly stood to shake my hand enthusiastically as the penny dropped. Luckily for me, and despite knowing every other important person in the world, Emma has a quicksilver memory and had recognised my very unimportant name.

"Do you mind if I take a photo of you with Jani?" Lynda asked.

"Of course not!" they both answered as I moved behind them and Lynda snapped us with her mobile phone.

"Keep us in touch with how the books are going," Emma said after some small talk as we made our farewells. "You must come to see us at home in Dorset soon."

Lynda and I walked back to the car as if we were floating on a little pink cloud. Jeremy was still suffering, but I promised he would get his chance to meet Julian and Emma, which he did the following year. Only as we got to know them better would we discover what an amazingly generous spirited couple they were.

As soon as the manuscript for *Sarah Sparrow the Scullery Maid* was finished, the publisher wasted no time in finding a layout designer and a printer in Wales. I had designed the cover with the logo and asked him to follow my wishes as to the size of the book – small enough for little hands to hold easily – and the colour of the paper, a gentle ivory tone known as English White. I wanted a silk marker ribbon so young readers could mark their place easily and not feel daunted by the prospect of having to read the whole book in one go. The publisher asked for forty illustrations, some cameos of the characters and a cover image; this was not quite what I was expecting, but I was over the moon at the prospect of my books being published at last. I think I would have sold my soul to the Devil at that stage.

Summer had crept up on us and the landlocked Cotswolds were suddenly hot and dry, the parched fields looking even flatter and less interesting than before; as well as being desperately homesick for Corfu, Jeremy and I also missed the sea and the rolling South Hams countryside, from which we had rarely been parted for long. The larger sitting room in the cottage, with its partially glazed roof, had turned into a tropical hothouse; it was far too hot to use at all during the daytime and not noticeably cooler after the sun had set. My publisher had asked for a series of twelve books, one for each month of the year. The list of the titles, with a short précis of each, was to be printed in the front of *Sarah Sparrow* and all the other eleven books. I duly sat down in the courtyard before the sun reached it, wrote a few lines to describe each of the twelve stories and sketched a cover image for each one. That was the easy part; I didn't dare multiply forty-plus pictures by twelve to work out how many paintings I would have to complete in very short order. This was getting serious.

Jeremy set up my portable wooden easel and a folding chair under the shade of the carport, with a tiny garden table beside it for my paints and brushes. At eight in the morning it was pleasant enough; each day the village postman came by to drop off our mail, stop to look at my work and ask me about the books. But by eleven, when Jeremy brought me an iced coffee, the low English sun was directly on me and I was sweltering. Jeremy then brought out the garden umbrella, which made some difference, but by lunchtime the temperatures had soared into the high eighties and there was not a breath of air anywhere. I was wearing a strappy camisole and shorts at this stage, with a wet flannel around my neck; I then resorted to wringing out a tee-shirt in cold water and wearing that until it dried fifteen minutes later and the process had to be repeated.

(This wet tee-shirt trick, I hasten to add, had not been acquired after participating in a lewd competition during an 18–30s package holiday in Magaluf; rather it had been my saviour in Cyprus, living on our first catamaran, Aries, when I was expecting Rory and the temperatures soared past 102 degrees. I was alone on the boat for the month of July while Jeremy was skippering his old yacht, Valdora, on charter in Southern Turkey; one morning an urgent announcement from the loudspeakers at the marina office warned all the yachties that a severe sandstorm was fast approaching. The sand was being blown straight from the Sahara and we were told to close all doors, windows and hatches and stay inside our boats. Within minutes the sky turned orange and the wind rose until it was howling in the rigging as the sun disappeared. I thought I had closed everything, but red sand soon began funnelling through the static air vents until I stuffed kitchen paper into them and closed off the last vestiges of fresh air. The storm raged for two days and the boat became a furnace – not funny when you're four weeks pregnant – but the wet tee-shirts saved me. When I eventually decided to venture outside, I found I couldn't open the saloon door because the cockpit was banked up with its own dune of red sand, which had to be shovelled away by one of the marina staff. The entire boat was covered with a thick layer of fine, sticky sand, which took repeated attempts over several days to hose off.

Worse still, my only way of keeping in touch with the outside world in 1981 was through the single telephone line in the marina office, a rickety shack in those days. A secretary would announce incoming calls to yachts in the marina over the tannoy; wind direction alone decreed how many yachts would actually hear these messages. '*Yiat Aree-ess, Aree-ess, Dzaini Tsaplin, Teeleffono!*' she would shout above the general commotion, and I would leap on my folding bicycle and pedal like crazy to the office before the caller decided to hang up. Aries seemed to get far more calls than any other yacht, mostly from my parents, which was slightly embarrassing. But it was positively humiliating for Annabel on her converted motor torpedo boat, 'Viking Girl,' given the inadvertently indelicate Greek pronunciation which regularly echoed around the marina: '*Vucking-ell, Yiat Vucking-ell, Annabel, teeleffono!*'.

Happy days.)

Beneath the carport Jeremy set up a large electric fan from our bedroom, which had turned from fridge to oven with the changing seasons. This made a big difference when switched to the highest setting and placed inches from my face, but it disturbed my art paper and vast quantities of masking tape were required to secure it to the easel. It was rather unfortunate that the carport also housed our dustbins. The plastic 'wheelie bins' brewed up their rotting contents as the day wore on, the smell emanating from them becoming an intolerable mixture of rotting vegetation and fetid cow pats. Jeremy moved them hither and thither, but the miasma lingered on. I lit a scented candle, which promptly blew out in the breeze from the fan. At this point Jeremy lost patience.

"For heaven's sake!" he exploded, "You can't have everything absolutely perfect, you'll just have to get on with it!"

I tried my best to think of Leonardo da Vinci and his fellow great masters of the fifteenth century, such as Michelangelo, Titian, Raphael and Botticelli, just getting on with it. Did they have to work in such insalubrious and uncomfortable settings? I am sure Michelangelo found it very painful laying on his back on wooden scaffolding planks for the four years it took him to finish the ceiling of the Sistine Chapel, but he did have a group of hardworking young apprentices to help him. The principal of my finishing-cum-art school, known to her pupils as Auntie Vicky, AV, often told us of the time she was commissioned to paint the ceiling of a dining room in a modern seaside villa in Torquay. The owners were a fanciful wealthy couple from the Midlands who had retired to the English Riviera where they had built their dream home, complete with a large collection of reproduction Italian marble statuary surrounding a kidney-shaped swimming pool overlooking Torbay. AV, who was possessed of a far from sylph-like figure, spent weeks lying on her back on scaffolding put up for the purpose. She was required to paint a sky of fluffy clouds tinged with sunset pink interspersed with chubby cherubs. Biting her tongue at the request and trying to imagine herself as a modern day Michelangelo, she reluctantly painted the seriously overweight winged babies complete with miniature bows and arrows, even if she was tempted to have them pointing the arrows at each other. AV was pleased when her clients raved about the finished ceiling until the gentleman proposed to put in lights above the ceiling, with a switch concealed on the floor at the head of the table with which to alter the mood; thus the sky would turn from daylight to dusk and thence to night, when little lights drilled into the ceiling would twinkle like stars. AV had to try to keep a straight face and, given her fiery temper, it was a wonder she didn't explode. I can't actually write her preferred answer when she was asked where the holes should be positioned.

"You're lucky you don't have to work in a garret on the Rive

Gauche as so many artists did," continued my husband helpfully. At least they would have had a nice view of the Seine, I mused.

After a hectic five weeks, working eighteen hours each day, the illustrations for the first book were finished and sent away; a few weeks later the publisher brought the first copy of *Sarah Sparrow the Scullery Maid – A Fine Romance* for us to see. I could hardly bring myself to look at it lying on the coffee table, partly as I was overwhelmed that it had finally been published, but mainly because I was so nervous that the colours reproduced from my original paintings would not be accurate – which they certainly weren't. My publisher stayed for lunch and stressed the importance of producing the next books in the series as quickly as possible. He had always been honest about his intention to sell the completed series to a mainstream publishing house, but I didn't much like this feeling of being forced to work to a deadline. A formal schedule of completion dates for each book was hardly conducive to creativity, particularly in such challenging circumstances, physically, mentally and financially.

Chapter 4

Palaces, Parties and a Prince

Courage isn't having the strength to go on –
it is going on when you don't have the strength.

Napoleon Bonaparte

"I shall order five hundred copies from your publisher to start with and make a special place for them amongst our Below Stairs display in the shop," said the young lady buyer at Blenheim Palace encouragingly. "Can you sign them all for me? We could even host a book launch here if you like."

The interior of the vast new gift shop had been very attractively and imaginatively designed with different areas themed on the life and workings of the Palace; at one end of the shop the original dairy had been sensitively converted into a large café with some tables spilling into the main shop. Here was an ideal spot to set up a table for my book launch.

My publisher came from London on the day of the launch and drove me to Blenheim to help prepare my signing table. A queue began to form at my table a few minutes after the shop opened and didn't diminish until late afternoon. One visitor from China asked me to sign my name and add a message in Chinese. She wrote it down for me and I had to copy it as accurately as I could; she showed it to her family who seemed to think I had done a good job and clapped daintily. Hearing the wonderfully familiar sound of Greek being spoken, I was thrilled to speak to a family from Cyprus in their own language, much to my publisher's astonishment. The day was enormously encouraging and, as I would soon learn, there were so many interesting customers to meet from all corners of the earth wherever I attended book signings over the following years – a surprising number of whom became friends and pen pals.

Following such a promising launch at Blenheim my publisher suggested a book tour of England. I reminded him that I was at my easel for over twelve hours a day as it was, but eventually I caved in and agreed to attempt one signing day each week. Predictably enough it fell to me to send off a few hand written letters to places I thought might host a book signing. One of the first to reply was Castle Howard in North Yorkshire, the fabulous location for the original 1981 television adaptation of Evelyn Waugh's wonderful *Brideshead Revisited.* Mrs. Howard was happy to agree and a few days later we left Oxfordshire at four in the morning, arriving at the castle in time to set up my signing table before opening time at nine. This meant setting my alarm for an ungodly hour to pre-pare myself, a task which took so much longer than it had when I was modelling in my twenties. While I was applying my make-up and wishing I had a tub of Polyfilla for the laughter lines, Jeremy made a flask of coffee and packed our picnic bag with Marmite and marmalade sandwiches, cold drinks and snacks. Much to my husband's disgust I came downstairs with my hair in heated roll-ers, covered by that good old standby from my modelling days, a chiffon scarf; I reminded him that nobody would see me flat out on my fully reclined seat. I promised to remove the rollers before we got to Castle Howard and suggested he stop the car as soon as we glimpsed the great house, exactly at the spot where Sebastian had shown it to Charles for the first time. I could take a photo then as the sun should be up. With a small rug over my knees and a feather pillow behind my beautifully warm head, I slept most of the way to Yorkshire, Dash snoring on my lap as usual. I woke up when Jeremy eventually stopped the car beside the massive black wrought iron gates at the head of the very long private drive.

"Where's the lake with Castle Howard in the background?" I asked tetchily. "I wanted a photograph of that view."

"I've searched the map and there's no such place with a road on it," Jeremy insisted. "They must have shot that sequence with the car on some private track, but I'm sure we could easily plough down to the lake over their formal lawns if you're determined."

I was disappointed but told him he could take photos later while I was signing books. Dash would enjoy a nice walk around the grounds after this long journey, I suggested more cheerfully. A table was already set up for me by the gift shop, situated in an enormous cobbled courtyard which used to house the stables and coach houses. The buildings had all been tastefully converted into the café, bookshop, gift shop and a visitor centre where tickets were bought for tours of the house. Personally I would rather have seen horses and coaches in the courtyard, as there would have been a hundred years ago.

It was going to be another very successful day; the queue for tickets had to pass by my signing table, presenting me with a captive audience. At lunchtime Jeremy fetched some more boxes of books from the car before taking the opportunity to walk down to the great house.

"Well? What was it like? Did you get any good photos?" I asked hopefully when he returned.

"I didn't bother much," Jeremy replied forlornly. "The fabric of the building is frightfully shabby when you get close, crumbling away in places. It was quite upsetting actually, but probably not as much as it is for the unfortunate owners."

I bought postcards of the house as a poor substitution and as we drove away that evening I glanced behind me to snatch the smallest view of the great dome in the far distance before it disappeared altogether. I wrote a letter of thanks to Mrs. Howard and received invitations to do book signings on four more occasions; the last one involved a drive from North Cornwall and after that we decided it was altogether a Tamar Bridge too far.

* * *

The Manor House Stories quickly came to the attention of the National Trust, in particular their South Devon properties. Officially labelled the Trust's Riviera Portfolio, I was invited to arrange book signing days at three of the properties. Compton Castle was under this collective umbrella and Geoffrey and Angela were delighted that my little book would be promoted at their home. They invited us to stay for the three days of signings and once again welcomed us warmly. Dash was super excited to be staying in the west wing and he obviously thought we had come to our senses at last and booked a really splendid hotel to stay in. Like me, he was nervous of the ancient spiral stone staircase that led up to the first floor, but more concerned about the steep and slippery oak stairs that climbed to our bedroom, where I had to carry him.

One of the other signing days was hosted by Greenway, the gorgeous former home of Agatha Christie on the River Dart, where I was placed by the window inside the attractive gift shop in the old courtyard. Agatha Christie's antique writing table had been readied for me with a pile of my books ready to sign. Above me the smiling face of Agatha looked down from a framed photograph on the wall and I just hoped to goodness she would bring me lots of customers rather than some scheming murderer. I needn't have worried. As I laid out my pens, blotting paper and a small vase of fresh flowers from the gardens at Compton, a tray of coffee and biscuits arrived from the restaurant before the first customers came into the shop. Visitors appreciated the fact that I was a local girl and it helped that the model and inspiration for the Manor House in my stories was actually in a small hamlet upriver from Totnes.*

I had been invited for coffee by the owners of Kingston House in Staverton, soon after we had returned from Spain and moved into our converted barn in Broadhempston in 1987. They had recently bought the house, which was in need of a great deal of renovation and repair. Coming from London, they confided that they might have bitten off more than they could chew with the dilapidated Queen Anne mansion. On a chilly February morning in their cavernous kitchen, they asked me for recommendations for a roofer, a blacksmith, a carpenter, a glazier and a plumber. Luckily there was a blacksmith working from a forge in their village, but I couldn't help with the others as Jeremy always did the maintenance on our houses.

"Well, I have always thought Kingston looked like a perfect dolls' house, as if you could open the front and see all the rooms inside." I answered, the words coming out of my mouth as if someone else was speaking, I'm convinced it was my Father. "I can imagine the whole estate being run by birds and animals,"

"Oh Jani, that would make a lovely children's story," said Michael as he turned away from the Aga, steaming kettle in hand. "Why don't you write it for your little ones?"

Bless that man! On the way home I invented the first story in my head, about a little sparrow called Sarah who was the Scullery Maid at a Manor House and wanted to wear a clean dress for just one day. It was a 'Cinderella' story where she would meet Jeremy Jackdaw the Chimney Sweep who had come to clean the chimneys at the house. Romance begins, a spring wedding is planned, Delia

---

*I was thrilled to be invited as a guest author and speaker at the very first Greenway Literary Festival in 2019.

Duck the Cook makes a fabulous wedding cake, Lord Peregrine Falcon sends for Miss. Nimble-Thimble the Reed Warbler who makes a beautiful wedding dress for Sarah, other characters erect a tent for the party and the happy couple leave for their honeymoon in Junket the Dairyman's cart. Before supper I scribbled the story on a bit of paper and read it to Rory and Miranda at bedtime. From their expressions I didn't need to ask if they approved.

"You could have lots of other birds and animals working at the house too, a robin for a gardener and someone called Rory!" suggested Rory.

"And I want to be in it too!" squeaked Miranda.

"You can both be in the stories, but first you'll have to help me choose the names of all the birds and animals." My answer pleased them but their reaction pleased me more. I knew that if the story of Sarah had appealed equally to a seven year-old boy and a two year-old girl and they both wanted more, I could be on to something. Rory chose Radish as the name for the gardening robin; Rory became the handsome Footman, Rory Redshank. My tiny blonde daughter was transformed into Miss Miranda Mistlethrush, the teenage daughter of the family who loved pink and spent hours in the bath – that was definitely a premonition!

* * *

Waiting for me on our return from Castle Howard was an email from my publisher firmly asking me to get on with the next book he wanted to publish. He was keen to have the Christmas story ready in time for the winter season. So as Jeremy was still unloading the car, I went straight back to work on the illustrations. I found it so very hard to envisage Christmas at The Manor House when the temperatures were still soaring in the Cotswolds. One hot morning the telephone rang; it was an old friend of mine who was shortly going abroad on holiday and wondered if Jeremy and I would care to house-sit for her while she was away; her regular sitter had fallen ill at the last moment.

I accepted immediately; this was one of the smartest and most luxurious houses I knew, right by the river in a Devon village where we had spent several happy Christmases. Beautifully and tastefully decorated, the house was as immaculate as ever and we decided simply to shut the doors on the three elegant reception rooms and restrict ourselves to our guest suite and the huge kitchen while we were there. We didn't want to risk any of Dash's silky hairs being shed on any of the furniture in the other rooms; the kitchen had perfectly comfy chairs for the evenings, as well as a long wooden table where I set up my painting things; the light streaming through showroom-sized glazed doors to a large courtyard would provide a perfect place to paint. This inner courtyard area resembled a *giardino centrale* in Tuscany with vast earthenware pots large enough for mature ornamental trees, some young olives and flowering plants; towering above them, a date palm soared skywards. This was more like it!

The weather was perfect for the whole ten days and I quickly realised I could paint outdoors in the garden, right at the river's edge, where Dash would lie patiently on the wooden jetty, staring at the water and waiting for me to take him swimming. It was most conducive to painting; the only sounds were the creaking of oars in rowlocks, the faint putter of engines as launches passed by, and the distant murmur of surf where the river met the sea. Some evenings we invited a few of our Devon friends for supper, a suggestion that had been generously made by our hosts. It was wonderful to see them again after our time in Oxfordshire, but I was so busy during the days that I had no time to cook for our guests. Luckily there was a farm shop nearby which sold excellent frozen ready meals by a firm called *Cook Shop*. All we had to do was pop them in the AGA and serve them with fresh vegetables. They made delicious puddings too, so for the first time in my life I could actually sit and talk to our guests instead of constantly jumping up and down from the table to deal with yet another culinary disaster. Back in the 1980's when it was the normal way of entertaining, my friends and I used to bemoan how much time and effort it took to give a dinner party, even a small one for six or eight people. I loathe cooking and work myself into a state of panic at the thought of having guests for dinner, so these evenings were a constant worry to me as I never knew how my dishes would turn out. Consequently I stuck to a few old favourites that I had more or less mastered; our hapless friends must have taken bets on whichever of these was going to be trotted out for the umpteenth time.

Nevertheless, as Din and I used to complain to each other, it would take four full days to host a dinner party, bearing in mind we both had two young children at home at that time. In between preparations the children had to be hauled out of bed, helped to dress, breakfasted, driven to two different schools some distance away, whereupon the whole process would be reversed six hours later. The first day was taken up with cleaning the house from top to bottom, as lady guests would always go upstairs to leave their coats in our bedrooms and frequently use the en-suites during the evening, rather than using the downstairs loo in the boot room used by the men. Day two would be taken up with shopping for the food and wine, involving an hour's drive to the nearest decent supermarket, then ironing the white linen napkins, cleaning the silver and polishing the glasses. Day three, the day of the dinner party, was always the time I dreaded most – often to the point of wanting to cancel the whole thing. Prepping the food and laying the table, picking and arranging flowers for the table, the hall and in all the rooms the guests would use, making two different puddings and preparing the coffee tray always took far longer than I had planned. After the ponies and dogs had been fed and watered and the children tucked up in bed, I would be completely exhausted, racing to the bedroom to have a quick shower, dress and tidy myself before cooking the meal.

As the guests arrived my feet would be hurting from standing all day, my head would be aching from the stress and all I wanted to do by then was to go to bed. For the rest of the evening my time was spent running backwards and forwards to the kitchen throughout the meal, never tasting the food, hardly having time to snatch more than three words of the conversations missed while taking out the dirty plates and loading the dishwasher in between courses, knowing a third load would have to go in after everyone had left. The fourth day would be spent putting everything away again, washing the linen and trying to find an hour for some family time. Why did we put ourselves through it? Because it was the 80's and 90's and it was expected. Our wealthier friends, (or those without children at expensive schools), would hire a cook for the evening if they didn't already have a resident chef, but Din and I and most of our other friends had to just battle on and put up with it. No wonder those decades passed me by in an eternal blur of fatigue.

In Corfu during our early years with Sarava, before the proud Greek drachma was so tragically ditched in favour of the Deutsche mark, (sorry, Euro, but that's what you are), it had been so much easier to entertain; we could afford to take our family to a taverna once, twice and occasionally three times a day without a second thought; the cost was no different to cooking at home in Devon. One of the only good things that had come from our association with our architect Spiro was the discovery of his favourite taverna in Corfu. *Maistro* was quite literally on the beach at the western end of Almiros, the four mile long, pale gold sands that looked across the sea to the island of Ereikoussa. A simple rustic structure resembling an oversized beach hut, your feet scrunching on the fine sand liberally coating the timber floor, this unpretentious taverna served fare less commonly found on the island. Beetroot and roasted garlic dip became a staple regularly copied on Sarava; but my favourite was a small wheel of mild goat's cheese, fried in breadcrumbs until the middle ran hot and creamy when it was cut, served with a home made blackberry coulis.

The very best thing about Maistro was the anticipation of a spectacular sunset visible from every table in the restaurant; the view over the beach and glassy sea made it almost impossible to look away and eat. Miranda and I would often slip away from our table and run onto the warm sand to watch the oversized crimson sun turn our world into a radiance of glowing coral pink as it fell below the horizon. Jeremy had often told us about the green flash that would appear as the last sliver of sun vanished, usually adding it was probably just a trick of the retina. We never saw it properly and, being colour blind himself, I suspect he must have made the whole thing up.

One particular Devon dinner party remains etched in my memory and still does nothing for my culinary confidence. In the early 90's I had been an exhibitor at the Spring Fair at the National Exhibition Centre in Birmingham – a vile, soulless, draughty, concrete and steel car park of a place that in January used gigantic blow heaters to warm it up. If your stand happened to be near one of the fans you boiled in the constant blast of recycled, smelly, germ-laden hot air; if it was more than a few feet away you froze for the five days of the Fair.

I was selling my own designs of greeting cards and prints from one of the smallest stands available, which was still extortionately expensive even though it was no larger than a broom cupboard. On the way to the Ladies one morning, I passed the biggest stand in the card hall. It was decked out like an ancient Grecian temple, a completely irrelevant excess of white pillars, swathes of lilac chiffon and plaster statues. I stared at it with my mouth open like a goldfish; it was the Andrew Brownsword stand, world famous at the time for a design concept called *Forever Friends* – Disney-style teddy bears doing 'cute' things. The company, based in Bath, was worth almost £200 million at the time; all this success came from these teddies that had originally been doodled, some say, by a secretary whose name never appeared on any of the lucrative merchandise.

I sighed enviously to see it bustling with deferential trade customers who had made their pilgrimages from all over the world, as I made my way back to my own little stand the size of a small larder. To disguise its white plastic partitions that lent it the air of a lavatory cubicle, I had decorated it with brown paper on which I hung my framed prints. Jeremy had made a very realistic 'flat pack' imitation Welsh dresser and sideboard, to which his mother had hand painted delicate, rosy apples on the fake drawers to match my *Orchard House* brand, named after the converted barn we had owned when we started the company. To add a distinctive rural touch I had also placed a bale of straw at the entrance, together with my green Hunter wellies; a blue and white vintage pottery jug brimming with Cornish daffodils had been brought fresh from the flower fields of Penzance by my friend Peta, who had come to help me.

Later that morning while I was taking an order, a group of five men in smart dark suits stood looking with great interest at my stand from the aisle. They were there for several minutes discussing my cards and prints, but they had walked away before I had finished with my customer. Having just seen his photo in the Times Rich List, I had instantly recognised one of the men as Andrew Brownsword himself. I raced down the walkway after the men like a demented stalker, catching up with the group to accost Andrew.

"Excuse me, are you who I think you are?" I asked breathlessly.

"Who do you think I am?" he replied with a charming smile; he was rather handsome actually and I felt a hot blush creeping up from my neck.

"Andrew Brownsword? You were just looking at my stand, the one with the bale of straw."

He was very complimentary about my designs and the stand, which he said was the only one in the whole place that brought an air of the countryside to the show. Andrew had recently bought a beautiful estate on the River Dart that had once belonged to an old friend of my mother's. I rashly asked him if he and his wife would like to come to dinner when the trade show was over and he was back in Devon again.

"I'd love to!" he said. "Just call my secretary anytime to arrange a date."

I started panicking for the rest of that day, worrying about the menu and who else I would invite for the evening. When I told Jeremy about it he was sceptical and told me, as usual, not to worry about it as he thought Andrew probably wouldn't come. There was method in my madness, I very much hoped that Andrew might take my designs under his wing and bring them out as a new range. He had all the expertise and resources to make them as world famous as his teddy bears. My cards and prints sold well enough from the trade shows and I had customers all over the world, but the marketing was difficult as I was up against the big card companies who employed teams of representatives. These merchandisers would make regular visits to the shops who bought their cards, re-stock the shelves and keep checks on the stock levels, so the shops had to make no effort whatsoever to re-order; it was all done for them. A few of my loyal retail customers bothered to ring me to re-order, but I could count them on one hand and they were always small independent shops – the high street card shops and chains would never bother. The Brownsword team would have been able to sell my cards by the millions, instead of the thousands I struggled to manage myself.

A date was set for dinner at our manor house a few weeks after the trade show. Now the panic began for real. I invited four close friends who I knew were used to the mindset of successful business-men; then I asked our stalwart housekeeper, Margaret, if she would come in for the evening to help with the dinner party. Margaret had two young granddaughters who were mad about *Forever Friends*, so she was only too happy to see Mr. Brownsword in the flesh, promising enthusiastically to wear a black dress and white apron for the occasion, just like one of the 'Nippies' from a Lyons Corner House. Bless her.

I thought I should make a bit of an effort with the food, searching through my recipes from friends until I found an unusual starter of artichoke mousse. It had been really delicious when it was served to us at our friend Peta's house in Cornwall years before, but I soon wished I had chosen a far less ambitious and fiddly dish; the horrid knobbly things took hours to peel. Before our guests arrived I successfully pressed the mousses (mice?) out of their circular moulds and was certain they would impress. We were all having drinks in the drawing room when Margaret caught my eye and beckoned me frantically from the shadows beyond the doorway.

"You'd better come and look at your mousses," she whispered. "They've been leaking!"

I flew into the kitchen to find all ten plates containing what could only be described as slushy green islands melting by inches into a sea of thin pea soup. Most unappetising.

"I've been mopping it up with kitchen paper as I go along," Margaret said in her matter-of-fact Devonian way. "So I'll just have to serve them up as soon as I've done the last bit of mopping!"

So much for *haute cuisine*. I should have stuck to half a grapefruit with a cherry on top. The rest of the dinner passed well enough and nobody seemed to notice the sloppy starter, although I did vaguely overhear the word 'interesting' as one of the guests tested the consistency. With what I thought was great self control, I didn't mention my artwork at all, although it was on my mind and I had hoped Andrew might ask me about it at the end of the evening, which he didn't. I mentioned it to Jeremy as we flopped, exhausted, into bed that night.

"Don't worry about it," he said in his usual way. "I expect he'll mention it when his wife writes to thank you."

I waited and waited for a letter, a card or even a phone call, but nothing ever came. Perhaps they had noticed the miserable mousses after all; or on the other hand perhaps neither of them had been properly brought up. Either way I have never risked that recipe since.

But that was nothing compared to the most disastrous party we had ever thrown. It had taken Jeremy over two years of backbreaking labour to build our new house, following the devastating fire that had destroyed our first home in 1983. For the housewarming party we chose mid-summer's day, imagining the weather would be splendid and that we could feed our sixty guests *al fresco* in the garden, from where there were stunning views over our fields bordering the Salcombe Estuary. Sure enough the appointed day dawned warm, sunny and bright with clear powder blue skies and not a breath of wind. Jeremy had built a wooden pergola above a large part of the terrace on which we were training ornamental vines; he had spent a couple of hours that morning covering the pergola with polythene sheeting to prevent the dew falling on the heads of our guests.

For once in our lives, I thought as I drove to the other side of the estuary to the artisan bakery in Frogmore, we had chosen a perfect day. Returning with a dozen of their speciality giant baguettes, I prepared them with garlic butter mixed with fresh herbs from our garden and wrapped them in tin foil. Then I turned my attention to assembling sixty lamb kebabs with onion, a rainbow of peppers, bay leaves and chestnut button mushrooms, leaving them to marinade in a mixture of olive oil, lemon juice, balsamic vinegar, crushed coriander seeds, ground black pepper and freshly squeezed orange juice. The starters were a simple standby from Jeremy's student days – baby cherry tomatoes stuffed with cream cheese, finely chopped chives and lots of seasoning – easy finger food. I had also made two giant Pavlovas the night before, leaving them in the cold oven to crisp up overnight. All I had to do later on was to cover the meringue in whipped Devonshire double cream and add the fresh raspberries delivered by our local grower down the lane.

Everything was ready well before seven, so I went to change into my party clothes and do my hair; after all I wouldn't be cooking, so I could glam up. Then the first clap of thunder came out of nowhere. I walked back towards the kitchen to find Jeremy shouting, blaspheming and shaking his fist like Basil Fawlty at the gathering black clouds overhead. As the thunder rolled ever nearer, the first fat, tentative drops of rain splattered onto the paving stones; minutes later this gentle summer shower had turned into a tropical monsoon. As we looked out towards the drive a torrent of mud-red water was gushing down the slope like a deluge of tomato soup into the lower courtyard, where the storm drains were already beginning to overflow. Neither of us had ever seen anything like it beyond the tropics.

"Bloody marvellous! I might have known it, sodding awful English weather!" yelled my husband. "Now everyone's going to get soaked to the skin before they get to the front door".

I was more concerned about our new carpets, a delicate shade of pale honey, which had recently been laid throughout the house. Jeremy had mown an acre of the field beside the garden for the thirty or so cars to park; tinder dry an hour earlier, it would soon resemble the Somerset Levels in wintertime. I quickly spread some old towels by the front door. An hour later the house was packed with sodden, gently steaming partygoers whose rictus grins betrayed a thoroughly British determination to enjoy themselves. With hairstyles flattened and dripping, makeup streaked, light summer dresses rendered transparent wherever they clung, their shoes and hems caked with mud, this barely recognisable scrum now expected to be fed. On the terraces the awnings bulged and swelled like engorged udders between the timberwork of the pergolas and – with a little encouragement from Jeremy's old friend Tim, helpfully brandishing a broom handle – they burst spectacularly over the tables beneath; in turn the trestles collapsed under the weight of the cataract, smashing most of the bottles and sluicing trays of nibbles and uncooked kebabs onto the lawn beyond.

The barbecue was awash by this time so I had little option but to begin a heroic struggle to cook sixty large grass-flecked kebabs under the electric grill in the kitchen, remembering too late that one of my Pavlovas was still inside the top oven. My carefully blow-dried hair was now frizzy and smelling of charred roast meat, my face was scarlet with the heat from the eye level grill, the acrid smeech making my eyes sting and water, but at least one lady friend was heading in my direction to help. Or so I thought. Handing me one of the outsize loaves she complained that the garlic bread wasn't hot enough and that I should pop it all back into the oven. The kebabs produced large volumes of oily smoke that quickly spread throughout the house and soon our miserable guests began ferreting furtively for car keys as they made their excuses and headed lamely towards the door.

Half asphyxiated, drenched to the skin, famished and badly in need of alcohol they might have been, but our guests' contentment was not yet complete. The field beyond the garden had turned from manicured grass to quagmire in the interlude; now their cars were slithering over the heavy red clay soil like a shoal of stranded fish, desperate to escape from the shallows of this hellish party. Some did manage to make it back onto the lane, but many had to wait for our neighbouring farmer to go home, change out of his best tweeds and return with his biggest tractor.

A handful of our closest friends stayed on to help clear the debris, scraping the worst of the mud from our carpets and sweeping up broken glass from the terrace. Only then did the storm abate, having settled over us so vindictively for precisely the three hours of our evening party, vanishing as quickly as it had appeared. We later found out the roads a mile away were bone dry. Outside the stars sparkled brightly from a deep midnight blue sky and the still air was heavy with the sweet smell of flattened, new-mown hay in the surrounding fields; from the depths of our valley a fox barked, interrupting the plaintive calls of curlews and oystercatchers drifting over the water. The cruel fates of timing had often worked in our favour, but when they decided to throw a tantrum they certainly upset the apple cart. From that day on Jeremy in particular would be looking for the first opportunity to move to a warmer climate.

Never mind Andrew Brownsword, probably one of the most exciting moments of my life had also occurred at the Birmingham Exhibition Centre, where I was again exhibiting my greetings cards and prints at the Summer Gift Fair. I was staying near Northampton with Lynda, who had been my saviour during the year we lived in Spain when I so missed the company of my parents and girlfriends. On the first morning of the fair I took the train from Northampton to the NEC, but our train stopped about ten minutes shy of the exhibition centre. Peering through the window there was no obvious reason why we had stopped in the middle of nowhere; British Rail, like airlines and anyone in charge of a tannoy system, are seemingly incapable of providing any useful information, preferring instead to stick to the trivial. Then I noticed a siding where two shiny black Range Rovers were parked next to another train waiting on the adjacent line. Looking more closely I noticed it was black, very glossy and sporting the Royal coat of arms on the side.

There and then I made a plan; I wouldn't go straight into the NEC as I had intended. Instead I would wait outside the main entrance to see who amongst the Royals was visiting. It was a gloriously sunny day and a small reception party of local dignitaries and Mayors were already waiting in a line when I arrived; two rows of steel barriers kept us common folk corralled away from the main thoroughfare where royal feet would tread. I managed to squeeze amongst a group of press photographers, all with cameras at the ready, whereupon I put my smart leather briefcase on the ground by my feet and waited; but soon a policeman came up to me and politely asked if I would mind crossing to the other side of the road. I was rather embarrassed as all the reporters' eyes seemed to be on me, so I scuttled over and positioned myself a few yards from the Mayoral party, still clutching the bunch of flowers I had picked from Lynda's garden that morning to put on my stand. Suddenly there was a flurry of activity amongst the police and security guards as an armoured Land Rover from the Bomb Disposal Unit screeched to a halt, blocking off the entrance from the main road.

"Has anyone left a briefcase here?" one of the officers shouted sternly, pointing to a large clear area where the paparazzi had scattered a safe distance away from the suspicious object. I glanced down at my feet where my briefcase should have been.

"Oh Lord, it's mine!" I shouted back, as I felt everyone rolling their eyes and breathing sighs of relief.

I was escorted by two robust men from the bomb squad, their radios crackling urgently about the imminent arrival of the royal visitor, to retrieve my case. They asked me to open it and had a quick look inside to make sure of its innocence, although they must surely have realised I wasn't really terrorist material. I was then told to return quickly to my place at the opposite side, the police having somehow got the idea I was one of the dignitaries.

Minutes later the two black Range Rovers pulled up at the entrance to the NEC and my heart almost stopped as His Royal Highness The Prince of Wales stepped out of the first car. I have to admit here that I had always had a bit of a crush on Prince Charles since my schooldays in Devon; what horse mad young girl wouldn't have a crush on a handsome Prince in jodhpurs? I even had a photo of Himself in polo kit sellotaped inside the lid of my desk. The Prince was making for the usual line-up of stuffed shirt dignitaries until he spotted me hanging back behind the barrier. He veered away from the official welcoming party, whereupon I impulsively thrust my bunch of flowers towards him, grinning like the proverbial Cheshire Cat, with heart thumping and knees knocking as I managed a little curtsey and handed him my posy.

"But I should be giving these to *you*!" he laughed, his cornflower blue eyes twinkling with good humour. "Are you exhibiting here?"

he asked with seeming genuine interest.

The low morning sun was behind him and shining directly into my eyes; I must have been squinting because he most considerately shifted a few inches to his left to shade me from the glare. The waiting Mayoral party were looking daggers at me.

"Yes I am! Do come and see my cards," I blurted, handing him one of Philip Pheasant the Gamekeeper that I had retrieved from my briefcase earlier on, just in case.

"Would Your Royal Highness give this to Prince Philip?" I asked, "It is named after him."

The Prince looked a little surprised and I was mentally kicking myself for not having designed a character with *his* name.

"Most certainly, and very good luck!" he said, shaking my hand as I prayed my palm wasn't sweaty.

All the while the press cameras opposite had been clicking away and I desperately hoped one of them had got a good photo of me with His Royal Highness. I watched Prince Charles meet his reception committee and disappear into the building. I would be late to open up my stand, but who cared; certainly not me. I had shaken the hand of my future King and I wouldn't be washing it for at least a week. As I approached the main doors all the reporters came running to surround me, asking my name and firing a dozen other questions in their boisterous way that must drive celebrities to drink.

"Jani, what did the Prince say to you?" They asked amidst the whir and clatter of shutters. "Jani, what did you say to him?"

"Did any of you get a good photo?" I asked, hoping at least one of them would have got a reasonable shot of me with the Prince.

"No we couldn't, you were obscured by a pillar," several of them answered as one.

But a photographer from the Daily Express did promise to send me whatever he had managed to get. As I made my way to my stand in the card hall, I was walking on air, smiling idiotically to myself and quietly singing a song I remembered Mummy singing when I was a child:

"I danced with a man, who'd danced with a girl, who'd danced with the Prince of Wales ...".

I waited all day for Prince Charles to visit the card hall, which was miles away from the main entrance. Then I realised HRH was there to see young members of The Prince's Trust who were exhibiting in the hall nearest the entrance. The Trust had been created to help young people start their own businesses and as they all had to be under thirty years old I wouldn't have qualified anyway. Another twenty-five years would pass before I met Prince Charles again; on that occasion, a few years before they were crowned King and Queen, I would also have the pleasure of meeting Camilla, Duchess of Cornwall.

A press agency did eventually send me a photograph showing Prince Charles holding my flowers and card, seemingly in animated conversation with a concrete pillar. I framed it anyway and added a little note and arrow under the photo saying Prince Charles had really been talking to me – honestly he had! Later that year, in the brochure advertising the next Spring Fair, a postage stamp sized colour photo showed me standing behind Prince Charles before he and his entourage turned towards the proper welcoming party. The huge smile on my face said it all.

Chapter 5
Every Mug has a Story to Tell

The one important thing I have learned over the years is the difference between taking one's work seriously and taking one's self seriously. The first is imperative, the second is disastrous.

Dame Margot Fonteyn

Eventually all the completed illustrations for the Christmas book were sent to my publisher, who passed them to his layout designer before the press files went to the printer in Wales; as Jeremy had already completed the page layout there was little work for the designer. For reasons best known to himself my publisher had managed to arrange a signing for me late in October at a bookshop in Penrith, Cumbria of all places. It was a long way to travel, even from Oxfordshire, so I booked a small Bed & Breakfast nearby. To make the journey worthwhile I had tried very hard to arrange signings at every one of the National Trust properties in the Lake District; given our connection to the Trust and Beatrix Potter I thought it would be a perfect fit. However I seemed to be banging my head against a brick wall; my phone calls were never returned and emails went unanswered. I wasn't too surprised; after all if I sold any books and gave them a healthy profit for doing so, I would have to give them an invoice for the wholesale price. That in turn would mean opening a new account in my name, which would involve a moment's light concentration for one of their book keepers – maybe as much as two minutes' worth. I don't suppose they would be such slackers if their own business was at stake.

So after a tiring summer of painting we left for Cumbria in Rory's Jeep with Dash, a boot full of books, an overnight case for Jeremy and me, not forgetting the outfit I would wear for the signing the following day. I had chosen the gorgeous Austrian traditional *dirndle* dress, complete with matching silk flower covered hair combs, bought in Innsbruck on one of our skiing holidays years ago. It would be Halloween and the lady who owned the bookshop had invited local children to come along in fancy dress – I was fervently hoping nobody would pop the 'who have you came as' question. As usual I had slept most of the way, having missed the hours of delays and road works, to be awoken by torrential rain battering at the windscreen and roof. We had arrived in the Lake District with the first of the storms that autumn, which inevitably was described as 'The Great Storm' by the BBC the following day. As we slopped our way along the twisty narrow road next to Ullswater, the waves were breaking over the low stone wall beside the lake and flooding the road; fallen trees scattered on either side hindered our progress further.

The B&B turned out to be right beside a main road into Penrith, entirely different from the impression and misleading image given on the website. In my head I had pictured a delightfully quaint whitewashed cottage, roofed with blue-green Lakeland slate, nestling in a lush valley of ancient oak trees, their leaves burnished with autumnal shades of red and gold, with views of a lake and charcoal grey Herdwick sheep grazing contentedly on the surrounding heather covered hillsides. I do this all the time and am inevitably disappointed; I don't know why, I just can't help myself. Everything from a beach picnic to a night at the opera is played out in my mind's eye and it is always picture perfect.

"Oh that's just terrific!" cursed Jeremy sarcastically as he pulled across the cattle grid into the car park.

The cottage *was* whitewashed and old, but there were no delightful views or even a garden. Jeremy grumpily took our bags out of the boot and I tucked Dash under my arm to keep him dry. As we approached the entrance we noticed what could only be described as a large wooden raft, wobbling on a deep pool of water that lapped against the front door.

"Wonderful! And all this for the price of good London hotel," Jeremy muttered as I reassured him the B&B would be delightful inside.

It wasn't. The smell of stewed cabbage was only surpassed by the odious décor, a relic of the worst of the early 1970's, combining tangerine, lime and chocolate brown swirly patterned carpets with primary coloured furnishings from the same period. There was nothing vaguely Lake District about it. I had been hoping for a few choice pieces by the famous craftsman Robert Thompson, who carved little mice as his trademark on all his furniture; here we were more likely to see a mouse scuttling from beneath the bed.

We signed in and were led upstairs along a narrow, dark landing with a creaking floor so uneven that I felt I was on the deck of a ship in heavy seas. Jeremy looked over his shoulder at me and rolled his eyes. It was going to be a long night. Our room was disappointingly shabby but at least it had an en-suite bathroom. I unpacked while Jeremy tried to doze on the double bed to recover from the journey. I decided to have a nice hot bath and wash my hair after ringing reception to ask what time their advertised traditional Cumbrian dinner would be served.

"We don't do dinners at this time of the year, just breakfasts," said the landlady bleakly. "There's a pub just a couple of hundred yards along the road, but you'd better book as they get busy with coach parties. Loads of people come to see the autumn colours."

I thought of all the disappointed visitors to the Lake District who would be unable to get a single glimpse of the deciduous trees through the torrential rain; in any event most of the branches had been stripped bare and the leaves were already rotting in sodden plies on the ground. But perhaps all those coach parties queued up instead to delight at the colours of our landlady's lurid carpets.

I had just stripped off for my bath when I noticed a gaping crevice in the wall next to the loo. Peering through the void I was horrified to see two partially dressed people moving around in the bedroom next door. I stuffed a bath towel into the gap and hoped it would stay there. This should have been the last straw, but that was provided later by the pub, a charmless roadhouse where everything was off the menu except flabby sausage and soggy chips in a basket. Oh for Corfu!

Thankfully the bookshop and its owner were delightful. While Jeremy struggled outside the shop to hang my bunting, (each pennant bearing a felt capital letter spelling out THE MANOR HOUSE STORIES), which he loathes almost as much as scatter cushions and fairy lights, I prepared my signing table. Dash and I settled ourselves at the far end of the shop, surrounded by the children's titles. Unfortunately the shop door was kept open and a freezing draught blew in all day; my hands were so cold I could hardly sign my name and I couldn't feel my feet at all. The very first copies of *Lady Davina Dove – A Christmas Story* had been delivered to the bookshop directly from the printers; I was so worried about the finished colours of the printed illustrations that I couldn't bring myself to open any of the new books beyond the first page, where I would be signing my name. Instead I determined to wait until we were in the car on the way home to examine the colours; that way any disappointment wouldn't ruin the entire day.

Only a handful of the invited customers successfully battled through the filthy weather and there was no passing trade that day in the soaked and freezing streets of Penrith. The first customer was a little boy dressed as Spiderman, so the local newspaper reporter had a good subject for his photo. It was pitch dark as we began the long journey home, but I was so relieved to change back into my warm travelling clothes. Dash acted as a hot water bottle on my lap and after eating the remains of our picnic from the previous day, I opened a copy of *Lady Davina Dove*. Even in the dim glow of the map light I could see the appallingly reproduced acid tones of my gentler greens and yellows and burst into tears.

"Don't worry about it," said Jeremy rather crossly, obviously losing patience with my conscientiousness. "Nobody but you would know the colours were a bit out; they looked perfectly alright to me!"

"Yes but you're colour blind!" I sniffed into my hankie.

This was not an unkind criticism, because he really is colour blind. During our honeymoon sailing from Salcombe to Cyprus in 1980, and all subsequent night sailings for that matter, Jeremy always woke me up whenever we were approaching a port. He could readily distinguish a red port-hand light, but the green of a starboard light looked white to him. The same applied whenever a huge supertanker or cruise ship loomed into our path, although fortunately the red (port) light was always the most important one to recognise. Don't ask – it's complicated. I might have thought twice about sailing 3,000 miles with him if I had known this beforehand.

Falling into a troubled sleep I determined never to paint anything light green or yellow in the next book, as these were the colours that had been so distorted in the printing process. By three in the morning when the car eventually nosed into the drive of our cottage I was beyond caring.

* * *

It was a happy coincidence that Oxfordshire had its first heavy snowfall of the year on the very day in early November when I started writing the January story, *Cream & Sugar the Milkmaids*. Ice had formed inside our bedroom windows overnight as soon as the central heating went off, which was most of the time as it was too costly to keep running. When Jeremy went downstairs to make tea he had let Dash out into the garden for a quick run in the snow to do what was necessary, but he had scampered back upstairs to our bed again before the kettle had boiled. I knew how cold he was because he burrowed under the duvet and curled up in the crook of my knees – his favourite spot – and I could feel the snow on his paws. I put on my dressing gown, switched on my electric blanket and told Jeremy I was staying in bed all day, asking him to bring our laptop upstairs with my breakfast tray of Marmite toast and tea.

"You'd make a good butler," I joked, as he shrugged and asked if I really intended to stay put all day.

"I might come down for supper to watch *Downton Abbey*," I replied. "I feel rather like The Dowager Countess of Grantham."

"I'm thinking Barbara Cartland actually!" Jeremy replied, as he scraped the ice from the inside of our French windows.

Like most of England's housing stock, our cottage had the insulation properties of a bus stop. Jeremy had paid great attention to insulating the home he built for us after the fire in 1983; but in Corfu our architect had contrived to frustrate Jeremy's plans to make The Lion House a comfortable home throughout summer and winter. When Jeremy had to break open an exterior wall to increase the dimensions of one particular window, he discovered broken fragments of polystyrene no thicker than a slice of toast inside the wall cavity; there should have been three-inch thick slabs of high density foam he had bought at great expense from Germany. On closer inspection Jeremy discovered the roof of The Lion House had also been insulated with the same miserable fragments. Perhaps our builders had taken the expression 'warm as toast' altogether too literally. More importantly, where had our proper insulation gone?

The new story flowed easily and by suppertime it was finished. Next morning there was a thick blanket of snow over the countryside, so we went for a walk and took snapshots that would come in handy for my illustrations for this new book, subtitled *Snowfall and Snowballs*. Wearing my ski suit and après-ski boots, I painted all the illustrations at my architect's easel in our bedroom, beside the ice-encrusted French doors that led onto the balcony. The glass roof above me gave excellent light but also dripped condensation on me; a rain hat was called for and Jeremy rigged up a large sheet of polythene to keep the water off my easel, but I didn't dare complain. As soon as I finished an illustration I would take it downstairs to Jeremy, who would scan it before sending it to the publisher. Sometimes I managed to complete two small pictures in one day, but those with the most detail took an entire week. In these delightful conditions our long and very cold winter was quickly passing, but it was becoming ever clearer that I couldn't continue to work under such a pressure of deadlines for an entire year without rest.

A partnership made with the best of intentions had run into the buffers; my publisher and I agreed to part company and my books were once again mine alone. Only then did I realise that a great weight had been lifted from my shoulders. In the eventuality it would take me nine more years to finish the illustrations for the series and publish all twelve books off my own bat; but never again would I have to work like a slave on an incessant production line.

Three of my books had been published to date and suddenly we had several thousand copies to collect, store and market by ourselves. During the next eleven months Jeremy and I would travel to every corner of the land to complete over one hundred book signing days, many of them at National Trust properties. There was money to be earned from my books, even if every penny of it would be earmarked for the printing of the next books in the series.

For various reasons there was a great urgency to liberate my books from the warehouse in Birmingham where my ex-publisher had stored them. Jeremy could collect them in a lorry without too much difficulty, but exactly where several tons of books could be kept was quite another matter; there would only be room in the cottage for a token working stock of a few hundred. I called a friendly National Trust manager at Greenway and asked her which distributors supplied books to their gift shop. She gave me details of a firm in Cornwall and I called them immediately to explain our unusual position. Fortunately they agreed to store them free of charge for a year until we could organise a more permanent solution.

Responsibility for marketing the books was now mine. I decided the best way forward was to roll out my offer of free 'Meet the Author' signing days. Only one venue in the whole of England turned down my offer – Chatsworth. In the first instance I had sent a sample of the first book to The Duchess of Devonshire, the last surviving Mitford sister, known universally as Debo, with a covering letter asking if my books might be considered for the Chatsworth gift shop. The Duchess had been Chatelaine of Chatsworth for over fifty years and was solely responsible for creating the estate's farm and gift shops. Before the second World War, her sister Unity's infatuation with Hitler led to young Deborah being invited to tea with the German dictator in Berlin, although the visit made little impression on her. 'If you sat in a room with Churchill,' she wrote, 'you were aware of this tremendous charisma. Kennedy had it too. But Hitler didn't – not to me anyway.'

'Debo' knew everyone worth knowing, including that greatest of hellenophiles Paddy Leigh Fermor, so I felt most fortunate when I received a handwritten letter of thanks a few days later, signed *Deborah*, saying how she had thought the book absolutely charming and ordering a few dozen as a trial order for the gift shop. A fortnight later another letter from the Duchess informed me the books had been very popular and had already sold out. She asked me to get in touch with the manageress of the gift shop to set up an account and enable her to place orders. Immediately I telephoned Chatsworth and was transferred to the gift shop, only to be told the manageress was 'in a meeting' … I wouldn't mind so much if these people told the truth and said 'she's outside having a fag,' or 'she's sitting opposite me right now filing her nails but simply can't be bothered to pick up the phone'.

I telephoned at different times every other day for the next three weeks without success. On the final attempt I caught the elusive lady and explained that Her Grace had asked me to get in touch to arrange a complimentary signing day at any time of her choosing; I could even bring a quantity of books with me on a sale or return basis if needed.

"Oh, we only have *really* famous authors for signing days," she said. "People like Mary Berry. Her books arrive by the pallet load!" The line went dead before I had a chance to reply.

I contemplated writing to the Duchess again but thought better of it; the manageress would be reprimanded and then, even if I had been invited to arrange a book signing, the atmosphere would be unbearable. I wish I'd had the chance to meet Deborah, as did Jeremy. I'm sure we would have got on well, being fellow commercial animals, as well as having many interests and even a friend or two in common; but sadly Deborah Devonshire died soon afterwards in September 2014. Her imaginative vision had taken a tiny farm shop from its humble beginnings in a garden shed to a business boasting a turnover of millions.

After that disappointment I was thrilled to be invited to do a book signing at Polesdon Lacey in Surrey, in my opinion the most beautiful of all the National Trust properties. Stunningly gorgeous in warm marzipan yellow and white, the Edwardian mansion is, amongst many things, where the then Duke & Duchess of York, later to become King George VI and Queen Elizabeth, spent their honeymoon. It was a very cold, blustery and rainy March day, but our welcome in the large gift shop from the young lady Retail Manager was as warm as toast. She was aware we had set off from home very early in the morning and for once we were offered coffee and even breakfast if we felt like it. I discovered over the next few years how unusual such treatment was; at some places I would be offered nothing at all. One Trust property in Cornwall completely forgot I was coming; everything was locked up when we arrived and I had to set up my table in the car park like a bookie at the races.

My table at Polesdon Lacey was opposite a display of enormous hand-decorated Easter eggs made especially for the National Trust; all day long the smell of chocolate made my mouth water. At the end of the afternoon the manager told me they had never sold so many books by a visiting author; she was so pleased that she handed me one of the huge Easter Eggs in gratitude for my efforts. I was invited back four times over the next two years, but although I always was given some token of thanks, I never got another Easter egg – much to my family's disappointment.

Dozens of National Trust managers all over the country began inviting me to appear for book signing days that summer. Jeremy and Dash always enjoyed exploring the grounds while I was meeting customers and signing the books. At Overbecks, a pretty National Trust property overlooking the Salcombe Estuary, the history of the house was particularly fascinating for me. Although Jeremy had been brought up within a couple of miles, and I was from Torbay and had spent many days with my parents picnicking across the water at East Portlemouth, neither of us knew the story of Overbecks.

An Edwardian house with seven acres of landscaped gardens overlooking the mouth of the Salcombe Estuary, Overbecks was named after its last private owner, Otto Overbeck. He bought the property in 1928 and later bequeathed it as a public park, a museum and a Hostel for Youth. Its bequest to the National Trust stipulated it was not to be used as a brothel, unlike so many houses in the surrounding area. This was certainly news to me. Who could have imagined the picturesque fishing village of Salcombe, long since a hollowed out carcass of holiday homes for the wealthy, had once been a hotbed (sic) of ladies of the night? It seems laughable to remember that in our youth, the luxurious Marine Hotel in Salcombe was tainted by a reputation as a 'dirty weekend' location for locals and Londoners alike – as Jeremy and I were reminded by our horrified mothers when we were considering it for our wedding reception.

But this was not the most intriguing part of the house's history. Otto Overbeck studied the sciences at Bonn University and later, whilst working at a brewery in Grimsby of all places, he discovered that a waste product of brewing was actually a nutritious food, which he somewhat misleadingly called *Carnos,* the latin for meat. A company was formed, which unfortunately didn't last long and Otto's patent expired. Almost immediately a very similar product appeared on the market under the registered brand name *Marmite.* No wonder I felt right at home there.

Probably the most enjoyable signing was set at St. Michael's Mount, the Cornish equivalent to Mont St. Michel in France. Our old friends from South Devon, Mary and James St. Aubyn, had inherited the Mount and the title from James's uncle, Lord St. Levan. Mary and I had been expecting our daughters at the same time and astonishingly they were both born on the same day in September 1987. Almost to the hour, my close friend Vanessa also gave birth in Munich to Sara, who would become one of my goddaughters. Two surreal telephone conversations were exchanged within minutes of each other between the three new fathers that day:

James in Cornwall: "Hello Jeremy, it's a girl!"

Jeremy in Devon: "Yes, isn't it wonderful! How ever did you know?"

James, after a short pause: "Well, I was there at the birth!"

Jeremy: "WHAT?"

Then, a few minutes later, Stefan in Munich: "Hallo Jeremy, it is a girl."

Jeremy: "I know! A little baby Miranda."

Stefan: "No Jeremy, she will be Sara!"

Eventually the penny dropped and they realised all three wives had given birth to daughters on the same day. From the age of two, after we returned from our year's sabbatical in Spain, Miranda shared many birthday parties with her two new friends, Louisa and Sara.

Mary was delighted I would be bringing my books to the Mount, which had been made over to the National Trust by James's uncle in 1954; like the Gilberts of Compton, James and his heirs would never be short of a castle to occupy. You could hardly see the Mount from the sleeping village of Marazion as we drove into the empty car park very early in the morning; a thick mist hung over the sea and everything looked decidedly spooky. I could imagine marauding Barbary pirates rowing ashore from their corsairs at any minute…

Cornwall and Devon's history records some terrifying descriptions of cut-throat Barbary pirates regularly crossing the seas in their corsairs to the coastal villages of the West Country and kidnapping men, women and children to take back to Morocco as slaves for Sultan Moulay Ismail, known as Bloody Ismail. One 11 year-old cabin boy from Penryn, Thomas Pellow, was able to buy his freedom and escape after 23 years and return to Cornwall. His story, included by Giles Milton in his extraordinary book, *White Gold*, is quite astonishing. Thomas also wrote his own account, *The History of the Long Captivity and Adventures of Thomas Pellow*. Who today would have thought the gentle, picturesque Cornish harbours and villages so beloved by holidaymakers could have been sacked by these vicious raids? Quite properly there is a lot of commotion about the slave trade at the moment, statues of those who had made their fortunes from slavery being torn down all over the world; but nobody ever mentions the white slave trade. Thousands of 'slaves' were captured from Cornwall alone and precious few ever returned.

My instructions had been to wait on the jetty at nine o'clock, when a launch from the Mount would come over to collect me. Jeremy dropped me off and disappeared towards the main car park; he would walk Dash across the Causeway to The Mount when the tide had gone out. I covered myself in every possible piece of waterproof clothing – I had a wheelie suitcase containing my summery book-signing outfit (which included pristine white cotton jeans) but had to wear my signature boater as it wouldn't fit in the case. I must have looked rather odd with a scarf tied over the straw hat, although I have recently seen a wonderful piece of archive film of Her Majesty Queen Elizabeth the Second on board *Brittania*, wearing full evening dress and a fabulous diamond tiara kept firmly in place by a silk scarf as she ventures onto a windy side deck. I waited and waited for what seemed hours, but in fact was only twenty minutes, straining my eyes for any sign of an approaching craft. The little I could see of the seascape through the fog was empty, so I called Mary's number on my mobile. James answered.

"Hello Jani, where are you? The launch has been over twice and couldn't find you!"

I told him I was on the jetty and was wearing a peach coloured raincoat.

"Hang on, I'll get the binoculars," said James, "Ah, now I've got you! You're on the wrong slipway!" he laughed. "Stay there and I'll get the boys to come across for you." Minutes later, out of the mist and mizzle a small launch drew up to the landing where I was waiting.

"Step aboard, Mrs Tully Chaplin," said a burly fellow in a thick navy Jersey and a natty wool cap, as he offered his hand.

"I've got a few bits and pieces …" I explained, pointing to the large box of accoutrements for my signing table, my wheelie case, a picnic bag and eight heavy boxes of books wrapped in polythene. Another sturdy fellow jumped out of the boat and deftly scooped up my luggage, loading it onto the boat. I was glad to be wearing short wellies as the bilges were slopping over the floorboards.

"I should tuck yourself under the cuddy," advised the skipper, pointing to the flimsy canvas shelter at the bows. "It's a bit choppy out there today and you might get wet."

How little he knows about me, I thought smugly, realising he had no idea how much time I had spent on boats. I sat meekly on the thwart in the shelter of the cuddy and we set off. The skipper was right; 'choppy' was an understatement. The little boat bounced around like a bath toy in the confused seas, but our voyage only took a few minutes and as we approached the Mount I could make out a little group huddled under umbrellas in the rain. I was helped

The Austrian Tyrol 1990

We Three Puffins

Me after sketching some details of the Salcombe Lifeboat for another RNLI card

Addy and me at a Temple in
Chiengmai. 1970

With Dame Margot Fonteyn in 1975

All the nice sailors love a girl – on board HMS Torquay, 1975

My Glamis Castle, Scotch House and Scone Palace cards, all commissioned in the 1990's

Writing with Dash in a cold climate

Original cover idea from 1990

With Emma and Julian Fellowes at Althorpe Literary Festival 2013

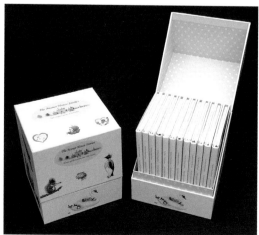

Thirty years and 500 illustrations later, my Manor House Stories were finally completed

Dressed to promote my cushions at Blenheim Palace

With the 11th Duke of Marlborough, Blenheim Game fair

Mug shot – a selection of my successful designs

With Angela Gilbert at Yialiskari, Corfu, watching the filming of My Family and Other Animals

Beside Gerry's statue with Lee Durrell, Jersey Zoo 2016

Me on Adonis at Devon County Show

Book signing at Holkham Hall, Norfolk

End of a day's book signing at St Michael's Mount

Constantine Bay, North Cornwall, our local beach

With Their Royal Highnesses The Prince of Wales and The Duchess of Cornwall, Port Isaac 2016 © Arthur Edwards

… and how I really looked on that day, with Martin Clunes

ashore and greeted with hugs by James and Mary, who handed me another very welcome umbrella before introducing me to their retail manager.

Almost exactly at the spot where I disembarked I noticed a tiny, weathered bronze footprint set into the stones. It was the print left by Queen Victoria when she visited The Mount; she had placed her shod foot in a sand box which was then taken away to be cast in bronze. This tradition has continued with every visiting monarch since, including Queen Elizabeth II.

I had a stream of customers all day and my hand was aching after writing so many personal messages in the books. Jeremy walked Dash across the causeway to join me before the afternoon tide covered it again and Mary came in to collect us for drinks as soon as the shop closed. Jeremy, Dash and I prepared to follow Mary up the steep path to the Castle. After some welcome drinks, James and Mary asked if we would like to go up to the very top of the Castle to admire the view. The paying visitors weren't allowed up to the great terrace, which was only accessible by the family's private lift. Winding our way through the Castle corridors we came to the elevator, which was only just big enough for the four of us to cram inside like sardines. James drew the metal grill across and we rattled upwards. From such an altitude the views over Mounts Bay were beyond description; Jeremy peered briefly over the high battlement to the rocks far below and advised me not to look.

I could have stayed there for hours but we were meeting my cousin and her husband for supper at The Godolphin, a small and attractive hotel overhanging the beach at Marazion. There was going to be full moon that night and we would have a stunning view as it rose over the Mount as we dined. As we said our fond farewells Mary handed me a large carrier bag from an exclusive gallery in Marazion; it was a wedding present for Miranda, a pretty salad bowl from one of the local potters. To Dash's delight we climbed into the launch and puttered away towards the mainland as the evening sun sparkled on the water, now as calm as a millpond.*

By the end of August my tapestry cushions had just been completed in Oxford and one of the first retail customers was Blenheim Palace. Over the years, Hines of Oxford had supplied them with their range of Flemish tapestries, including a bespoke design for Blenheim. However they were not having any luck persuading the buyer to stock my *Country Gentry Collection*, probably because it was themed on fox hunting, shooting and stalking; evidently she was nervous that her clientele might be offended. I tried to explain that the designs were in fact a role reversal: the fox was the huntsman, the pheasant was the gamekeeper and the grouse was the stalker, instead of the other way around. But the buyer was not a country girl and she was still hesitant, although I knew for sure these very British designs would sell brilliantly to the hundreds of thousands of international visitors at Blenheim.

I felt compelled to take things into my own hands; luckily I can be very devious. So one day I put two of the cushions, *The Hon. Freddie Fox* and *Philip Pheasant the Gamekeeper,* in a large carrier bag and set off for the Palace gift shop. The buyer was upstairs in her office when I arrived, but I felt sure I could persuade her to buy my cushions if she saw them in the shop setting. I asked the girls at the main tills in the centre of the shop if they would look after my cushions while I went to the loo.

"Perhaps you could prop them up against the glass screen behind you," I suggested innocently, "and see if they create any interest."

---

*You can see Mary and James in Series 1, Episode 3 of Martin Clunes' *Islands of Britain* where he visits St. Michael's Mount and conducts a hilarious interview with them.

They did so very enthusiastically without a moment's hesitation.

I went to the very smart Ladies, where every window in the cubicles on the east side has the most fabulous open views over the park and lake, and put my cunning plan into action. Two well dressed visitors were washing their hands as I spoke to them.

"Excuse me," I began, "I would like to ask a small favour."

They looked a little surprised but smiled politely as they agreed to help if they could. I explained about the buyer and my cushions and asked if they would mind going to the counter where my cushions were on display and asking the assistants if they were for sale. I reassured them both that they wouldn't be able to buy them because they were not yet part of the stock.

"Leave it to us," they laughed and disappeared towards the counter.

Just to be on the safe side, I accosted an elderly couple who were looking at books in the children's section. I explained that *The Manor House Stories* on the shelf were mine and told them about the issue with the cushions.

"We'd be delighted," said the husband, "I'm sure we would actually like to buy them if they do ever stock them here. A great friend of ours is Master of the Quorn!"

I left it for a few minutes before going to retrieve my cushions and found the buyer by the tills where she was cuddling one of my cushions.

"The girls have been telling me how several customers have inquired about your cushions already," she said.

"Another lady has just asked for a set!" said another assistant – that enquiry was genuine.

"Well, I guess we'd better order some," said the buyer, as I tried to avoid the eyes of my willing decoys.

The tapestry company were delighted with the order placed later that day; it was the first of very many they would receive for my 'Country Gentry Collection,' which soon grew from cushions to upholstered stools, fire screens, draught excluders and tapestry covered waste paper bins. For the next few years they remained some of the best selling items in the shop, which confirms my feeling that I would have made an excellent buyer.

The buyer regularly invited me to do book signings surrounded by a display of my cushions. One December day an extremely tall and very elegantly dressed man was looking closely at my cushions, so I explained that they were my designs. He looked awfully familiar but it wasn't until I heard his deep, resonant voice that I realised he was Jim Carter – Mr. Carson the butler from *Downton Abbey*. I was quite star-struck and asked if he would mind having a picture taken with me. I barely came up to his chest, but he sweetly put his arm around me and I got my photo, just as a petite lady came up to us.

"This is my wife; we're Christmas shopping together," he said, turning to her and explaining about my cushions.

"How lovely," she smiled charmingly.

I knew her immediately but simply couldn't remember her name. Not only was she a very famous actress, but I had last seen her in 2005 on Yialiskari beach in Corfu when she was filming a television adaption of *My Family and Other Animals*. Angela Gilbert and I had been lucky enough to be invited to watch some of the action at close quarters.

"Hello," I said. "I last saw you in Corfu. We were often on neighbouring tables at Agni that summer."

"Oh yes, I adored Corfu!" she answered, as I racked my brains to put a name to the face.

"I am *so* sorry," I apologised, "I know your name as well as my own, but I just can't recall it now."

"It doesn't matter, at all," she replied modestly as she smiled up at her husband towering above her.

"Oh, but it does! Please put me out of my misery or it will drive me mad for the rest of the day."

"Imelda Staunton,"she said meekly.†

* * *

In April our children had given Jeremy and me annual passes for Blenheim, which allowed us to wander the extensive grounds whenever we wished; their generous gift was a godsend that probably kept us relatively sane for the remainder of our time in Oxfordshire. We had both just become senior citizens – indescribably ghastly terminology that really means we were supposed to be entirely invisible for the rest of our lives, probably a nuisance if not an entirely useless burden on society. Our state pensions had come not a moment too soon, but the bus passes, zimmer frames, cardigans and slippers would just have to wait for the time being. Dash adored being taken for long walks in such manicured parkland; we were often the only visitors early in the morning and could easily imagine ourselves once more the owners of a small country estate – this time without the work. Of course for me it would have been better if I was on horseback; however, in all seasons Blenheim was our saving grace during those years in deepest, landlocked Oxfordshire when we so missed living by the sea in Corfu and Devon.

There were crisp and sunny winter mornings when the parkland was crystallised with glittering frost and the gossamer spiders' webs glistened with a million diamonds; there were short autumn

---

† Amongst numerous other acting triumphs, including *Sense & Sensibility and Harry Potter,* Imelda played the part of Queen Elizabeth II in the final seasons of the Netflix series *The Crown.*

days when the deciduous trees were burnished red and gold and squirrels scampered around gathering nuts; there were bright, blue and white windy days of spring when the lake was surrounded by nodding daffodils and the fluffy chicks of waterfowl took their first swims. Then in summer, when the fountains in the formal gardens splashed and sparkled and the Rose Garden was in full bloom, you could pick up the heady perfume as it wafted around the park. The only pity was that dogs were not allowed in the café, so we took a flask of coffee most days. I was also a regular visitor to the Rose Garden during the summer before Miranda's wedding; armed with several Tesco carrier bags, I gathered all the freshly fallen multi-coloured rose petals to dry and scent for use as eco-friendly, organic confetti … I might just possibly have accidentally coaxed some of the attached (but obviously ready to fall) petals into my bags too.

We came to know every pathway and every tree in the Blenheim Park, in fact I painted one particularly enormous oak tree as the one in which Sgt. Simon Squirrel the Quartermaster has his store-room, 'Nuts & Co.' in *The Manor House Stories.* (Just a few weeks after I painted the tree, we were horrified to see it had been felled and only the vast stump was left – no doubt it had some sort of disease or was considered dangerous, but I consoled myself that it had been preserved for posterity in my little books.) Another tree at Blenheim had found universal fame since it was featured in the fifth *Harry Potter* film; hoards of children and the young at heart from all corners of the globe come to visit and pose in front of it; this venerable Cedar of Lebanon is completely hollow, but has been expensively stabilised and preserved for future generations. At the time Blenheim allowed free entry to visit this tree, which I thought very nice of them.

My tapestry designs were proving so successful that I decided to contact other British homeware manufacturers about my designs. I began by sending out a few emails with images of my artwork each morning before I started painting. In particular I hoped to find a pottery to revive a very popular series of mugs I had designed in the 1990's for a well known pottery in Stoke-on-Trent.

Back then, on a bitterly cold day in January 1994, I had taken a train to Stoke-on-Trent, where I was met at the station by the Managing Director. The Lowry scenes around me were brought into sharp focus by the snow already lying on the pavements and grim, brick buildings with strangely shaped pottery chimneys in silhouette against the dark sky. Although Lowry famously painted the industrial areas of his home, Lancashire, this area seemed so typical of his 'matchstick men' paintings. I had never visited Staffordshire before and it was unlike any place I had ever been. I was given a tour of the factory and was astonished to see how labour intensive the process was. The afternoon meeting went well and I was confident my designs would soon be in production as I was taken back to the station and caught the train for Devon. It was snowing more heavily now and the feeble daylight had disappeared altogether. I was glad to be in the warmth and light of the train and was just about to settle into a cosy snooze, when to my horror the guard announced over the tannoy that all passengers would have to disembark at Wolverhampton – no explanation given. Obviously it was either the wrong kind of snow or the wrong kind of darkness. Bloody British Rail!

Given my hopeless sense of direction, coupled with a patholog-ical inability to read railway timetables, I began to panic. I would have no idea which train was bound for Newton Abbot, I would likely get accosted on top of a bridge between platforms and drop my large portfolio of artwork onto the lines below, after which I would definitely miss the last train home. Then I reassured myself that a porter holding a placard for Mrs Tully Chaplin would surely be waiting to escort me to my new carriage. The reality was somewhat different.

At Wolverhampton I stepped out of the stuffy train onto a platform slippery with a thick layer of wet snow. As I feared there was a bridge, so I stuck with the crowd and struggled up and down the steps to an unprotected platform resembling *Wuthering Heights,* bitterly cold with half a gale blowing along its length. Snowflakes stung my eyes as I tried to pull my suit jacket tighter around me, wishing to goodness I had brought a big coat. Eventually the tannoy crackled into life. There were lots of words, but I couldn't understand a single one; they seemed to be delivered by a man shouting underwater from Jamaica in a thick Birmingham accent. There were no porters or guards to be seen, but I remembered an old ploy of my my mother's. During the war all signs at railway stations, sea ports and crossroads were removed to confuse the Germans when they invaded. My newly married mother travelled all over the country by train to join my father wherever he was stationed; she would always ask the train driver where he was going, as he would probably be the only one who knew with any certainty.

After an eternity a train appeared through a flurry of snowflakes, the engine pulling up miles down the platform from me. I thrust my head inside one of the carriage doors and shouted 'Does this train go to Newton Abbot?' at nobody in particular. Several men shouted back that it did, so I clambered aboard, found a seat and sank down gratefully in the steamy warmth beside a window dripping with condensation, rivulets of water running onto the grubby table. It was unfortunate that I found myself in a carriage with a tribe of football fans celebrating victory with as much beer as they could afford. Their language and lewd comments shouted in my direction made my damp hair curl even more; when the bawdy songs began, tired as I was, I felt I could no longer stay put. I gathered up my things and went in search of a guard. A few carriages and jeers later I found a steward in the cafeteria – better known as the Last Resort, where taste-free butter-free sandwiches and coffees made from acorns are sold to desperate people. I explained my situation to the steward, who had a kind face, and hoped he would take pity on me.

"That's all right luv, you can sit in First 'til you get to Newton Abbot; it's empty anyway."

I sat in splendid and comfortable isolation for the rest of the journey and was delighted when the refreshment trolley came rattling along the carriage, as I was longing for a cup of tea.

"Sorry luv, before you ask, there's no hot water. It's the snow," said the steward. Before I had time to work out how snow could possibly prevent water boiling, he spoke again.

"You can have a bottle of water though. It's free in First and you can have a newspaper too if you want."

I was tickled pink by this unexpected bounty and gratefully accepted a bottle of water, but as he only had copies of *News of the World* I politely declined the kind offer of a paper.

However this nightmare journey was worth it in the end, as the well known pottery commissioned three of my designs for fine bone china mugs, '*The Gamekeeper*,' '*The Fisherman*' and '*The Golfer*,' which immediately went into production. The mugs sold all over the world and I thought I was onto a winner, but sadly this relationship went pear-shaped shortly after the company's sales representative for Australia and the Far East came especially to find me at the next Spring Fair in Birmingham. My visitor was a tanned, tall and handsome man in his late thirties and spoke with a delicious Australian accent – basically *Crocodile Dundee* in a suit.

"You must be Jani Tully Chaplin," he said confidently.

I was pleasantly surprised; I was more often called 'that bird lady'.

"Well I just wanted to come over and shake your hand! Your mugs have sold all over Australia, they just fly off the shelves. I've taken orders for thousands this year!"

I was flabbergasted, my royalty payments had certainly not reflected orders like that. Furthermore, he added, many of his customers had asked for mugs with native Australian birds as characters. He had certainly brought a ray of Aussie sunshine and friendliness into the hideous exhibition centre and I wished he could have stayed longer.

Back at home Jeremy quickly discovered there was no mention of Australia on my royalty statements. Obviously the firm had been omitting these orders from the sales sheets they sent me. Eager to get some hard evidence I telephoned my Aunt in Sydney. The next day she popped into David Jones where she found my mugs prominently displayed in the china department.

Jeremy confronted the pottery owners as politely as he could – which was polite in the same way as a bull would gently hint when you're not wanted in his field – demanding to know why sales to Australia hadn't appeared on my royalty statements. Naturally they denied everything and threatened to sue me for defamation. After a flurry of solicitors' letters we decided my only course of action was to withdraw my designs from the company, citing failure to provide full disclosure; the temptation to sue them was overwhelming, but would have been fruitless unless we could afford a full audit of the company. But it was a matter of principle: I was being cheated and felt I would be sticking up for the rights of artists and designers everywhere, much as I did when my Scotch House designs had been copied. On that occasion I received compensation far in excess of the original design fee, so I was paid twice for the same designs. I'm rather hoping to be copied again by another wealthy company.

However all was not lost. The discontinued mugs came to the attention of Royal Doulton who asked me to create designs for a collection of their bone china mugs. I made detailed pencil drawings of six gardens of the world, entitled *Classical, Seaside, Cottage, Indian, Mediterranean* and *Caribbean*. These designs were commissioned and were selling well until Royal Doulton was once again taken over, along with so many of our great English china manufacturers such as Wedgwood.

All this previous experience with the potteries stood me in good stead and within a year of our arrival back in England from Corfu, my designs had been licensed to several new companies manufacturing items from cufflinks to silk scarves; Hudson & Middleton, the pottery now making my mugs, was the oldest in Stoke-on-Trent. At my suggestion their mugs featuring my designs soon arrived at one of my very favourite places in the whole of England – Dartington Hall in South Devon. (I have left instructions in my will for my some of my ashes to be scattered in the formal gardens, on the grassy terraces overlooking the amphitheatre where, with Rory and Miranda and their friends, we have enjoyed many magical summer evenings of 'Shakespeare in the Gardens'. In autumn numerous squirrels scamper about to collect the sweet chestnuts that fall from the trees on the uppermost terrace.)

At nearby Shinners Bridge, the old stone buildings that once housed a cider press, the famous Dartington Tweed mill and the Dartington Glass works, had been converted years ago into a cluster of small eclectic shops, as well as the first 'Cranks' vegetarian restaurant outside London. The original title of *The Manor House Stories* had been launched in the bookshop at Dartington in 2013, so it was exciting to return for the day to launch my mugs in the smart kitchen shop. Beside my table the manageress had made a display of my books, so sales were very good on both counts. The mugs were sold in bespoke cardboard boxes which I could sign, as I obviously couldn't sign the china. But the English potteries were once again suffering at the hands of cheap Chinese imports and the agreement eventually came to an end when the company changed hands for the umpteenth time.

Nevertheless the cottage soon began filling up with samples of my different licensees' products. I would certainly never have to buy another mug, nor indeed another silk tie or pair of cufflinks for Jeremy. But royalties take time to accumulate and we decided the only way forward with *The Manor House Stories* was to publish the rest of the series ourselves. However the cost of producing such high quality, traditional hardback books, complete with dust jackets and silk marker ribbons, was exorbitant. I briefly toyed with the idea of finding a printer overseas, which would have been far cheaper, but then my integrity and patriotism got the better of me – I had always wanted the books printed in Great Britain. It had been a shocking disappointment to discover Beatrix Potter's books were now printed cheaply in China; I felt she must be turning in her grave at the thought.

All too soon I was working on the illustrations for the fourth book of *The Manor House Stories*. It was already so cold in the cottage that I had to wear my ski suit over thermal underwear and two jumpers, with hat and après ski boots, as I beavered away at my easel in the bedroom. I could hardly remember the summer when I had sweltered in the garden.

It was this month that we received another financial blow, a very minor one to most people, but to us it was almost the last straw. Shortly before Christmas I had been invited to three book signing days in Yorkshire. Our second port of call at Fountains Abbey was blessed with a large gift shop and café courtyard complex where the crowds kept me busy all day. In the afternoon a well-dressed elderly lady came to my table and was admiring *The Manor House Stories*.

"These are absolutely gorgeous," she said, "and the illustrations are fabulous! My daughter is a children's editor at Random House and I would love to show them to her."

I practically hugged her! This was surely the miracle to prove my salvation. If Random House took on the books they would be marketed worldwide and I would be in a very different position, no longer having to chase all over the country at our own expense to sell the books. At that precise moment Jeremy came into the shop and I introduced him to the lady.

"Can we give you the three books?" he asked.

"Oh no, thank you; I'm very happy to buy all the titles you have for my grandchildren and I'll show them to my daughter when I visit her in London next week," she replied.

On the way to a very pleasant B&B that evening I kept thinking about Random House; it was my second favourite publisher for children's books, Harper Collins being my first choice because of the wonderful range of co-ordinating merchandise they had arranged for Jill Barklem's *Brambly Hedge* books – merchandise being the real money-spinner for any books; somewhere I could also hear Jude Law's handsome character in *The Holiday* saying: 'My mother is an editor at Random House'. I was convinced this meeting was meant to be. Just over a week later I received a charming email from the daughter saying she loved the books and would be taking them into the office the following week to show the Random House picture book team.

A fortnight later I got my answer.

Hi Jani,

I hope you are well. I have now had a response back from the picture book team, which I am copying in below for you:

The Manor House Stories is a really marketable and promotable idea which clearly speaks directly to the sorts of customers who visit National Trust properties. The 'Downton Abbey' trend is clearly here to stay! Having said that, though, I'm afraid that I wouldn't see these working so well with our more traditional retail routes – high-street bookshops and supermarkets, so it would be a difficult proposition for us to take on at Penguin. The picture-book market is increasingly squeezed, and dominated by a very few well-known authors and licensed brands such as Peppa Pig – or classic characters such as Peter Rabbit. Without the backing of an established author or character brand it is really difficult to launch a new series into the picture-book space and I'm afraid that ultimately we didn't feel that your series was commercially robust enough to compete in the standard bookselling channels.

That being said, you clearly have found a fantastic niche for your books and I do hope your success continues. I'm only sorry that there won't be a place for the series at Penguin at this time.

I'm sorry to be the bearer of bad news, but I wish you all the very best with your books and will look forward to reading the ones I have to my daughter when she is a little older!

Best wishes, etc

Supermarkets? Are you joking? I never would have countenanced the idea of selling my books in supermarkets. I had given them a list of the book signings I had arranged in the past year, along with sales figures; it ran to sixty-six signings at various National Trust and other far more prestigious locations all over the country, which I had hoped would impress Penguin Random House. At the time I had already sold many thousands of books all by myself, without any advertising and without help from a publisher. The

reply seemed most obtuse and contradictory; moreover the publishers were obviously closed to the idea of my gentle, traditional
children's stories that weren't illustrated with amorphous primary
coloured blobs or angry pen and ink scratches. I am considering
another series featuring a multi-racial gang of inner city children
playing in a disused car park, as had once been helpfully suggested
to me by an editor at Hodder Headline.

My final signing event in North Yorkshire was Harewood
House, the ancestral home of the Earl of Harewood, whose mother
was Princess Mary. Once again I was asked to sign my books outside the gift shop, in a dark and draughty corner of the cobbled
courtyard. I wore everything warm possible, from a thermal vest to
my Shearling coat with a hood, bought very reasonably in Corfu,
fur-lined boots and the woolly hat I had bought at my first signing
at Ripley Castle, but I was still freezing all day. It was so difficult to
sign my name and write inscriptions in the books when my fingers
were numb and my eyes were watering in the icy wind. Jeremy
came out of the shop carrying a pair of brown, fur trimmed, sue-
dette fingerless gloves; he had cleverly chosen the colour to match
my outfit – amazing considering he probably thought they were
green, but perhaps he asked the assistant for advice.

In the afternoon some young parents with a five year-old daughter asked me to inscribe her name in some of my books. The little
girl, cuddled in her father's arms, was bundled up in a ski-suit,
hat and mittens but looked pale and rather unwell. I talked to her
for a few minutes as I wrote a special message in her book and
she smiled shyly, waving goodbye as they left. The next customers
came forward and I had almost forgotten about the little girl when
I noticed her mother running back through the archway into the
courtyard. She waited patiently for a lull in the queue of customers
before coming forward.

Quietly she explained that her daughter had leukaemia and this was her first outing since she had left hospital, following long and gruelling treatment. The little girl adored books and her parents had read to her constantly in hospital. They had brought her along specifically to see me and she had been excited to meet a 'real' author. The young Mum was crying and my eyes were so full of tears that I feared my mascara would run and make me look like a panda for the rest of the day. I muttered something about it being my privilege and pleasure and told her I hoped the little girl would soon make a full recovery. I gave her a hug and thanked her for sharing her story with me; I could feel her shaking body through her coat. For the rest of that day I had such a warm glow inside and wondered what on earth I had to moan about – just being a bit cold. When I was a girl, constantly complaining about my freckles, curly red hair, matchstick legs, knobbly knees and so on, my mother would often reprimand me severely with her 'Don't you dare complain / God has given you eyes that see, legs that work and ears that hear / Think of all the poor children that don't have those gifts / You should be thankful and never, ever complain!' routine. And quite rightly too.

The young retail manager at Harewood was delighted with the number of books going through her till and at the end of the day she asked if we could send her an invoice to include the stock we had left for her shop. We drove home in the dark and got back well after midnight. Next morning Jeremy counted the few books we had brought back and realised we had sold a record quantity of books, most of them at Harewood. My invoice was emailed to the manageress that morning and we waited for payment; and waited and waited, without as much as an acknowledgement. After a couple of weeks Jeremy telephoned Harewood House, having had no reply from their shop.

"Oh yes, the shop went into liquidation the day after your wife's visit," replied a disinterested voice from the estate office. "They're nothing to do with us; it was a franchise. Sorry, cheerio."

Naturally there were no contact details available for the manageress and evidently no chance of getting any satisfaction from the company involved. In time honoured fashion they would simply pocket the money at the end of a lucrative trading season, declare bankruptcy and leave a string of debts before reopening under the new banner *Thieving Bastards 2016 Ltd*. Jeremy was livid when he told me.

"The manageress must have known full well what was happening!" he exploded, "She could have paid us in cash from the till before we left. All that way, all those books sold and not a penny to show for it!"

It was a hard lesson and a horrid experience, but I will always remember that lovely young mother from Leeds. I didn't make a note of her name, but hope her daughter is healthy, happy and thriving now.

Chapter 6
Needs Must ...

The key is to learn from failures, and then to keep going.

Sir Ranulph Fiennes

After another arctic winter in the Cotswolds, spring finally arrived and Jeremy, Dash and I were on the road again; thrice weekly book signings at stately homes and castles in every corner of the land became our tiring routine until the end of August.

In September I bought tickets for Blenheim Palace Literary Festival, where Julian Fellowes was a guest speaker. Jeremy opened the questions from the floor – the audience having apparently lost their voices and the ability to raise an arm – and Julian's answers were a fascinating insight into his writing and creative processes. By coincidence I had arranged a signing at Kingston Lacy in Dorset the following day, following which Emma had invited us for tea. We warmed ourselves in front of the fire as Emma made the most delicious cinnamon toast, a mixture of caster sugar and powdered cinnamon sprinkled on hot buttered toast; it was a teatime treat both Jeremy and I had altogether forgotten from our childhood.

"You must use the cheapest sliced white bread or it doesn't work!" she told us; we have copied it ever since and I keep a jar of the mixture in my kitchen with a label marked accordingly.

Julian wanted to know all about my plans for *The Manor House Stories* and I told him I would ideally like a large publisher to take them on.

"Which publisher would be your first choice?" he asked.

"Harper Collins," I replied without a moment's hesitation,

"because they had arranged such a fabulous range of merchandise for Jill Barklem's *Brambly Hedge* books."

"Who publishes the scripts for *Downton Abbey*?" he asked, turning to Emma.

"Harper Collins," Emma confirmed as she poured the tea.

Julian promised to get in touch with his contact and suggest they might like to publish my books. It was a typical act of kindness and generosity, Julian having given a helping hand to many young actors and writers over the years. The result, sent from Harper Collins to the literary agent with whom I had also signed a contract at Julian's suggestion, was disappointing. Their team found my children's books very charming, enjoyable and beautifully illustrated and written, but they did not have list space to properly support a brand so similar in style to Jill Barklems's *Brambly Hedge* collection. None of us could understand why Harper Collins did not want to publish a new range of children's books, considering thirty years had passed since they first published *Brambly Hedge* and the books were no longer to be found in most bookshops.

So even with Julian's backing and recommendation, it appeared I would have to go it alone. He did try to cheer me up by telling me that before the runaway worldwide success of *Downton Abbey*, he had so many rejections from publishers that he seriously considered slipping a fifty pound note between each page of his submitted manuscripts. Naturally, as soon as *Downton* became so popular, publishers were all clamouring to jump on his bandwagon and sign contracts with him.

Two signings we had very much enjoyed that summer were at Holkham Hall and Houghton Hall in North Norfolk; I was invited a few times each year and they could be done consecutively, with an overnight stay nearby. Holkham Hall, (pronounced Hoecum) was built by Thomas Coke, (that's Cook to you and me), 1st Earl of Leicester, in the 16th century. The nearby long stretch of beach at Wells-next-the-Sea can be seen at the end of one of our favourite films, *Shakespeare in Love,* where Viola (Gwyneth Paltrow) is washed up on 'a strange and distant shore' as the survivor of a shipwreck, thus setting the scene for *Twelfth Night.*

Built in the 1720s for Great Britain's first Prime Minister, Sir Robert Walpole, Houghton Hall, (that would be Horton), is one of Norfolk's most beautiful stately homes and remains one of England's finest Palladian houses. During the eighteenth century, Walpole also amassed one of the greatest collections of European art in Britain, and Houghton became a museum to the collection. Two generations later the picture collection was sold to Catherine the Great of Russia to settle debts. It was only when the future 5th Marquess of Cholmondeley, (pronounced Chumley), took on the house just after the First World War, that it was restored to its former glory. Another family name of the Cholmondeleys is the fabulously expressive Rocksavage, but I daresay that's pronounced Rossidge, or some such.

The current Chatelaine loved *The Manor House Stories* for her young twins, who delighted in the mischievous Willow Tit twins, Arthur and Sebastian – characters who appear in all the books. One of my signings at Houghton coincided with the twins' fifth birthday and they came to meet me with their mother, Lady Rose. I was delighted that she gave each of the twins' party guests one of my signed books as going home presents. (I feared Prince George might have said he had already got it, but hoped he wouldn't open the bag until he was on the way home.)

In the summer at another signing day at Houghton Hall, I noticed many of the visitors wandering about carrying large bunches of sweet peas. I asked one lady where they had come from and she told me all the visitors were invited to pick as many as they wanted from the walled garden. As soon as my day was over and the gift shop closed, I left Jeremy to pack the car and raced to the walled garden where I almost bumped into one of the gardeners standing by the gate.

"I'm sorry madam, we're closing up now," he said.

I explained what I had been doing all day and why I didn't have a chance to go to the garden for some Sweet Peas. I added that they were one of my favourite flowers and I wanted to dry the petals for my daughter's wedding in September.

"Oh well, that's different," he said. "Go on then, I'll wait here for you."

To say I was greedy is an understatement; there were rows and rows of the flowers in between each of the vegetable beds, all climbing six feet high on rows of bamboo canes as far as the eye could see. Every colour of Sweet Pea imaginable sparkled in the late afternoon sunshine and the scent was divine. I felt as if I had flown over the rainbow and landed in Oz; I picked as many as I could carry. Time flew by before I heard a loud whistle, which I ignored and carried on picking. There was another more urgent whistle and I heard Jeremy's voice calling my name. I made my way quickly back to the gate with my flowers to find a very annoyed husband and an equally patient head gardener waiting for me.

"For heaven's sake!" Jeremy urged. "This poor man's waiting to lock the gates and go home; just look at the time!"

I apologised to the gardener and thanked him for waiting.

"That's all right madam," he smiled, staring wide eyed at the bale of sweet peas bulging in my arms. "I was quite tempted to lock you in, but I feared for the garden's future!"

Then one morning I learnt that I could no longer sell my books at any National Trust properties, excepting those that fell within a twenty mile radius of my home. (There's just one.) The directors had in their wisdom changed the buying policy. Retail Managers would not be allowed to buy from independent producers, authors, artists, crafts people, potters and other artisans; they could only buy from the Trust's favoured wholesalers. Had I supplied any wholesaler with my books, they would take their considerable commission and I would be selling them at a loss. This affected all the small local businesses and cottage industries whose unique products, not available on the high street, made the Trust shops so interesting. Visitors loved buying souvenirs from the different properties: honey and preserves made at the property or in the nearest village, pottery and paintings by local artists; from woodcarvings to gloves there was always something different and unusual. Sadly this new policy put paid to any further signings at National Trust properties and shops; obviously they could do without the considerable profits that sales of my books had already earned for them.

Jeremy composed a pithy letter to the acting Chairperson at Their Wokenesses' headquarters, stating all the reasons why this change of policy was so contrary to the Trust's founding principles. He described how all the gift shops now looked identical and sold the same products; how you could buy the same mass produced jams, chutneys, chocolate and biscuits made in a factory on some industrial estate in Manchester, all of them branded for whichever Trust property was selling them. He also complained that many gifts, greeting cards, ornaments and mugs were made in China, including the newly published Beatrix Potter books. Scandalous! Poor Beatrix and Hardie would have been mortified; such policies were against all their beliefs, being way ahead of their time in their support of the arts and crafts. We waited weeks for a reply, eventually receiving a standard letter from some aspiring politician that addressed none of our points, but answered lots of other questions we hadn't asked. Of course this disappointingly inadequate response could have partly been due to the final sentence in Jeremy's letter: *Perhaps it would be simpler in future for the National Trust to source all its stock from John Lewis.*

On the other hand Jeremy's mention of the Rawnsley connection might have stirred up unwelcome memories amongst the new breed of directors, who seemed to have forgotten the original ethos of preserving properties for *successive* generations, rather than attempting to curry favour on some trendy whim. Hardie's grandson Conrad, who launched the Neptune Campaign in 1965 to preserve the Cornish coastline, was undoubtedly better remembered by the Trust for his push to make its officers more democratically accountable. But equally it could have been his suggestion that the Trust headquarters should open blocks of three separate toilets – namely Gentlemen, Ladies and Queers – that probably cooked his goose.

I kept that farcical letter from the trust, if only to remind me to tear up all further correspondence from them, but I have kept many far more precious letters too. The first came from HRH The Prince of Wales – as he then was – when I sent him the first of *The Manor House Stories* books to be published, to congratulate him on becoming a grandfather to HRH Prince George. He must have received lorry loads of presents and I was not expecting any reply; but within a week I received a charming handwritten letter, thanking me for sending him the book. I was particularly impressed that the letter heading was Birkhall, the house on the Balmoral Estate which had been left to Prince Charles by his grandmother, Queen Elizabeth The Queen Mother. For His Royal Highness to write His own letter at all was wonderful, but to do it while on holiday in the Highlands was beyond the call of duty. A silver framed photocopy of this precious letter has come with me to all my book signings ever since.

I am never in any danger of becoming conceited though, despite the thrilling letters. My experiences seem to go from the sublime to the 'gor blimey,' in rapid succession. One such incident occurred during a book signing day at Bolsover Castle in Derbyshire. The fairytale castle was created as an extravagant retreat by playboy, poet and courtier, Sir William Cavendish. With elaborate medieval-style turrets and towers it was a building designed to surprise and delight the Cavendish's guests, who included King Charles I. In 1634 Sir William spent a staggering £15,000 (try 4 million today) on banquets and entertainment for the Royal party when they visited the Castle.

The building I most wanted to see was the magnificent indoor Riding House, which is amongst the finest in the country. It's easy to imagine dashing William Cavendish back in the 1600's training his horses in their stately exercises, chiefly for use in battle situations, which was the forerunner to the dressage we know today (a horse that could leap and lash out both hind legs on command – the Capriole – could be an asset). Once riding master to the future King Charles II, William Cavendish built the Riding School and stables for the fine horses he imported from as far afield as Turkey and North Africa. Of all the riding disciplines in which I have competed, dressage has always been my favourite. When I was seventeen I was chosen to represent Devon at the National Dressage Championships at the British Horse Society Headquarters at Stoneleigh, Warwickshire. On my gorgeous Palomino, Adonis, we were placed third individually in the Prix Caprilli. I was the youngest rider to be placed that day.

However my duty at Bolsover was not to go sightseeing but to meet the visitors and sign books. Jeremy helped me set up my table, chair and garden parasol, being a very hot, sunny day, in the sheltered and airless cobbled inner courtyard. I was wearing my customary boater with a summery outfit. On the far side of the courtyard two elderly ladies looked in my direction before entering the Castle arm in arm.

"Oh look, she must be selling ice creams!" one exclaimed to the other in ringing tones that could have been heard in Edinburgh.

I have kept a list of many other useful comments about me and my books over the years, such as 'These books are too wordy'; 'Our grandson is only six and he's already translating Chaucer into Swaheli'; 'Are they made up names (pointing at Seymour Swansdown the Ferryman) or are they their real names?'; 'We've got more than enough bloody books'; ' Our children would trash them in seconds'. The more obscure 'I've come for binoculars' still baffles me. A comment I never really understood came from a young woman visitor at a National Trust property near Norwich: 'I don't like these books because I'm anti-establishment'. Another prize response came from an intimidating teenage girl in Port Isaac, dressed as a Goth, who was glaring at me and my table of books. I had politely asked if I could help.

"I don't talk to strangers," she replied, talking to me.

Most often I am asked for directions, usually when I am visiting somewhere for the first time and I don't have a clue. Early one morning at a summer festival held in the landscaped grounds of the Port Eliot estate, a purple-nosed and very inebriated old roué staggered in my direction.

"I've got two questions for you, m'dear," he slurred between hiccups, leaning towards me far too close for comfort. "Where are the loos and what's a ha ha?"

I tried my best to explain that a ha ha was a deep, steep-sided ditch that acted as an effective barrier to cattle and sheep, whilst preserving views which would otherwise be interrupted by a wall or a hedge. The man didn't appear to understand and I never saw him return. I realised later that I hadn't warned him that the loos were beyond the ha ha, so I think he probably fell straight into the ditch on his way to relieve himself.

By and large my signing days have introduced me to the most charming customers. From an elderly Romany – dapper in a pin-stripe suit on a very hot day in Padstow – who wanted to buy the original of my illustration of a gypsy caravan, to an inconspicuous looking young father of twins, who turned out to be an international investment manager with a basic salary of seven million. Many have become friends or pen pals, while others have sponsored publication of *The Manor House Stories.* Occasionally, inevitably perhaps, a handful have been offhand, rude or even insulting; one unfortunate man had to be restrained from hitting me and over-turning my table. (He obviously felt very strongly that my shoes clashed with my slacks.) Some customers make a point of coming to see me just to chat and make sure I haven't published another book since we last met. This was all very encouraging, although there was one elderly gentleman who gradually became rather too frisky for my liking. Years ago I remember my aunt suffering from the same unwanted attention from an acquaintance in Sydney. She had asked a friend, an Irish Nun who worked in a nursing home, at what age men stopped thinking about sex.

"Not until they're dead, dear – and then give them another ten minutes!" she had advised.

Sometimes the managers of venues were unsympathetic. For one property in deepest Cornwall we had left Oxfordshire at three in the morning in order to arrive in good time before the property opened to the public. On my lap as usual, Dash looked longingly from the car as we boarded the King Harry Ferry five hours later, obviously remembering the much larger Minoan ferries that had sailed us from Venice to Corfu and back three or four times each year. His enthusiastically wagging tail told us he was hoping this little craft would once again be taking us to the warm waters of the Ionian. Eventually we arrived to find the venue locked and bolted, my appointment completely forgotten. As the first visitors of the day began to arrive in the car park, Jeremy set up my table in the shade of an oak tree near the entrance, where we decided to remain after the staff finally deigned to open the grounds, rather than move closer to the shop.

As we packed up later that afternoon Jeremy totted up my sales and informed the manager. I had sold sixty-one copies, but the shop had only taken payments for forty-five. Evidently some customers had conveniently forgotten to walk to the till in the shop.

"So you've obviously been selling them yourself instead of sending the customers to pay in here." she snapped, making Jeremy immediately see red.

"How dare you accuse my wife of selling her books under the table!" he exploded.

When I saw her face turn purple I grabbed Jeremy's arm and dragged him away before he really got stuck in.

* * *

At a pre-Christmas signing day at Blenheim Palace, a freelance journalist whose articles and photographs were used in *Cotswold Life* and other such magazines came to interview me. He made notes as he asked questions, then took a few photos of me holding a copy of *Lady Davina Dove – A Christmas Story,* in front of the enormous Christmas tree in the gift shop. This photo also appeared in colour on the front of the *Oxford Times* and generated quite a few sales from my website. Unfortunately they spelt my name wrong, so I telephoned the editor and he kindly offered to put in a correction, so I received an extra bit of publicity.

When I started modelling way back in 1969, my parents kept a scrap book of newspaper and magazine cuttings; I still have it to this day, but sadly there is one particular event for which I have no photograph. In the early 70's I had been a finalist in the *Miss Great Britain* contest and in May 1975 I had won the *Miss Torbay* competition. My last national competition was in 1976 when I was crowned *Miss Heineken* – part of the prize was a trip to Amsterdam to tour the lager factory. I loathed Heineken so I skipped the tour altogether and visited the art galleries instead.

I had only entered these outmoded competitions as a shortcut to furthering my career as a fashion and photographic model; nevertheless a year of fun and a little glamour followed as Miss Torbay. A full diary had been arranged for the year of my reign and a white Rolls Royce Corniche, complete with liveried chauffeur, had been provided to carry me to the first month's various functions. In June I was asked to be the mascot of the Third Royal Tank Regiment who were coming to Torbay on a promotional tour. In the early evening they were hosting a cocktail party for the Mayor of Torbay and local dignitaries to which I was invited. I was told the regiment would arrange transport for me to the party and I was to be ready at 5pm. I wore a cream silk cocktail dress and at 5pm on the dot the doorbell of my parents' home rang. Mummy answered the door to two young soldiers in army fatigues. We invited them in and they handed me a green boiler suit, advising me I would need to wear it over my dress. I must have looked very puzzled but did as I was told – not liking to question the polite uniformed chaps. I soon found out why I had to cover up.

At the bottom of our drive my transport awaited me; the two soldiers looked highly amused as I gasped at the sight of two colossal tanks parked in the avenue. Gamely I clambered aboard the first and was asked to stand, upright and unsupported, in the

Commander's hatch on top of the gun turret, where I would have to remain for the drive to the seafront. As the tank started to move onto the main road I hadn't been prepared for the very jerky way a tank turns on its caterpillar tracks and I was thrown forwards and back quite violently. My young soldier escort standing next to me gallantly offered to hold me tightly around my waist; he was obviously enjoying himself and I had a suspicion the whole exercise had been planned well in advance. He confessed a little later that 'the lads' had drawn straws for the job.

After a very enjoyable party in a large marquee on Paignton Green, my transport home was a smart staff car, which thankfully was far more comfortable than the tank and didn't require me to wear the boiler suit again. However nobody took a photo of me in the tank and I so wish they had. My darling Pop dined out on the story for years, recounting with glee how he had driven into our quiet tree lined avenue to be staring down the barrels of two neatly parked tanks and saying to himself, 'This can only be something to do with my daughter!'

A few days later I was on a trip from Plymouth to Torquay on the anti-submarine frigate HMS Torquay. I was to be entertained to lunch in the Officer's Mess after being shown around the warship. I thoroughly enjoyed being piped aboard and thought I had chosen my outfit perfectly; considering the amount of ships' ladders I would have to climb below decks, a skirt was out of the question. Instead I wore white leather hotpants with over the knee white leather boots and to add a nice nautical touch, a red and white spotty top trimmed with navy blue piping; the sailors seemed to like it too, oddly enough. Stuart, a photographer from the local paper who accompanied me to every event that year, assembled some of the ship's company on the foredeck to take photos of me being held horizontally by four of them like a beached mermaid, wearing one of the officer's caps, much to their amusement.

Unfortunately as soon as I went below decks I began to feel decidedly seasick. Warships are not designed to be comfortable; nor, for that matter, do they smell like a bed of roses. My queasiness became progressively worse as the ship ploughed into open water, which was distinctly rough that day. I did my best to take an interest in the hot, fume laden engine room and to ask sensible questions, nodding wisely without understanding a word of the answers. I was escorted into the Mess where a table was laid for 12 officers and myself, the smell of cooking making me feel even worse. I have never liked poultry and was horrified by the plate of bony chicken casserole before me. I drank glass after glass of water and tried to hide the chicken under the mashed potato, just picking at the vegetables. I politely refused the spotted dick and custard for pudding as the ship rolled to the swell. It was a nightmare and the kind officers must have thought me extremely boring and dull; I hardly dared speak for fear of throwing up all over the table. Pretending to be fascinated by navigation, I asked if I could be taken up to the bridge for the last leg of the trip. I imagined I would feel better if I could at least see where we were going, but I hadn't reckoned on the height of the bridge, which accentuated the ship's fearful rolling. After this experience it was even more surprising that I dared to set out from Salcombe five years later with Jeremy on our first catamaran *Aries* to sail the 3,000 miles to Cyprus for an extended honeymoon.

During that memorable Miss Torbay year I had suddenly developed chronic hay fever. This came as a shock, having never even sneezed during all the years I had been riding and dealing with hay on a daily basis. However 1975 was the first year oil seed rape had been grown as a commercial crop in Devon; thousands of people began to suffer badly from allergies to its pollen and many more baulked at the sight of the foreign, bright yellow crop covering the countryside. My duties included personal appearances every evening – seven days a week during May, June and July – at various hotels and venues in Torbay. On stage I would be given a microphone to introduce myself and the Carnival Committee volunteers, who would then sell raffle tickets to the audience. The considerable proceeds were distributed amongst local charities at the end of the year.

As soon as flaming June began, being the hottest and driest summer on record, so did my hayfever symptoms. Mummy and I swam every day on the beach, a couple of minutes walk from our house, but I would always have to get ready for the evening as soon as we had finished our afternoon tea. Blow drying my long hair in my very hot bedroom, before putting on full 'stage' make up, was almost impossible with watering eyes and constant sneezing. My outfit was always a long white evening dress, turquoise satin sash, very high white heels, a long red velvet cloak and of course the large, heavy, sparkly crown.

I would arrive in my MG Midget and be escorted into the building, then onto the stage and into the unforgiving spotlight. With a red nose, watery eyes with false eyelashes clinging on for dear life – tissues tucked inside the top of my dress – I would attempt to greet the visitors. But before I had uttered a few words the violent sneezing would start again, throwing my head forward and toppling the crown onto the floor before me. To my surprise, as I apologised and explained about the hayfever, there was always a ripple of sympathetic murmuring amongst the audience, many nodding and others sneezing, to reassure me they too were suffering. Many years later a doctor suggested I took non-drowsy antihistamines from February each year, in the hope this would build up my immunity before the pollen season. It worked! Strangely I never had hay fever whilst living in Cyprus, Spain or Corfu; but none of those countries grew oil seed rape.

Towards the end of May I had been a guest at the Devon County Show; after many years of competing there on Adonis, I should have known that it invariably rained, turning the walkways into a sea of liquid red mud. However as a beauty queen I could hardly appear in jodhpurs, wellies and a raincoat during my television interview. The cameraman asked the interviewer and me to step off the raised floor of the trade stand because we were too shaded, so we both stepped down straight onto some very soggy turf. It took just a couple of seconds for my five inch high cork platform wedge sandals to sink and the cameraman shouted 'Cut!' as my head slid out of shot. The well known presenter began the process for a second time but only got as far as the introduction before I started sinking again. Much to his embarrassment I asked if I could hold on to his shoulder as he continued. This didn't help at all, as we both began to sink into the quagmire, whereupon he became rather cross and cut the interview short, complaining loudly about the wet mud on his shoes and trousers.

I adored my platform shoes because they raised my modest height to a respectable 5ft 11inches, but couldn't be seen under a full length evening dress or the fashionable wide leg trousers; they were very nearly my downfall on another occasion that summer. One of the venues was approached by a very steep ramp from the car park to the entrance. I got out of the Midget as usual in full regalia and began my descent towards the entrance, where the carnival committee were waiting for me at the bottom of the slope. I quickly realised I had no control over my progress and was gathering speed at an alarming rate. Faster and faster down the incline I tottered, in great danger of falling flat on my very made-up face.

"I can't stop!" I yelled, in a most unladylike fashion. "Catch me!"

Moving as one, a few volunteers raced forward with arms out-stretched as I crashed into them like a runaway train into the buff-ers. The crown flew through the air into a flower bed and gales of laughter assailed the Mayoral party who were waiting inside the hotel. It was only when one of the committee asked to look at my shoes that she discovered the front of the sole turned upwards, like Geisha shoes: it was like trying to balance without toes, so I had absolutely no chance of stopping on a downhill slope. I have kept these ankle breakers to show my grandchildren one day … they will never believe how I walked in them at all.

Without doubt my most enjoyable duty that year was to meet Dame Margot Fonteyn the day after I had seen her dance at the Festival Theatre. The official reception was held at Oldway Mansion, the stunning Palladian mansion originally built in the 19th Century by Isaac Singer, of sewing machine fame; it was later rebuilt in the style of the Palace of Versailles by his son Paris Singer for his mistress, the renowned dancer Isadora Duncan. From the moment Margot came on to the stage in the role of Juliet to dance the balcony scene, I would have defied anyone in the audience to believe she was any more than a fourteen year-old girl. Margot was in her mid-fifties at the time.

I was introduced to her at the reception and as we shook hands and I curtseyed, the photographer from the local paper was clicking away. Knowing I would be meeting her, my parents had bought me Margot Fonteyn's autobiography and I had kept it with me. I asked her to sign it, which she did as more photos were taken. I will never forget how gorgeous she looked in her little mink pillbox hat, her dark hair smoothed into a neat 'ballet bun'; she turned her beautiful smile towards me.

"I hate having photographs taken these days; it's all right for you being young and pretty, but I am far too old!" she sighed.

Nowadays I can begin to understand how she felt.

I couldn't believe how such a world famous dancer, prima ballerina of the Royal Ballet, could be so modest. Of course I remonstrated with her and told her most people would kill for her fine features, large eyes and high cheek bones. I couldn't bring myself to add that her sparkling personality and expansive smile would have given her a radiance even if she were a hundred – that really would have sounded too grovelling, even if it was plain for all to see. I remembered what Karen Blixen, author of *Out of Africa*, had commented after meeting Marilyn Monroe: '*I think Marilyn is bound to make an almost overwhelming impression on the people who meet her for the first time. It is not that she is pretty, although she is of course almost incredibly pretty, but she radiates, at the same time, unbounded vitality and a kind of unbelievable innocence.*'

Naturally I could not have known at the time that my future mother-in-law had been a friend of Margot Fonteyn for many years, although she remained one of the few stars of the ballet world not to have visited the Chaplin's farm in South Devon.

Chapter 7
Crossing the Tamar

Last night I dreamt I went to Manderley again …

Rebecca, Daphne du Maurier

In March 2015 we were given notice to quit our rented cottage in Oxfordshire, not because of the marijuana we were farming in the sitting room, but because the owners were returning to occupy it. After four years living under the same roof with our grown up children without killing each other – actually in a surprising harmony undreamt of by many families – it was quite a shock to realise we would once again be scattered to the winds of fate. At every available opportunity we scanned the internet for suitable and affordable properties; Miranda had to be as close as possible to the hunting stables near Chipping Norton where she exercised and cared for the pampered horses; Rory needed to remain in the Cotswolds where the majority of his wealthy clients were based. But Jeremy, Dash and I had the chance to return to our beloved westcountry again. After a month of searching, Miranda had decided on a tiny house in an unspoilt Oxfordshire village. Rory had very handily found himself a charming cottage and a warehouse, for his ever growing mountains of equipment, that were both on the same farm.

But Jeremy and I had seen nothing we could consider or afford in Devon, however far into the grass-in-the-middle-of-the-road wilds we ventured. Grim grey bungalows in some godforsaken settlement miles from as much as a postbox, or north-facing annexes in rundown farmhouses surrounded by rusting piles of corrugated iron and dead tractors were all we could find. Soon our search took us over the Cornish border, where the choice seemed little better. I was beginning to panic. Then, before dawn one morning I opened the computer and typed in *Converted barns to rent in North Cornwall*. Scrolling through the images, one leapt out of the screen at me: a long granite cottage with a low red door, a Grade 2 listed converted cowshed close to the North Cornish coast in a high village on the very edge of Bodmin Moor – Poldark Country!

I have adored North Cornwall all my life; my parents had a caravan in a farmer's field on the cliffs overlooking Treyarnon Bay, where we spent a summer holiday each year of my childhood and early teenage. Padstow was a traditional, unspoilt working fishing village in those days, boasting a butcher, baker, fishmonger, grocery shop, chandlery and Post Office. Sadly nowadays only the excellent Chough Bakery and a sub-Post Office in the local convenience shop remain, the rest of the premises long since taken over by pasty or fudge shops, trendy home decor gift shops and copycat clothing outlets found in most English towns. Every memory I had of Cornwall was happy; Jeremy and I had regularly taken Rory, Miranda and their friends for long days and short holidays by the sea from our home in South Devon. They had both learned to surf at Treyarnon and Polzeath and loved the area as much as we did. Martin Clunes summed it up perfectly when he reminisced that so many people had childhood memories of holidays in Cornwall, and how those old-fashioned holidays were hugely successful. Two of our oldest friends and one of my first cousins, 'Sue of the Roaring Candles,' lived near Penzance.

The little cottage must have been waiting for us and I knew instinctively we could be happy living in that magical and mystical land of a thousand legends across the Tamar. But I had yet to find out if it was still available and, more importantly, whether pets were allowed. It was an agonising wait until I could ring the agents.

Dash might well be welcome, they said, so I made an appointment to view the following day.

Jeremy studied the map closely and had to agree the position was perfect, the village itself overlooking unspoilt farmland undulating towards the coast between Port Isaac and Mawgan Porth; on the lane to the village there was even a spot known as Delphi – most propitious, given our passion for all things Greek. Could this be another sign? Would the Oracle greet us there? Leaving at dawn the next morning we eventually took a turning off the main road to Penzance four hours later. I had often noticed the little sign to St Breward on our trips to the beaches of North Cornwall; it seemed to point to nowhere but open moorland, not a building to be seen on the peaceful horizon. We crossed a cattle grid to find ourselves on an unkempt lane weaving across open moorland. Bordering the narrow road and growing in gay profusion all over the springy turf were bushes of gorse in full, golden flower, interrupted here and there by windswept hawthorns, granite boulders and outcrops. Here the high moors were above the tree line, apart from a few stunted oaks and stands of pine in the distance towards the twin granite tors of Rough Tor and Brown Willy.*

The sun blazed as I opened my window to breathe in the scents of coconut and honey from the butter yellow gorse blossom. There was ample time to take in the sights and sounds as we crawled between the sheep, ponies and Highland cattle who had decided the lane offered the best place to contemplate their good fortune, as they gazed immovable into the morning sun. A few minutes later Jeremy pulled off the lane and pointed out the Norman church tower at the farther edge of the village. I had with me a copy of a

---

*Brown Willy, the unfortunate butt of schoolboy humour, comes from the Cornish *Bronn Ewhella*, or Highest Hill.

charming passage from David Freeman's *St. Breward A History of a Cornish Village.*

> *Steeped deep in the ancient mists of history lies the ancient Cornish village of St. Breward. Set high above a green and enchanted land of legend and myth, lies the Cornish village of St. Breward nestling like a guardian above a timeless river, the Camel, where the valley's higher western slopes meet the great Moor of Bosvenegh.*
>
> *Here close by, rises the Camel river's moor born tributaries, the ice crystal De Lank, a haven for the playful otter and a world of rare fauna and flora. This too is where the picture book Jump and the Allen rise, quiet moorland streams where brook & rainbow trout and salmon have spawned since before the dark ages. Here too within the arms of St. Breward can be found ancient wells guarded in timeless glades by nymphs and faeries. These are places of great mystical power to which Celtic travellers and ancient pilgrims turned for cure and respite.*
>
> *Legend lives here amongst the mighty walls of St. Breward's shield. And beneath her cloak, for those who wish to seek it, if they look closely, find it they shall.*

Our first glimpse of the cottage quite took our breath away; it looked like something from *Hansel and Gretel*, snuggling cosily into the contours of its gently sloping garden seven hundred feet above sea level. The sagging Cornish slate roof resembled a gently undulating wave, showing the character of its great age and giving the appearance of having slowly settled into the hillside over the centuries. Stopping in front of the five-bar gate, we fell in love with the cottage on sight and prayed the interior would live up to expectations.

"Ah, lovely Cornish granite!" I exclaimed, patting the wall as the owner and his agent greeted us at the front door.

My enthusiasm seemed to please them as Jeremy and I admired the crystalline stone sparkling in the sun. I recalled Peta telling me how some granite even glittered in the rain. Inside, the cottage was even more delightful; vaulted ceilings gave a feeling of space and thick stone walls the colour and texture of clotted cream retained all their original curves, lumps and bumps from the 1540s, when Henry VIII was still on the throne. The owner beamed when I begged him to accept us as tenants: we would improve the garden – which had run wild – and never trouble him when a drain was blocked or a light bulb needed changing; Jeremy, I reassured him, had once built a house and was highly competent and practical. This must have struck a chord with him, as we later learnt that the previous tenant had been a young single mother who, quite understandably, couldn't manage to change the numerous recessed lights in the high-ceilinged kitchen.

We took the short drive to Port Isaac to get a glimpse and a sniff of the nearest seashore before driving back to landlocked Oxfordshire. After four years away from the coast, it was sheer bliss to hear the cry of seagulls as they wheeled over our heads and to inhale the tang of seaweed on the rocks mingling with salty ozone air blowing straight in from the wild Atlantic. Little could I imagine that within a couple of months I would become an accepted member of the small Port Isaac community and be affectionately nicknamed 'The Book Lady'. The following day a call from the agents confirmed the cottage was ours. It was the best possible news in four long years. As our eviction day approached, the cottage was gradually cleared and cleaned until it looked better than we had found it. Jeremy spent days on his hands and knees shampooing the carpets, only for the doltish landlord to trample all over them in his muddy wellies when we returned the keys.

On a glorious morning in May, Rory and one of his employees drove two of his events business vans to Cornwall, each one brimful with as many of our belongings as we thought would fit into the tiny cottage; our Georgian and Victorian four-poster beds and larger pieces of furniture would have to remain in storage for a little longer. We led the way in Rory's car, also full to the gunwales, Dash fast asleep on my lap as usual, only waking as our tyres rumbled across the first cattle grid on the moor. He sat up and looked through the windscreen, wagging his tail madly at the sight of a little river ahead; he was anticipating a paddle but we had no time to stop. The ancient granite clapper bridge, the Delphi Jeremy had noticed on the map, would become one of his favourite places in his final years, traversing as it did a deep river pool with a little spit of coarse sand where he could paddle up to his chin and fetch sticks to his heart's content. He never would swim properly in cold English water, he was far too used to the warm sea in Corfu where he had grown up. Opening the door to our new home we were delighted to find new carpets and freshly painted walls throughout, not that we had remembered anything shoddy before. We had certainly fallen on our feet.

Jeremy, Rory and his helper unloaded all our furniture and placed each piece in the cottage before bringing in the boxes of smaller items, which had been labelled with the different rooms into which their contents should go. I unpacked as much as I could and made our bed. Dash scampered around the garden and in and out of the cottage, eventually choosing the back of the sofa to take a nap. By early evening the vans were empty, so we decamped to the village pub for supper. Next to the church, The Old Inn, the highest pub in Cornwall, was quaintly traditional, cosy and busy with locals; the food was excellent and the portions more than the two boys could eat. Dash was treated to bits of sausage and from that night on, every time we walked past the pub in the following years, he would strain on his lead to try to get back in again.

The following day, our 35th wedding anniversary, dawned as

sunny and bright as our wedding day. I couldn't believe we were actually waking up in Cornwall; I dashed out of the heavy front door into the garden to relish the scent of moors and fields and to watch the gulls flying overhead towards the fishing grounds off Padstow and Port Isaac. There was so much sky! There was not a cloud to be seen, only the con trails of transatlantic aeroplanes leaving a cat's cradle of white streamers across the vast expanse of powder blue. Swallows flitted above my head, swooping and diving between the treetops. At the top of the garden was a bank which was a riot of wild flowers, overhung with honeysuckle; it made me think of the beautiful description from *A Midsummer Night's Dream* where Shakespeare refers to honeysuckle by the older name of woodbine.

I know a bank where the wild thyme grows, where oxslips and the nodding violet grows. Quite over-canopied with luscious woodbine, with sweet musk-roses and with eglantine: there sleeps Titania sometime of the night.... My two oldest friends, Tony and Peta, called to say they would be coming up from their home near St. Just to help us celebrate our anniversary; they had been at our wedding in 1980 when their young daughter Reseigh had been one of my bridesmaids. I explained that I had only unpacked a kettle and four mugs so far and couldn't promise much in the way of lunch.

"Don't worry!" they said, "We'll bring everything with us for a picnic in the garden."

I urged them not to set off too early, aware that I would have to make myself presentable after such a hectic twenty-four hours. I had retained a horror of guests arriving prematurely ever since Jeremy's parents had surprised us – and not in a good way – at our home in Spain many years ago.

Back in 1988 we had expected Liz and Michael to arrive at our remote *finca* near Jesús Pobre at least three full days after their ferry docked at Calais. I should have known that my inconsiderate father in-law would have different ideas. Scorching southward towards Spain in the Spring sunshine, the uncrowded *routes nationales* and motorways had gone to his head as he harked back to the pleasures of pre-war motoring in France. Once he was behind the wheel it was all Liz could do to persuade her obstinate husband to stop for fuel before the tank ran dry, let alone stop for lunch. Somewhere before the Spanish border, and only after threatening to open the passenger door and hurl herself onto the motorway, Liz finally persuaded Michael to stop for the night.

My mother-in-law's fondly anticipated leisurely saunter through the French countryside had turned into the Monte Carlo Rally and in consequence my dear parents-in-law arrived two days early, eventually telephoning us for final directions through the orange groves when they were less than ten minutes away. At the time my arm was elbow-deep in a blocked shower drain in the guest casita, baby Miranda was sleeping in her pram in the *naya*, five year-old Rory was haring around the courtyard on his go kart and Jeremy was in a trench, laying a new electricity cable to the pool house; but that didn't prevent Liz and Michael begging for something – anything – to eat as soon as they got out of the car. Painfully aware of her husband's driving habits, Liz had scavenged four apples and a lump of cheddar from their Sussex home and carefully rationed them out as they journeyed south. Later she proudly offered me the remaining sweaty morsel of cheese she had so carefully saved, in case I craved some wholesome English cheddar. I politely refused the offer, knowing from experience that it was probably covered in mould long before it had been salvaged from their fridge for the journey. Liz's larder had always been stuffed with carefully hoarded provisions, nearly all of which had been clumsily re-sealed and long since passed their sell-by dates. A bag of cashew nuts still stands out as a particular low point: originally opened seven years before she had offered them to our children, they were crawling with maggots. Then there was the lobster bisque she served to Jeremy when he had arrived late one night during our engagement, after which he was violently ill for three days. Rummaging through the dustbin four days later, Jeremy found the offending tin still carrying the price label from a shop in Salcombe that had closed twenty years earlier. Well, that's what living through the Blitz did to you, I suppose.

When Liz had first stayed with us in Devon after Jeremy and I returned from Cyprus, she insisted she would accompany me on my weekly trip to the nearest supermarket. Having successfully crossed everything off my long list and trundled gratefully to the checkout desk, I was surprised to find my trolley almost empty. Unseen, my dear mother-in-law had removed half of my grocery items as fast as I was picking them off the shelves, certain it was her duty to turn me into a frugal, or preferably parsimonious house-wife. '*Two* loaves of bread?' she had exclaimed in horror. 'What an extravagance! Surely you can come back again the day after tomor-row for another fresh one!' (And drive twelve miles there and back to get it, was my unspoken reply). Her accusation of profligacy was particularly hard to swallow, coming as it did from someone who chose to cross the Atlantic in Concord.

The most comical part of my mother-in-law's criticisms, now so fondly remembered, is that Jeremy and I are inescapably and irre-versibly turning into our parents. This is slightly depressing, even when we are grudgingly assured we have also inherited one or two of our parents' many virtues.

Increasingly often we catch ourselves mirroring their idiosyncra-sies, including their life threatening fridge and larder oversights, their determined refusal to master any remote control or admit to their deafness, their sham horror at the price of posting a birthday card and a pathological inability to watch the evening news without shouting at the television. We have even been caught repeating the same infuriating lines we had vowed never to utter to our own children when the time eventually came. Jeremy's hearing is certainly not what it used to be, in fact he becomes deaf as a post – and therefore somewhat unresponsive – in a crowded room or whenever background music is played. 'Retard?,' boomed a loud Irish lady at a wedding reception recently. My husband felt the hot lava of outrage beginning to rise at such an affront until the lady added 'Or do you still work?'.

Laden with baskets of food and a chilled bottle of Champagne, Tony and Peta arrived punctually for morning coffee, which they knew full well was always served promptly at eleven in any Chaplin household. After proudly showing them around our little cottage, we sat in the sun around a makeshift table of packing cases and ate our hot pasties with the bubbly, followed by perfectly ripe Cornish strawberries and lashings of clotted cream.

Keen to show us the area where they had spent many holidays as teenagers, they drove us around the neighbouring hamlets and sights – I would say beauty spots, but we were utterly surrounded by a beautiful rural idyll. Jeremy did comment on the great number of chapels and reading rooms that popped up wherever more than three cottages and a telephone box formed a settlement; he began wondering if after all Stella Gibbons' hilarious *Cold Comfort Farm*, with its cast of Quivering Brethren and the dysfunctional Starkadder family, was more properly set on Bodmin Moor. We learnt later that anyone in Cornwall who acts a bit strange is described as having 'gone Bodmin'.

The tranquil scenery and its miles of untouched moorland has looked very different in the past. It is difficult to imagine the scale of industrialisation that scarred this landscape a hundred and more years ago, when granite was quarried and clay was dried within a mile of our cottage. Vast granite blocks from the local quarries were exported widely from Cornwall; the Singapore docks, the Eddystone lighthouse, the Royal Opera House and Tower Bridge all incorporate our local stone. Older cottages in the village, tiny one-up, one-down buildings, would all have been occupied by the hardy men who prised and chiselled the granite from the ground. (To deter the incessant nuisance calls we endure, I sometimes answer the phone with 'Bodmin Treacle Mines, can I help?,' which confuses fraudulent and genuine callers alike).

At last Tony parked on the track below Alex Tor, from where we walked to the top to admire the even wider views before us; a patchwork quilt of fields and uncultivated moorland spread out until it reached the sparkling ultramarine swathes of sea. As we picked our way back down the slope, we heard a cuckoo calling from the direction of distant conifer woods. In deference to an age-old superstition we all turned on our heels to walk a few paces uphill again as the cuckoo sang. Another cuckoo replied from a copse nearby, quite a rarity as none of us had ever heard two cuckoos answering. To Jeremy's great discomfort I started to sing a song remembered from my kindergarten and Peta gleefully joined in:

> *The cuckoo is a pretty bird, she singeth as she flies;*
> *She bringeth us good tidings, she telleth us no lies;*
> *She sucketh all sweet flowers to keep her throttle clear,*
> *And every time she singeth cuckoo-cuckoo-cuckoo!*
> *The summer draweth near.*

On that glorious day we really felt the summer was around the corner; we were so fortunate to be in Cornwall and to have the whole county to revisit and explore at our leisure.

Finding our way around the neighbourhood during the following days, our first and very necessary port of call was a village shop; at the time there were several in the surrounding hamlets, each one useful in its own way – one stocked Earl Grey teabags, another provided the best sourdough loaves and so on. If we had doubted that Cornwall lacked any of Corfu's delightful eccentricities, we needed to look no further. The shop windows displayed the usual clutter of notices and advertisements that form the heart of any caring village community; evidently there were clubs and gatherings to suit all tastes, even if some sounded a little obscure to newcomers. One poster invited villagers to watch an evening of Short Mat Bowling. (We have yet to meet Short Mat.) A local pub shockingly announced its new Children Eating Area, while an eye-catching leaflet in bold letters advertised a new date for the Alzheimers Support Group Coffee Morning, with *please don't forget this time!* scrawled angrily in red beneath. (We have noted the contact number in pessimistic anticipation.) Another notice announced a meeting of the local bipolar group – Jeremy became quite animated at the prospect of meeting many intrepid explorers of the ice-capped wastes.

(Most of the modern, politically correct mental health terminology hasn't yet appeared over my husband's horizon; nor can he get to grips with the host of acronyms beloved of minority groups these days. However he doesn't want to be left out and has decided he is chronically HS2-minus and borderline WD40. As for me, I have decided to self-identify as a Cavalier King Charles Spaniel).

The first time we visited our own cosy little village shop at the bottom of our hill, we found it bustling with customers busily chattering like a flock of rooks and not doing much shopping. It was surprisingly well stocked for such a small community, but it made us yearn for the nearest supermarket to The Lion House. As you will probably know, any shop in Corfu boasting a floor area larger than a ping pong table is considered a supermarket; but boy, did they know how to cram in the stock. At Yianni's *oporopantopoleío*, (a wonderfully long name for a shop that sells a little of everything under the sun), in the hamlet of Siniés, you could buy anything from Bollinger Champagne and Beluga caviar to weedkiller and wellies.

As our turn came to settle up for our basket of groceries – including some excellent local cheese – a flustered little old lady poked her head around the door and spoke to the assistant.

"Mary, can you ask young Kensa to come and pick me up?" she asked in broad Cornish. "My key's stopped working and I'm locked out of the car."

The assistant was about to dial the number when the old dear reappeared at the door.

" Cancel that, Mary," she said sheepishly. "Wrong car!"

"That Morwenna!" muttered the assistant. "Shouldn't be on the loose without her carers."

At that point the community shuttle bus drew up outside the front door, blocking the road as the driver got out and came to the doorway.

"Anyone for Tesco or Aldi?" he shouted mischievously at the customers in the shop.

"BUGGER OFF!" shouted the assistant in mock fury, before adding that she'd be expecting him for the pub quiz night later on.

It's all very refreshingly Greek.

The next two weeks passed in a happy blur of unpacking. Delightful as it was, the cottage was undeniably small and would have easily fitted in its entirety within the two sitting rooms of our old manor house. Nonetheless our remaining furniture seemed as if it had been made for the cottage, when it had eventually been squeezed through the front door; while I could step over the threshold with a three-inch clearance above my head, Jeremy almost had to fold himself in half to get under the lintel. Our unpacking marathon was only interrupted whenever we ventured too close to the five-bar gate onto the lane, where a gentle trickle of villagers passed by every so often, eager to meet the new foreigners. Introductions made and, in our case, names as quickly forgotten, Jeremy and I tried to sweeten the pill of our immigrant status by insisting we weren't proper outsiders, coming as we did from just over the border in South Devon. That proved a resounding mistake which only served to stir up the age-old rivalry between the two counties. Second home-owning Londoners would have been the more palatable option.

Our new neighbours, and the Cornish folk in general, were most agreeably welcoming by English standards. Had we been in Corfu our arrival would have been somewhat different … Neighbours would have thrown a goat on the barbecue in our honour; basil plants, bottles of home made wine, baskets of vegetables and lemons, a pomegranate and a kilo of olive oil would have been left by our front door; the local priest, the mayor and a dozen others would have called by unannounced for a glass of ouzo and everybody within a ten mile radius would have discovered our life stories, political leanings and blood groups before we could say *Zíto i Elláda* – long live Greece!

Over the following months we came to learn some of the vagaries of Cornish pronunciation. St Austell, for instance, is Saynozzle, or occasionally Snozzell; Launceston is Larnson and Rough Tor is Rowter. We learnt to marvel at Cornwall's jewellery box of place names, every one an etymological conundrum: Boxheater, Playing Place, Barriper, Indian Queens, Grumbla, Cripplesease,

Hugus, Skinner's Bottom and Bessie Beneath barely scratch the surface.

We no longer had the use of our children's cars, so our first task was to buy a vehicle of our own. In the days of plenty we had bought several cars for our children, but they certainly couldn't return the favour now – nor would we have expected them to. Jeremy settled on a barely roadworthy, sludge green family estate car of French origin for the sum of £600. It looked very much the same from front or back and ate so many batteries we wondered if it was an early prototype electric car. The beastly thing had to be push-started in the mornings, (having first identified the right end to push), but it trundled us about for the next two years. It was big enough for all the paraphernalia I took to signings, even if it did handle like an obese slug and was barely any speedier. But the shabby wreck did earn us some Brownie points with the locals as we trailed its plume of oily smoke around the countryside. At least we didn't own a Chelsea Tractor.

As I took my ease at the top of the garden one Sunday afternoon I decided I wanted to bring some of the characters from *The Manor House Stories* with me to Cornwall. Knowing a little of Cornwall's mining history and heritage, I decided to weave this into a story about Chuff, a young Cornish Chough, the national bird of Cornwall which appears on the Cornish coat of arms. (Incidentally my adjective is correct, as Cornwall is proud to consider itself a separate nation from England and Cornish folk are pleased to say they are travelling abroad whenever they cross the Tamar.)

I began to write some notes, the bones of the story about a chough who is hatched on the clifftops, falls over the edge and is rescued by a passing seagull who happens to be coastguard. The little choughling is too scared to try flying again, but when the youngsters from The Manor House arrive in their gypsy caravan for a holiday, the kind hearted Miss Miranda Mistlethrush understands his fear and gives him confidence with her 'magical' scarf. More adventures follow and Chuff decides to become an engineer in the winding house of his local tin mine, following in the footsteps of his father and grandfather. It seemed like a good idea, but some research would be needed first.

On an unusually blustery day in June we drove through thunderstorms towards Land's End and found our way to the Levant Tin Mine, now owned by the National Trust. Copper and tin had been mined in the Pendeen area for generations, the mine workings of Levant reaching a depth of 2,000 feet and extending over a mile beneath the sea bed. The Phoenicians had sailed as far as Cornwall to buy tin thousands of years ago, but the Levant Mine first appeared on a map in 1748, since when fortunes have been made and lost from tin mining. Between 1826 and 1840 seven new engines were brought on site as the age of steam arrived; but in 1919 Levant was the scene of a mining disaster in which thirty-one men were killed when a link on the 'man engine' snapped, sending the moving ladders down the shaft. That engine was never repaired and the deep levels were never worked again.

Donning waterproofs and wellies we made our way in the teeth of a gale down the rough track from the car park. Inside the little building we asked to join in the next guided tour. We were the only visitors at that time and when I explained our purpose a friendly volunteer told us there would be no charge for the tour. The smell of hot pasties crisping up in a little heated cabinet by the till made our mouths water and I asked if I could reserve a couple for lunch after the tour.

"Good idea; we always sell out quickly," said the volunteer, who had been intrigued by our connection to a founder of the National

Trust. "What name shall I put on the bags? … Hang on, I'll just write Rawnsley, that'll do nicely!"

The tour was at once fascinating and horrifying: a timid glimpse over the edge of a vertical shaft that disappeared two thousand feet through solid granite, straight as a die and hewn by hand, was utterly petrifying. Jeremy was fascinated by the engine house of the resurrected beam engine, where we were treated to the spectacle of the engineer starting up the steam driven monster for our benefit; this was the winding engine, the machine that had once hauled countless tons of ore to the surface every day. Its colossally heavy iron flywheel – some twelve feet in diameter – gradually built up speed amidst a rumble of turning shafts and the hissing of escaping steam until the floor beneath our feet shuddered. I tried to look enraptured, not being at all mechanically minded, but my eyes were drawn to a high windowsill on which sat a flourishing red geranium in a terracotta pot. At the end of the demonstration I asked why there was a pot plant in such an unlikely setting.

"Nobody's noticed that before!" laughed the wiry old engineer. "You see, the operators spent so much time in the engine houses they liked to make them look homely. They always had a red geranium, which they thought lucky; they even whitewashed the inside walls and some of the engine houses had curtains too!"

We ate our piping hot pasties in the car while the Atlantic gale rocked us about and stair rods of rain battered the roof, as condensation ran down inside the windows like translucent tadpoles racing each other to the bottom. We had never tasted such delicious pasties and, me being me, I kept the bag as a souvenir of a happy and fascinating day, despite the weather. We counted our blessings as we considered the brutal hardships of life as a Cornish miner, men, women and children all, in the 19th century. Few of the miners lived to see thirty, even on such a spectacular stretch of coast as this.†

I had decided to offer a page at the back of the book to the Cornwall Chough Preservation Network, which protects the nests of the birds and charts their progress throughout the year. Throughout the centuries when mining had made fortunes for Cornwall's mine owners, choughs had been prolific. The Cornish name for chough is *Palores*, meaning digger, as choughs dig in the earth with their long, curved scarlet beaks, seeking out their diet of invertebrates. The miners grazed their livestock on the clifftops, thus keeping the vegetation at a low level and enabling the birds to reach their food source. As the local mining industry declined and the miners moved away, taking their livestock with them, a dense scrub of brambles and gorse soon covered the clifftops and the choughs could no longer dig for their food. They abandoned Cornwall and settled in Pembrokeshire. In recent years the Chough Network, in partnership with the National Trust, have reintroduced grazing animals to the clifftops of Cornwall and the choughs have returned to breed on the cliffs. At a meeting with the regional manager of the charity, I learnt that she and other volunteers guarded the nesting sites day and night during the breeding season to deter any despicable collectors from stealing the eggs.

It reminded me of the time, at the suggestion of Sir David Attenborough, I painted a picture of the Red Kite and donated it to an auction in aid of the birds, organised by the Royal Society for Nature Conservation. Red Kites were on the brink of extinction in Britain, only 60 birds remained in the wild, all of them clustered in

---

† A couple of years later we were invited by the PR manager of Geevor Mine to a service of remembrance at the Miners' Church, St. John the Baptist at Pendeen. It was a moving ceremony in which the names of the miners who had died in the Levant disaster were read out, after which a traditional tea of saffron buns was enjoyed by us all.

the hanging oak woods of Wales. Luckily I tracked down a female Red Kite in captivity at the Hawk Conservancy Trust in Andover, where I was able to sit in front of Blodwyn's aviary to make sketches and take photographs. She modelled like a true professional, even stretching her long wings so I could get a better view of the underside plumage.

Rory and Miranda were with us and we decided to watch the display of falconry with the other visitors. At the age of three, Miranda would not be parted from her favourite soft toy, Roger Rabbit, so he sat beside her on the bench as we watched the display. As an enormous Eagle Owl was flying back to its handler, it suddenly veered off course, swooped towards us with its six-foot wingspan, dived between Jeremy and Miranda, grabbed Roger and flew off with him! Poor Miranda wailed in horror and burst into floods of tears until the handler managed to extricate the lifelike rabbit from the bird's claws. She hadn't been alarmed in the slightest by the ferocious beak and talons that had come within inches of her face; her only concern was for poor Roger. Jeremy had caught the whole thing on his video camera, until he dropped it at the last second to shield Miranda. The attack looked compellingly horrific as the huge bird flew nearer until its body outgrew the viewfinder, but some choice expletives had to be edited out before the children could watch the footage.

An extraordinary thing had happened to me later that week, something to confirm my unshakeable belief in the afterlife and that our departed loved ones can help us from above. There was a very tight deadline for the painting to be finished, mounted and framed before the auction. My time for painting was also limited to the school day, when Miranda was at nursery and Rory was a young day boy at prep school. A kind neighbour in the village had given me her entire collection of back copies of RSPB colour magazines, thinking they might come in useful for research in those pre-internet days. I needed a picture of the hanging woods in Wales for the background of my painting, so I went into the office that had been my father's bedroom for the year before he died peacefully in his sleep. Looking at the towering pile of magazines my heart sank; I knew it would take me all day to go through them to search for what I needed, even if a picture of the hanging woods was by some miracle to be found amongst the hundreds of pages. So I closed my eyes and said out loud: 'Oh Pop, please help!'

Before he died my father had always assisted me with my art-work whenever he could; in those pre-internet days he must have spent hours trawling the local libraries for pictures and references I needed, sometimes painstakingly sifting through my own col-lection of natural history books for a particular specimen. With my eyes tightly closed I thrust my hand into the pile of magazines and drew out the first one my fingers touched. I let it fall open by itself and opened my eyes. In front of me was an article about Red Kites with a double page spread of a colour photograph entitled *The Hanging Oak Woods of Wales.* I raced into the kitchen with the open magazine to tell Jeremy, who looked at me as if I had finally lost my marbles, but he said nothing; he knew me better than to suggest it was just a coincidence. This was not to be the only time something inexplicably similar would happen to me; over the years we have been married Jeremy has learnt not to scoff, but to listen attentively and keep his counsel.

A month later Jeremy and I had attended the auction at Phillips in Cardiff; the previous evening we were invited to a reception and preview where the items for auction were on display. I was very nervous that nobody would want my painting, so I told Jeremy he must bid for it, even if we ended up buying it. Luckily the bidding went well and it fetched the highest price of the sale, being bought by a director of Rothschilds Bank. We eventually made greeting cards of the painting and sold the whole print run, donating a percentage from the sale of each card to the RSPB who were protecting the Red Kites in Wales. We were delighted to read in the press the following spring that Gurkha soldiers had been deployed to guard the nesting sites. The success of the project was astounding and a multitude of Red Kites now grace the skies over Britain once more. Whenever we visit Rory and Miranda in Oxfordshire these days, we spot so many Red Kites that I have driven my family to distraction by shouting through the sunroof 'I helped to save you!'

(Since then, on a blistering hot summer's day in Cornwall, I had been preparing some books at the top of the garden when a familiar call made me look up into the clear blue sky. I was astounded to see some Red Kites soaring high overhead on the thermals. At first I thought they must be buzzards, but as they swooped lower I spotted their distinctive forked tails. I watched them fly directly above me, one bird gliding a few metres over my head. I stood in disbelief as they disappeared towards the coast, thrilled to have seen no less than five of these beautiful birds in Cornwall for the first time. Similarly we had only ever seen one wild Chough before, at our friends' house which sits near the clifftops beyond St. Just; on a clear day you could see the Isles of Scilly from their garden. We had just been mulling over my idea for a children's book about a Cornish Chough, when one flew low directly over our heads – something our friends had never witnessed in all the years they had lived there. Naturally I took it as a sign.)

Whether coincidence or the paranormal, my experience with the pile of magazines was repeated a few months later, when I had awoken one morning and told Jeremy about the oddest dream I had just had. I didn't usually tell him about the really peculiar ones for fear he would summon the men in white coats. In this particular dream I was standing in a parched field of dry grass with a flock of baby ostrich chicks around my feet. Never very interested in my strange dreams, Jeremy grunted and went downstairs to make early morning tea.

"Just look at this!" he exclaimed as he returned five minutes later with my tray.

He handed me a postcard that had just been delivered by our postman. It was from my aunt in Sydney, with a charming colour photograph of a dessicated patch of Australian grassland covered in a flock of baby ostriches! I so wish I could channel these premonitions whenever important decisions have to be made; as Hamlet so famously said: 'There are more things in heaven and earth, Horatio, than are dreamt of in your philosophy.'

Jeremy, on the other hand, is certain that dreams are all connected to diet. For supper not so long ago I made my vegetarian version of *melitzana bourekia* and added a generous splash of Sossis Kiros' home made village wine; somehow the bottle had found its way into our luggage from Kassiopi and thence into the garden shed, where it had lingered for too many years. Idiotically I hadn't tasted the bottle first, otherwise I would have known its contents had undergone multiple fermentation cycles and turned into a dangerous mixture of rocket propellant and sheep dip. I had a splitting headache all night and eventually fell asleep just before dawn, when I dreamt a Greek priest, intent on killing me, was chasing me around the polished marble floors of Athens Airport; he was driving a bright orange plastic motor scooter in the shape of a giant lobster. Jeremy put it down to eating cooked cheese before bedtime, but I knew otherwise. Next time I'm in Athens Airport, I'll be on the lookout.

* * *

After much deliberation, we decided to take a risk and self publish *The Holiday – A Chough's Tale* in a glossy softback format, which would be far less expensive to produce than the top quality hardback books with silk marker ribbons and dust jackets of *The Manor House Stories* titles. Nevertheless, cost was an issue and we were doing this as a risky experiment. I wrote to a couple of Cornish companies, one selling coffee and tea and the other making pasties and biscuits, to ask if they would be prepared to help; luckily they both agreed but there was a still a substantial shortfall. I had almost given up hope until I decided to contact the very last company on my list – Specsavers in Bodmin. I didn't hold out much hope; it was such a large national company and I doubted anyone at the Bodmin branch would be interested. Later that day I took a call from the lady Director, asking me to put all the details in an email. I offered her an entry on the sponsors' page with the added enticement of having the Specsavers logo printed in a corner of the back cover. Within a couple of days I had my answer. A slot was immediately booked with the printers and I was about to become a publisher. Every journey begins with a single step.

In the meantime I wasted no time finding local outlets for my existing books. My first book signing in Cornwall was at Pencarrow, a privately owned Palladian mansion ten minutes drive from our cottage. The Cornish name Pencarrow means 'head of the valley' or 'high fort' and as you drive down the mile-long carriage road you pass through the remains of the Iron Age hill fort; there has been a dwelling on the site for centuries. I felt the atmosphere of the souls who have lived here as we drove through an mysterious copse of eerie looking tall, slim trunked trees that could have easily been one of Tolkien's inspirations for *Lord of the Rings*. I was shown to a little tearoom with charming vintage chairs and tables covered in chintz oilcloth. As I was setting up my display for the day Lady

Iona Molesworth-St.Aubyn, the elderly Chatelaine of Pencarrow, popped in to say hello. A cousin by marriage of our friends at St. Michael's Mount, Lady M admired my books over cups of coffee as we chatted about mutual friends and our pet dogs until the first customers began to arrive.

A few days later Lady M telephoned me and during our conversation she confided that she was terribly worried about one of her chickens; this hen had gone broody and wouldn't leave her eggs, although she had been sitting for so long that they must have addled. The rest of her white hens had been taken by the fox, so this hen was the only remaining white chicken in the flock; she had become rather lonely as the other common brown hens bullied her and left her out of their social gatherings. So, like the Ugly Duckling, she had trotted off all on her own to lay her eggs. Sadly she didn't turn into a swan but was obviously hopeful of hatching a brood of her own.

"She really needs to go to a good home where she'll be safe from the fox," said Iona.

The whole episode was beginning to resemble a theme for P G Wodehouse, in fact *Lady Molesworth's Chicken – The Feathers Fly at Pencarrow,* sounded like a story he had actually written. Lady M had a vast estate to look after and many staff to chivvy along, yet she was obviously most concerned about the welfare of one paltry chicken. I offered to pop up to our neighbouring farmer to see if he would take the bird. His farm was only fifty yards up the lane from us, a distance from our garden that his own hens found conveniently short; moreover they evidently thought our cottage had once been home to their ancestors and were intent on repossession. Jeremy, having been brought up on a farm with the most wayward and unruly animals imaginable, has caught and returned them many times. A few days later Dash and I spotted a white chicken pecking and scratching happily amongst the brown hens. According to her new owners, she had been delivered to them by Lady M in person, much to their astonishment, and had been happily accepted into the resident gang. The hen turned out to be a very good layer, which just goes to show that a happy chicken is a productive chicken.

Beyond Pencarrow in the quaint fishing village of Port Isaac I discovered a tiny bookshop tucked away in a courtyard at the top of the village. Taking my courage in both hands, which also held copies of the three *Manor House Stories*, I went in to look for the owner. I am by nature very shy. As a child I hid behind my mother's skirts if anyone approached and as a teenager I could never enter the local church youth club unless my cousins were there to meet me at the door. It was a disadvantage I had fought very hard to conquer, but on this occasion I need not have worried. I was cheerfully greeted by a delicious Cornish voice.

"Hello my love, how are you?"

A twinkly eyed gentleman with smoky white hair sat behind a little counter and peered at me over gold-rimmed half spectacles. I was greatly encouraged by the welcome and asked him if he would be interested in stocking my little books. I placed them on the counter. He wasn't sure; they were very nice, but he had too much stock already and had no room for more.

"Can I just leave you these three and see if you have any interest?" I suggested.

"All right my love, leave them here and we'll see. Cheerio for now."

I gave him a business card and left. Jeremy and I were halfway home when my phone rang.

"Well your books have all gone; a lady came in just after you left and bought the lot. So I fancy you'd better bring me some more!"

Mike said with delight.

Little did I know at the time how this single sale would lead to six years of weekly book signings outside Mike's shop, from early Spring to late Autumn – the year of the Pandemic lockdowns excepted. Hundreds of my books have been sold from this tiny shop in Port Isaac, where regular visitors from all over the world have returned year after year to buy the latest titles.

Mike was interested to know why my books had not yet attracted the attention of a major publisher; at the time I was still hoping a high-end publishing house would take them on. Mike suggested I had a word with Jon Cleave, the charismatic bass singer in the Port Isaac sea shanty group, *Fisherman's Friends,* who had also written some children's books. Jon was kind and helpful and over a coffee outside his shop he suggested I self publish, as he did. We had barely heard of the group but, discovering they sang some Friday evenings on the beach by the harbour when the tide permitted, we decided to go along. The following Friday Jeremy Dash and I sat down on the Platt, (for landlubbers that's the open space by the harbour where fishermen traditionally mend and store their pots and nets), with boxes of fish and chips and some local cider from the bar beside the slipway; soon the Platt filled with people and by the time the group had finished setting up on the beach there wasn't an inch to spare. We were entranced as soon as they struck up with *Santiana*, a rousing sea shanty to which the old lags in the audience sang along with gusto.

The small horseshoe bay set in its own bowl of high cliffs provided the perfect acoustics and the music reverberated around the lower village; by the time the group were winding up two hours later the crowd's singing almost drowned out 'the buoys,' as they have dubbed themselves. There was no charge for the entertainment, but at the end of the evening volunteers went around the audience with buckets collecting for local charities, (or as one of the band joked, to pay for his new kitchen.) I defy anyone listening live to the *Fisherman's Friends* not to join in and laugh out loud at their deliciously irreverent Cornish banter – ('Don't go driving in the lanes, you tourists, 'cos you'll only make fools of yourselves'). We went to many more performances every summer until worldwide fame put paid to such capers. Word quickly spread of an impromptu performance by 'the buoys' on the Platt, just after their first film had hit the cinemas; the ensuing traffic jams brought much of North Cornwall to a standstill. But we had been invited to the 'wrap' party on the last day of filming by one of the cast who had bought my books; it was a magical evening which ended as the sun set with each actor singing alongside the character they portrayed.

The village has a fascinating history with connections to smuggling that few will talk about, even to this day; but Port Isaac's other claim to international fame is through its location as the fictional *Portwenn* in the astonishingly popular television series, *Doc Martin*, starring Martin Clunes. Martin first played the part of a Cornish doctor in the hilarious 2000 film, *Saving Grace*, which was filmed in Port Isaac. The television series was a spin off from that film; it ran to ten seasons that were shown around the world and has an impressively wide following of fans who visit Port Isaac to do the 'Doc Martin Trail'. Over the years I have been lucky enough to meet some principal members of the cast at Port Isaac, including Martin himself, who is a natural comedian and friendly to everybody, especially their dogs. The famous actress Dame Eileen Atkins, who plays Martin's Aunt Ruth, came to the courtyard very early one morning as I was setting up my table outside Mike's shop. Coming up to me with a smile and a cheery 'hello,' she asked what my books were about. When I had given her the briefest description she bought both published books of my Corfu Trilogy and asked me to inscribe her name. They were a very happy cast and crew, who had intruded as lightly as possible, blending naturally into the local community and donating a great deal to the village.

The rest of the summer was a blur of book signings all over the country once again, so my Cornish book would have to wait until the winter before I could begin the illustrations. I was delighted to be invited to sign my books at Melford Hall in Suffolk, owned by the Hyde-Parker family, cousins of Beatrix Potter, where she had stayed regularly. The bedroom Beatrix always used can be viewed during a tour of the house and in the visitor's book is her signature and an original ink drawing of Jemima Puddleduck and the 'Foxy Whiskered Gentleman,' all from her stay in 1912.

Hever Castle provided an especially memorable location in the first week of July. I had always wanted to visit since watching the stunning 1969 Hal Wallis film, *Anne of the Thousand Days*, with Richard Burton as Henry VIII and the young, very beautiful Geneviève Bujold as Anne Boleyn. Hever was Anne's childhood home and much of the film was shot there; I was astonished to be shown the very prayer book poor Anne had taken with her to her execution. I should perhaps explain that although the locations for these book signings may sound glamorous, Jeremy and I had to travel many hundreds of miles, often leaving at three in the morning from Cornwall and eating a picnic breakfast of Marmite and marmalade sandwiches with coffee from a flask. Comfort stops were usually taken in a dew-damp field as there were no service stations on the minor roads we often had to travel. Occasionally a hasty stop at a roadside M&S convenience store would delight Dash with a meal of cocktail sausages if we had forgotten to pack his dried food. The signing days were all complimentary for the venue; our meagre profit came from books sold, but we only received the wholesale price and never any travelling expenses. Despite making far more out of my visit than I did, very few of the venues offered us as much as a cup of coffee.* Such is the self-publisher's lot.

One of my last summer signings at Port Isaac that year was particularly special. The morning rush of customers had tailed off when I noticed an elderly lady approaching Mike's bookshop. She looked very different to the usual visitors to the little village, dressed as she was in a tailored A-line skirt that matched one of the shades of her Liberty print blouse. With neat coiffure and manicured nails with the same colour polish as mine, I already knew we had a lot in common. She carried a stylish walking cane and a small shoulder bag matching her court shoes, looking as if he she had stepped straight out of Belgravia. I greeted her as she stood in front of my table and scrutinised my children's books.

"These are absolutely exquisite!" she said, picking one up and carefully turning the pages. "Who published them?"

This was a most unusual question and I wondered why she was interested. I explained the situation and quickly added that I was hoping to find a top publisher for the completed series one day.

"Who does your illustrations?" She asked. "They're outstanding!"

I was explaining they were all mine when her husband arrived to escort her to Nathan Outlaw's for lunch; she wished she had more time to look at the books and handed me her card, asking me to keep in touch and let me know if she could help.

At home that evening I showed the card to Jeremy and told him all about my meeting with this charming lady. A quick internet search revealed that Gina Pollinger and her husband Murray ran a world renowned literary agency. Gina specialised in children's

---

* Greenway, Coleton Fishacre and Compton Castle always gave us lunch which was highly unusual and very welcome.

literature, her authors included Michael Morpurgo, Jacqueline Wilson and Anne Fine, a Children's Laureate; among the adult authors Gina discovered was Penelope Lively, a winner of the Booker Prize. Gina had unearthed many of her writers in the 'unsolicited manuscript' pile – otherwise known as the slush bucket – which most agents and publishers refused to accept, let alone look at. It is a testament to Gina's vision that she broke the mould and had the imagination to look at the work of these unknown writers, which led to her reputation for talent-spotting. Gina was particularly good at matching illustrators to authors and it was her suggestion that Quentin Blake should illustrate the books of Roald Dahl, whom Murray represented.

(I am incandescent with rage to learn that Roald Dahl's books have just been rewritten to soothe the delicate sensibilities of the woke police, changing every word that could possibly be deemed offensive until only conjunctions and prepositions remain. White (as a sheet) has been removed as have the words black, fat, ugly, crazy and female – even if they referred to inanimate objects. What next? Shakespeare? The Bible? – they'd have a field day with that. Dickens no doubt (whoops, too late!). I am so glad I have kept the original books my children loved – all of them written long before offence was so gladly and easily taken. I hope I shall be allowed to read them to my grandchildren one day).

I wrote a letter to Gina and enclosed my books, to which she replied that my 'outstanding' books were 'sparkling on her desk'. I heard no more so after a few months I telephoned to speak to Gina. Murray answered and said that Gina had been taken seriously ill and 'was not the person she was when I had met her'. I said how very sorry I was and asked to be remembered to her. Tragically Gina died in 2017 having suffered from motor neurone disease.

I have since made contact with Gina's daughter Claudia, who, as it has most extraordinarily turned out, we had known well in Corfu. She and her husband Ben Philo opened a gourmet restaurant and upmarket catering business in the hills north of Kassiopi; Jeremy and I had attended the party on the opening night of *The Invisible Kitchen* and they in turn had visited us on board Sarava. I so wish I had been able to tell Gina about such a happy coincidence. What were the chances of that? Delve deeply enough and we will all surely find a connection to every other person in the world. Claudia and Ben now run the highly acclaimed *Owl Tearooms* at Holt in Norfolk.

October brought a dramatic change in the weather. As the gales set in I closeted myself in our bedroom to complete the illustrations for the next two children's books. My first solo venture into the world of publishing, with *The Holiday – A Chough's Tale*, had been unexpectedly successful. Suitably encouraged, Jeremy and I quickly decided the only way forward with *The Manor House Stories* was to publish the rest of the series ourselves. But the cost of producing such high quality, traditional hardback books was exorbitant. So at the suggestion of a friend I tested the water with a novel idea to help finance the project; Meriel had bought twelve copies of each title that had been published for her twelve grandchildren. How she happened upon my books in the first place is stranger than fiction; it was through an acquaintance of ours in Corfu who had recommended them to her when she was there on holiday. We had obviously been destined to meet. By an extraordinary coincidence Meriel had been 'the money' backing the purchaser of Jeremy's sought after waterside restaurant premises in Dartmouth, way back in the mid 1970's. Each year she held a charity sale at her spacious home in Somerset, where she had invited me to take a stall for my books. At the end of a very busy day she asked me how I was going to carry on with the series. I explained how the cost of printing was holding me back

"I would willingly give you £500 towards the printing cost," Meriel offered, already gauging my reaction. "Yes I know, Jani; you would need lots more people to do the same."

In the car on the way home I mulled over her idea; it could possibly work, I counted in my head how many people I would need to sponsor a new title and what I could call them, 'Sponsors' or 'Friends of The Manor House Stories'. I told Jeremy what I was thinking.

"You would need to give them an incentive, a signed original illustration from whichever book they sponsor," he suggested. "And some free signed first editions too, perhaps."

"And they could have a child's name printed in the back of the book as well. I think they'd love that," I added, surprised that my husband was not actually disagreeing with me about a business idea.

"But it could be difficult to get enough likeminded people," he mused, determined to inject his usual dose of reality before I drifted off to sleep for the rest of the journey home.

The following day we set about composing a letter introducing the *Friends of The Manor House Stories* which I would send to some of the customers who had already bought the first three books. I sent out dozens of smart letters, each showing the cover image from the next title we wanted to publish and a brief description of the story. Within three days, much to my surprise, I had received enough promises of sponsorship for the book to go full steam ahead. We took our courage in both hands, along with the promised sponsorship donations, and *Chesterfield Penguin the Butler – All At Sea*, was sent off to the firm in Wales who had printed the first three titles. I made a full page at the back of *Chesterfield* available to the Durrell Wildlife Conservation Trust to describe the work they do, which I hoped would raise their profile and to which I would make voluntary contributions each year. For the charity page they sent me some lovely photos of Gerry Durrell as a boy in Corfu and in later life as the world famous conservationist and author. The pattern for funding the books had been set for the remaining eight titles; I hoped I would be as lucky in attracting willing sponsors for them all.

As we were now beginning to feel settled in Cornwall, we thought it would be sensible to have the next two titles printed in the county. Once again I had secured promises of sponsorship to cover some of the printing costs; many of the original sponsors were generous enough to support every title in the series. I chose another two charities to support with these books, Children's Hospice South West and Michael Morpurgo's charity, Farms for City Children. We knew a large international printing firm in Padstow and gave them the order to print two titles at the same time, which was a great deal more cost effective. The printers were given samples of the existing titles to ensure everything matched the previous books and, as I had always insisted, I went to the factory floor to match the colours of the illustrations with my original paintings as the first sheets came off the press.

A book launch had already been arranged at the Duchy of Cornwall Nursery near Lostwithiel, owned and often visited by the Duke of Cornwall; the plant nursery and gift shop kindly agreed to host the launch and provide refreshments from the excellent restaurant for the invited guests. A few days before the launch Jeremy and I collected several hundred books from Padstow and as Jeremy loaded dozens of boxes into the car, I was asked to sign a form accepting delivery. It suddenly occurred to me that it might be a good idea to check the finished product for faults and asked Jeremy to open up a box of each title.

"You really don't need to do that after reading the proofs," he said, his arms straining under the weight of another two boxes.

Reluctantly Jeremy cut open a box of each title for me and continued loading the car. Skimming through the first book I was horrified to discover the pages of the two titles had been muddled up: half of *Miss Miranda Mistlethrush* had been printed in *Radish Robin the Gardener*. Sure enough the same confusion applied to *Radish Robin*, turning both titles into nonsense. I couldn't believe my eyes.

Reception was about to close for the day but I insisted the manager was summoned. Then I told Jeremy to bring back the boxes he had packed in the car. My heart was pounding, not least with fury at such a disastrous mistake, but also because the launch was just days away. All the arrangements had been made with the Duchy Nursery, advertising had been done weeks before, the press had been notified and invitations to the great and the good of Cornwall and beyond had been sent. I had to insist that they immediately reprint at least two hundred copies of each title, just to cover the launch.

"But it's Tuesday and you'd need them by Friday for your launch on Saturday," said the disgruntled account manager, without any hint of an apology. "We'd have to get extra staff in to work overnight!"

"Then so be it," I insisted furiously, jumping into the car. "This is entirely your fault and entirely your problem!"

The following Friday afternoon we loaded the freshly reprinted books into the car, having checked a few at random to make sure we weren't being fobbed off with the old copies. The launch went ahead very successfully and we thought our printing problems were behind us, until the bulk of the production arrived some weeks later. Pre-orders had already been sent all over the country, but a few days later a lady customer from Australia called me about the copies she had bought for her granddaughter at Blenheim Palace; neither book made sense as the two stories were muddled up. I was mortified to discover this had occurred for a second time and immediately replaced all the orders sent out.

Our cottage was turned into a production line as Jeremy and I checked through every single one of the 6,000 books – mountains of boxes obscuring all daylight in the sitting room. Naturally I claimed compensation from the printers for all the time and trouble their inefficiency had caused and they were compelled to organise yet another print run. Third time lucky we thought, but no: different faults appeared in the final print run. This time the firm's manager came to our cottage to see the boxes of faulty books for himself, still remarkably unapologetic and determined to find some means to blame us for his company's blunders.

Wild horses could not have dragged us back to their premises ever again and I decided to return to the printers in Wales for all the remaining titles. Then a very extraordinary thing happened: I sent an email to the young man who had always handled *The Manor House Stories* at the Welsh firm, informing him we wanted to publish another two books and asking for a quotation. Although we had never met him, Dai had been very efficient and always answered my queries by return; I was surprised I hadn't received any reply. A week later I received an email from Dai asking how we were getting on and whether or not I had decided to continue with my children's books. I noticed the email address was at a different firm, so I called the number and Dai answered. He had left his original printers and was now working for another company thirty miles down the road. He had never received my email, but our thoughts must have crossed in the ether – a theory we discussed a few years and a few thousand books later, when Dai came to stay for the weekend with us in our Cornish cottage.

The following two titles were perfectly produced under his personal supervision at the new firm, where we met in person for the first time. Printers generally hate their clients visiting the shop floor, particularly where colours are involved, but I always felt it was essential to watch the printed sheets come off the press and compare the tones against my original paintings. At that stage minor tweaks could still be made to the colours, even if the press operators thought them perfect as they were. To the technician's dismay I insisted on carrying the unwieldy sheets to and fro into the car park where I could fully assess each new colour adjustment in daylight, rather than under an array of unnatural neon strip lights. No wonder the press floor was usually out of bounds to all except the colour blind.

Chapter 8

Mistletoe and Wine

Those who don't believe in magic will never find it.

Roald Dahl

This was to be our first Christmas in Cornwall, but before I could throw myself into preparing for the celebrations, which I had started planning in August, Jeremy and I had to steel ourselves for the rounds of Christmas Fairs we attended each year. These were lucrative events we could ill afford to miss if we wanted to survive the New Year lulls; they also provided the last opportunity to catch a truly malevolent strain of flu before the holiday, a probability that easily outstripped the school carol services that had so often laid us low when the children were young. Many of these fairs were held in the Cotswolds, handily close for us to stay with Rory for their duration. Easily the biggest and best of these shopping fests was hosted over three long and arduous days at Lord and Lady Bamford's Daylesford estate in aid of the WellChild charity. For six consecutive years I was invited as a guest author.

A stone's throw from Stow-on-the-Wold in the heart of the Cotswolds, the November weather was always destined to be cruel; either bitterly cold or deluged with weeks of rain beforehand, the surrounding roads, grounds and car parks would be transformed into skating rinks, ski slopes or swamps, according to nature's whim. The riggers had set up the vast marquees for the event long before we wretched stallholders arrived; unhelpfully they had already churned the parking areas into mud baths, so the only way to get anywhere near our particular marquee entrance was to ignore the parking marshals, point the car at our chosen unloading spot and charge headlong across the field in a controlled slalom like Jeremy Clarkson – praying that nobody else had the same idea at the same time. Luckily this came naturally to my Jeremy.

My little stall of books, slotted in at the last minute wherever it could be fitted, was dwarfed by the professional exhibitors selling boots for £1000 a pair, cashmere jumpers for £500 each, or boutique gin for £100 a bottle. At ten o-clock sharp a flurry of the Cotswolds' finest, all dressed in the uniform of aspiring county landowners, whether they lived in Notting Hill or Northampton, streamed into the tents and began shopping as if life itself depended upon it. The young mums, painfully thin and glamorous in designer tweed jackets, tight white leggings and faux riding boots, all wore the same haunted expressions; the men in their red corduroy trousers, checked waistcoats and Barbour jackets becoming jauntier after each tasting of fortifying sloe gin. An hour later the car parks were bursting with row after row of identical cars and would remain so until the end of the final day. Think of Daylesford as a place where Range Rovers foregather to breed.

I was always frantically busy at Daylesford and I gained many loyal customers over the years. The same could not be said for other fairs, where organisers were eager to pocket the stallholders' fees, but not so clever at persuading the public to attend. One such, organised at a motor racing circuit in Wiltshire, had been heavily promoted and recommended; I only got in at the last minute after someone else had had the good sense to drop out. A vast hanger of a marquee with a roof dripping with condensation, minus seven degrees as Jeremy and I arrived in the morning, no heating because the diesel had frozen, not a paying customer to be seen and five hundred pounds to the worse. Well, you can imagine.

But that particularly luckless day had been redeemed by a

telephone call answered as I shivered beside my stand.

"WHAT did you say?" I asked in disbelief, straining to hear the faint voice on my mobile phone.

"Would you like to talk to Cliff Richard?" a producer from BBC Radio Oxford repeated. "He's appearing live on the programme this morning and we can put you on; we know you are one of his greatest fans!"

"Oh yes please!" I answered, my legs turning to jelly.

I was told they would call me in about half an hour and I could talk with my idol – the handsome singer I had fallen in love with at the age of six. The radio station already knew I had papered every inch of my childhood bedroom with his pictures and that I was one of the first members of his Fan Club. I had also owned a pillowcase printed with his face in monochrome which gradually faded in the wash; my mother decided it had become disturbingly reminiscent of the Shroud of Turin, so I forbad her to wash it again. I had even suffered a black eye on Cliff's behalf when my cousin John, ten years my senior and a committed Elvis fan, had insulted Cliff's music; knowing my worship of Cliff, John never missed an opportunity to tease me. One day when I was nine, he went too far with his insults and I threw one of my shoes at him. He ducked, picked up the shoe and laughingly threw it back at me, never meaning to actually hit me. The hard heel of the shoe caught me smack on my eye and I went running to Mummy in tears. John was almost in tears too, mortified that the shoe had hit me; we adored each other, he having become the brother I had lost just four years before. He shot out of the house, leapt on his motorbike and roared into the nearby town, returning with an enormous raw steak to draw the bruising from my black eye. Maybe that was the start of my vegetarian tendency.

I found a quiet corner of the restaurant marquee and waited

impatiently for the call.

"Hi Jani," said the familiar, meltingly soft voice, heard so often on radio and television.

I was dumbstruck. Cliff had spoken my name! There was only enough time to ask him if he would re-release a song I loved, *I Believe In You*, which had never been in the hit parade, but featured a lovely melody and the most beautiful words. He laughed and said he would think about it; I said it would make a fabulous Christmas song and suggested the accompanying video should be of him and a lady, wearing glamorous winter outfits, walking through a snowy pine forest in the Austrian Tyrol. I offered to be that lady but am still waiting for the call.

Heading home to Cornwall at last, exhausted after ten days of constant selling at the shopping fairs, I insisted we divert to Dartmoor to collect our holly and ivy. As far back as I can remember, my entire family used to meet on Dartmoor on the Sunday before Christmas to pick holly and ivy from the secret woods in the heart of the moor. I can still smell the rich, smoky, fruit cake scent of damp moorland earth and pine trees and feel again the thrill of seeing the shiny red berries sparkling like rubies amongst the glossy dark green foliage.

Christmas decorations were always a source of marital discord in our lives. I firmly believe you can never have enough of them and would happily leave the fairy lights up all year round; Jeremy, on the other hand, was brought up to believe that one string of lights on a small Christmas tree is quite sufficient. Jeremy and I always disagreed about the size required for the main tree, his argument being that he always had to lop off the topmost prickly shoot anyway, which accounted for another foot and therefore extra cost to the tree. Now we were in North Cornwall we had another problem, as the cottage sitting room left little room for all of us if a tree took up any floor space. Luckily, when pushed, my husband has a very inventive mind and made a platform to attach from the bannisters of the landing, on which the tree could stand overlooking the room and leaving the floor unhindered. The effect was most attractive and our flying tree drew much praise; oddly enough Christmas trees used to be hung upside down from ceilings in parts of Europe. Jeremy's other duty before Christmas was to cook a large gammon, boiled first in cider then liberally coated with honey before going into the oven; as soon as it had cooled he took it up to the garden shed, where we kept a spare fridge.

On Christmas Eve Miranda and her lively young Sprocker Spaniel Rupert arrived in the afternoon and I persuaded Miranda to come with me to our village church, where a service of Carols by Candlelight was to be held. Jeremy insisted his church days were over; he had been compelled to attend several thousand interminable services during his schooldays, enduring the discomfort of stiff starched shirts and collar studs throughout, and refused to leave the comforts of home on such a wild moorland night. Stinging rain blew in from the sea, threatening the fairy lights Jeremy had strung outside the cottage. It took Miranda an eternity to find a parking space near the church, in a village designed for horse and cart, for it seemed every single car and tractor from the surrounding moors had turned up before us. We were the very last to arrive in the little church, the heavy oak door being closed firmly against the weather after we entered. Inside we were warmly greeted by the churchwardens who offered us mince pies and glasses of mulled wine. Every pew being full, the vicar walked us down the full length of the aisle to the only empty seats in the choir stall, much to Miranda's horror and embarrassment.

"Oh God, Mummy, now we'll have to sing with the choir!" Miranda hissed as we carried our wine and mince pies before us, absorbing unflinching stares from the seated congregation.

I assured her in my best stage whisper that there would only be a couple of carols and tried to draw her attention to the beauty around us. Apart from the fairy lights on the Christmas tree, the only illumination in the church glowed from hundreds of candles flickering in every nook and cranny, from the lowest pediments to the highest capitals, and amongst the festive greenery on every windowsill. The crystal in the ancient Cornish granite pillars and mullions reflected the warm glow, sparkling like dancing fireflies. Sipping our wine, we browsed the festively decorated carol sheets, which listed thirty Christmas favourites; after the vicar had welcomed his flock, the organ struck up *The Holly and the Ivy* directly behind us, drowning out the noise of the rain drumming on the roof.

To see Miranda singing beside me, after all the years since we used to attend the Christmas Morning service as a young family, it suddenly struck me that she was now a good head taller than me and I had to look up instead of down to see her face. Where had that time gone? I noticed the two candles either side of the bible on the lectern were burning down to the last inch as the service progressed, the flames flickering dangerously close to the pages. Twenty minutes into the service Miranda started looking at her watch; she was getting hungry and our glasses were already drained.

"I think we're going to sing every carol on the sheet!" she whispered, darting one of her 'what have you let me in for' looks.

Perhaps she was right; in the middle of Bodmin Moor, some folks probably liked to make the most of their single appearance of the year in church. The lectern candles had already burnt down to stumps, their pools of spluttering wax threatening the pages of the open bible. Miranda groaned as the vicar announced carol number seven. At the worst that left twenty-three more to get through, I thought as I noticed Miranda pointedly picking up her empty wine glass, ever hopeful of a top-up. The bells rang out joyously as we eventually left the church an hour later; we could still hear their peal carrying across the village as we reached the cottage. Miranda had the grace to admit the atmosphere at the service had been very special; for me it was an evening I would relive in my mind many times, especially during the pandemic when, for the first time in my life, churches all over the countryside remained closed at Christmas.

On Christmas morning, amidst all the flurry of opening presents, Jeremy had gone to the shed to retrieve the ham, so he could slice it ready for our cold supper. It had vanished. Another argument ensued as I accused him of forgetting to put it in the spare fridge, certain that a team of rats from the farm must have carried it away and eaten it. Jeremy was walking around in a daze, muttering to himself about the ham, which Rory – who had arrived in the small hours, having set up a Christmas Eve dance at a hotel in Knightsbridge – was trying to help him find.

Much later that evening Jeremy took some wet dog towels to the garden shed where the tumble dryer was also kept; he opened the door of the machine and there was the ham. He will never live this down and every time we lose something – which is increasingly often – I ask him if he's looked in the tumbly. (I don't know the Cornish translation for tumble dryer, but I can tell you the brilliantly onomatopoeic 'pop-ti-ping' is Cornish for microwave oven).

By tradition we always indulged ourselves with an Austrian breakfast on Boxing Day, recreated as best we could from our skiing holidays in the Tyrol when the children were young. Unlike anything I have tasted since, the fresh round rolls, the traditional *Kaisersemmel,* from the bakery in our tiny mountain village were absolutely delicious.

Always too excited to sleep longer, I could smell the baker's oven from four in the morning as soon as I ventured out onto our balcony, wrapped in my duvet as I inhaled the crisp, icy mountain air while the rest of the village slept. Sipping my tea as I gazed up at the snow covered peak high above, I cherished the extraordinary silence and absorbed the atmosphere of the snowy, pine-clad bowl in which the village was enfolded. A winking red light at the mountain's summit, looming five thousand feet above our hotel, shone out amongst the stars; how strange it was to think we would all be up there, almost at the very top in a few hours time. Our family run hotel served a buffet style breakfast with platters of thinly sliced Austrian cheeses, wafer thin ham, Mortadella and salami. Alpine breakfasts were always served with a selection of preserves, my particular favourite was lingonberry, also known as mountain cranberry; add some or all of these ingredients to fresh warm buttered rolls – appetisingly soft within, yet crusty enough to be toothsome without actually breaking your teeth – and we would be ready for the ski slopes. Or even for the beaches of Cornwall.

Luckily the Cornish weather had improved and an impotent sun peered through the early morning mists on the moor. In the far distance the strip of sea beyond Padstow sparkled sapphire blue, so we loaded the dogs, bundles of towels, coats, hats, a bottle of sloe gin and a tin of Scottish shortbread and headed for my favourite beach at Treyarnon. The surf was rolling in and some hardy souls in wetsuits were already paddling out on their boards. Dash instantly made for every single rock pool as usual, soaking his long coat up to his neck, while Rupert careered around in circles on the wet sand chasing his tennis ball. That evening, suitably mellowed by the bracing sea air, my family enjoyed the prodigal ham. It was none the worse for its couple of days in the tumble dryer; the nights had been cold and it had matured nicely.

In hindsight it was a miracle we ever returned to Austria after the unpromising start to our first skiing holiday in the Tyrol. Heavy snow at Bristol Airport had seriously delayed our flight to Salzburg where, to our young children's intense dismay, not a flake of the white stuff was to be seen. As the transfer coach wove its way through the mountain passes, visiting a string of rain soaked resorts along the way, it soon became obvious we would be the last tourists to be dropped off. A little after midnight the four of us were ordered to disembark beside a crossroad in the middle of nowhere. Our considerable protests fell on deaf ears as our suitcases were thrown out beside us, although we were assured in a mixture of sign language and raised voices that we would only have to wait two minutes for the connecting minibus to our hotel. As the door hissed shut behind him, the driver left us to the silence of the mountains. Twenty minutes later, frozen solid as marble statues in the sub-zero air, we were saved from premature death by a passing motorist who very kindly strapped our luggage onto the roof of his car and drove us the last ten miles to our hotel.

It got even worse.

Our family room had been double booked, the concierge regretfully informed us as we struggled up to the lofts where the staff lived. Our miniscule double room had just enough floor space for the children to stretch out on a couple of camp beds, leaving no room for our suitcases except in the loo. Exhausted by the interminable journey and thoroughly disheartened by the lack of snow, we could not even summon up the anger to complain and gratefully fell asleep.

At six in the morning Jeremy got up to answer a call of nature, stepping carefully over our sleeping children before attempting to reverse into the loo. I must explain. The toilet was located in the eaves at the farthest end of a very narrow twelve-foot long corridor, reached through a low doorway that led off the bedroom; in itself that presented no insuperable problem, until the diminishing height of the sloping ceiling was taken into account. Unfortunately it was impossible for Jeremy to stand up anywhere near the loo, so his only means of approach was to crouch over double and shuffle backwards with pyjama trousers round his ankles, avoiding our scattered luggage as best he could. Once comfortably seated he noticed the skylight less than a foot above his head; being incurably inquisitive he released the lever and pushed the glass wide open, whereupon a cascade of snow landed squarely in his lap. Fortunately his curses had been mollified by the mere presence of real snow and, able to stand up at last with his head and shoulders poking out of the hatch, the dim glow of dawn revealed more than a foot of snow had fallen during the few hours we had been asleep. Our holiday was perfect from that moment on: the sun shone for the rest of the week and the skiing conditions were the best the village had seen for years. We were moved directly to the best family room in the hotel, given a bottle of Champagne for our inconvenience and promised a generous discount if we booked directly for the following year – which we happily did for the following three seasons.

By the last of our skiing holidays in Austria I was experiencing frequent hot flushes due to the 'change of life,' as men like to call it. This was exasperating when bundled up to the chin in skiwear, especially as my suit was an all-in-one, making it almost impossible to remove quickly whenever my temperature shot up to what felt like 104 degrees in seconds. I had recently bought a tiny but very powerful circular magnet in pink glittery plastic, which was guaranteed to prevent these flushes and other unpleasant symptoms. It came in two halves which you attached to your pants, so one half was against your skin and the other half was on the outer fabric, the two magnets clamping it tightly in place. The first time I went to the loo in our ensuite bathroom in the hotel, I leapt out of my skin as my pants flew across the bathroom floor and attached themselves to the metal waste bin under the wash hand basin. I had forgotten all about the magnet and was convinced there was a poltergeist in the loo with me, until I shakily retrieved them and found the magnet clamping my pants to the bin like a limpet to a rock.

As a family we had always loved the snow, particularly the Austrian variety which always seems so excessively sparkly and glittery. We have only experienced heavy snow once in Cornwall; it fell thick and fast one dark afternoon in the February of 2018 and was quickly dubbed the 'Beast from the East'. We watched from inside our cottage as the deep slate windowsills gradually disappeared under thick white blankets. By early evening the snow was half way up the windows and the garden resembled a scene from Narnia. Dash so enjoyed playing in the snow we couldn't stop him constantly ringing his little bell that hung from a ribbon on the door handle, asking to be let out. Snowballs formed instantly around his paws and we had to put him in a shallow bath of tepid water to melt them. I made some little 'booties' from old pairs of tights and tied them on with ribbons; they worked really well and I thought I might go into production on the distant day when I had absolutely nothing better to do.

The snow settled heavily and next morning Jeremy had to shovel away the drift before we could open our gate onto the lane. All my potted plants in the garden were in danger of dying and Jeremy covered the pots in bubblewrap to stop the roots freezing. I was worried about my summer flowering shrubs and decided to cover each bush with a colourful sarong, securing them with pegs; the garden looked as if it was full of highly coloured balloons, until we awoke next day to find them all covered with snow and transformed into igloos.

We put on all the warmest clothes we could find and attempted to walk up the lane onto the Moor, knowing how beautiful it would look in the snow. Before we reached the cattle grid we could see the lane ahead was impassable, blocked up to waist height with snowdrifts. We were fast running out of fresh food, so Jeremy thought he would take our Austrian toboggan to the village shop for supplies; we had bought it in the Tyrol for Miranda when she was three and somehow it had survived our many moves. He only got halfway down the hill when he found it impassable without crampons and an ice-pick. We were utterly marooned.

I found it quite exciting, thinking we could easily survive on pasta and tinned tomatoes, until Jeremy reminded me about the power cuts that would invariably strike the moors and leave us without any heating or means of cooking. I ran around gathering all the candles I could find and filling flasks with boiling water, wishing I had not left our trusty little tilley stove in Corfu.

For a few days at the end of February the mercury was regularly dropping to –6°C overnight, remaining below freezing all day. Far away we could hear the happy shrieks and laughter of children as they played snowballs and sledged on the blanketed fields at the farther end of the village. In the daytime when the sun was out, we sat in the car in front of the cottage to have morning coffee, lunch and afternoon tea; it was so much warmer than the cottage, where the heating was severely rationed until a fresh delivery of oil could get through to us.

During my childhood, snow would blanket most of South Devon as regularly as clockwork every winter. Dartmoor communities were cut off from civilisation, sheep were rescued from deep snowdrifts, ponies sought the shelter of lower ground, schools were closed for days on end and we used our wooden surf boards as makeshift toboggans. Great swathes of Bodmin Moor were left entirely inaccessible except by helicopter during the freeze of 1962, which lasted for many weeks.

Shortly before Christmas one year I received an invitation to the Hunt Ball at Drogo Castle on Dartmoor. I was seventeen and had passed my driving test that spring, so Mummy agreed to let me borrow her new Mini Countryman for the evening. (It was so stupid of me not to take our Land Rover in which I had taken my driving test, but I thought the Mini would be more comfortable.). At the time we had a Thai girl staying with us while she studied English. A family friend of Addy's, Neng was the same age as me and it was her first visit to England, so I had asked her to come along to the ball with another riding friend. It had been bitterly cold all day, with leaden skies that held the promise of snow. However, having spent most of the day getting ready in my bedroom, and despite my parents trying to dissuade us from venturing onto the moors when snow had been forecast, I was not listening. My dressmaker had made a gorgeous long dress for me and I was determined to wear it to the ball.

The haberdashery assistant had warned me that the moss green velvet I had chosen for my dress was actually curtain material; knowing nothing about dressmaking I insisted it would be fine, unaware the finished dress would be as heavy to wear as a roll of woollen carpet. We set off well after dusk on the journey that would normally take about an hour from Torbay; my father had insisted I needed to allow extra time if we wanted to arrive before dinner, as the dark moorland roads might be a little icy. By the time we reached Newton Abbot snow was falling quite heavily. Brimming with the deceitful confidence of youth, I decided we should carry on regardless; we had come this far and I reckoned we were definitely beyond the point of no return. I knew the road well as I had several friends who lived on the moors, but beyond Moretonhampstead the road became indistinguishable from the verges. Then as the Mini's tyres scrambled and spun their way to the top of a hill before Chagford, I suddenly remembered there was a steep descent over the brow. I put the car into first gear, remembering how my father had taught me to rely on the gearbox instead of the brakes in snowy conditions. The first few yards were easy as we began to creep slowly down the hill.

"This is a doddle!" I told my silent, ashen faced, friends.

Sitting petrified in the back seat, Neng had never seen snow before and was already certain the world was about to end. Then the Mini started to slide, its speed increasing uncontrollably until we were hurtling down the hill like a toboggan. The snow drifts at either side of the road were several feet high, reducing the road between the hedges to the width of the Cresta Run. I couldn't steer, or brake, but I sat there grasping the steering wheel for dear life. At the bottom of the hill the car veered violently to the right and crashed heavily into a deep drift by a gateway. The snow had looked soft enough, but in fact it camouflaged a stone wall and a row of iron railings.

"Are you all okay?" I asked my passengers.

They nodded in speechless terror as I tried to reverse, quickly realising the car was stuck fast and wouldn't budge an inch.

"We'd better get out quickly," I said, worried that steam from the bonnet meant the car would soon burst into flames, just as I had seen in so many James Bond films. Stepping out into two feet of snow in our flimsy evening pumps beneath our long gowns was challenging to say the least; there wasn't a single coat or shawl between us. (Why do teenagers hate wearing coats?). We gathered our dresses up to our knees and started to plough and slip our way back up the long hill in total darkness, aiming for the crest where Rose had spotted a cottage with lights on. It seemed to take forever, although the recent journey down the hill had been accomplished in a couple of hair-raising seconds.

"Jani, I can't feer my feet!" said Neng miserably.

My heavy dress had come into its own, but my two girlfriends shivered uncontrollably as we stumbled up to the cottage and rapped on the door. An ample woman in fluffy slippers and a flowery apron came to the door.

"Oh my Lord, just look at you!" she exclaimed, turning away and yelling over her shoulder before we could utter a word.

"ARTHUR, 'ENRY, come 'ere!"

Two burly young farmers soon filled the doorway either side of their mother; backlit by the warm glow from the fireplace they appeared to be ten feet tall and wider than haystacks. I hastily explained about the car being stuck at the bottom of the hill. Dumbstruck at the sight of three gifts sent from above, the haystack twins sprang out of their trance and disappeared into the snowstorm to look at the car. Mother ushered us towards the open fire and very thoughtfully made us mugs of tea; fortunately we had no time to finish the fearfully strong brew before her sons returned.

"Yer bumper be stuck fast in yer front wheel," the hairier haystack mumbled, still unable to look away from us in case we vanished into thin air. "So you'm be going nowhere in that car tonight!"

Seeing our crestfallen faces he asked where we were headed.

"The Hunt Ball at Drogo Castle," I answered disconsolately.

"Be jiggered!" was his response, "You'm never be fetchin' up there in this weather."

Terrified at the prospect of being compelled to pass the night with only the haystacks for company, I turned to the mother and asked to use the telephone, called Drogo (thank heavens for 'phone books) and explained why and where we were stuck.

"Hang on, I'll see who's got a Land Rover," a voice reassured.

Twenty minutes and an eternity of awkward silences later there was another knock at the door. It was a Pony Club chum's boyfriend who had come in his Land Rover with two eager friends, a length of rope and an admirably chivalrous attitude.

"Hello Jani, we've got the car out of the hedge and I can tow you to the Castle. We should just about make it up there in time for the dinner."

Assisted by our knights in shining wellies we three girls slid back down the hill and climbed into the Mini, which had undergone some remedial bumper surgery with a pick-axe. Arriving on the end of a tow rope at the Castle was not the way I had intended to make my entrance. As soon as we were inside I called my parents to tell them the sorry news, adding that all three of us would have to spend the night in Chagford until we could get the Mini to a garage the next morning. I felt terribly guilty of course and apologised profusely for damaging Mummy's car, but it didn't prevent me galloping around the ballroom dancing the Polka in my new dress. The logs blazed in the vast fireplaces as the heat from the crowded room and my heavy dress forced me to retire to the lower steps of a draughty granite staircase to eat supper with my girlfriends. Poor Neng was still in shock, made even worse when she was presented with a plate of venison casserole. The colour drained from her face when I explained what she was eating.

"Oh no! You mean rike dear rittle Bambi?" she wailed in horror.

At midnight my new best friends gave us a lift to the Three Crowns in Chagford where we were given a comfortable room with a large double bed, sleeping fitfully side by side in our evening gowns like the three bears. To their credit the hotel didn't charge us anything and arranged for a local garage to collect the Mini from the Castle. Poor Neng has nightmares to this day about snowdlifts, Dlogo Castle, The Thlee Clowns and Bambi stew.

Rory, Miranda and Rupert went back to their homes in Oxfordshire with cars laden with presents; Jeremy and I took a last look at the beautiful tree before Twelfth Night when all the decorations had to be taken down and packed away for another year. The cottage and garden looked strangely bare and forlorn but we told ourselves that a New Year was about to begin and we had the thought of a Cornish spring and summer to look forward to.

As the January storms set in, hurling rain horizontally against the front of our Cornish cottage with the force of a fire hydrant, the door that led from our bedroom onto the terrace began to leak. I had to roll up a couple of old towels and squash them against the threshold where the water seeped in; by morning the rolled towels would be frozen stiff. We had joined the real world, unable to afford to turn on the heating for more than a couple of hours a day. But I cheered myself up by thinking, 'but it's Cornish rain!,' which inspired me to write this ditty and send it to Radio Cornwall, whose presenter read it out one morning.

> *I love the rain 'cos it's Cornish rain*
> *I love the wind in the willows,*
> *I love the snow as it covers the ground*
> *I just sink back into my pillows.*
>
> *I love the mist 'cos it's Cornish mist*
> *As it lays a veil over the Moor,*
> *Creating a feeling of mystical charm*
> *It wraps itself round every tor.*

I love the sun 'cos it's Cornish sun,
I love the surf on the sand,
I love the stone hedges all covered in flowers
And watching my little dog run.

I love the cream 'cos it's Cornish cream,
I love the strawberries in summer,
I love the pasties and star-gazey pie,
Fresh lobster and shellfish and bream.

I feel the enchantment of magic around,
I know there are fairies close by
And wizards and piskies and all kinds of folk
And goblins that live underground.

I am sure there are mermaids who swim in the sea
And dragons who live in the caves,
There are legends and myths wherever you go
Of Cornish kings, pirates and braves.

My wish is to leave this fine county never
My wish is to make it my home,
And if Cornwall feels the same about me
I'll love it forever and ever.

Although we loved the cottage dearly, it was built of granite, albeit with three-foot thick walls of the stuff. Granite, a byword for sturdiness, is surprisingly porous and sooner or later the driving Cornish rain soaks into the stone during wintertime and acts like a perfect evaporator to cool the house. There was no open fire or wood burning stove to leach away the damp air because there was no chimney. Originally converted merely for use as a summer holiday let, our landlord had not been permitted to add a chimney to the listed building; after all, no cowsheds Tudor or otherwise ever boasted a fireplace to keep the animals cosy during the winter months. However I am not so sure of the building's origins. At the front of the building is a very narrow vertical slit, set deep into the thick wall and now glazed, which looks exactly like a medieval arrow loop. Henry VIII was busy erecting castles and fortifications all around Cornwall at the time, lest the French attacked. As in our cottage, the interior walls around an arrow loop are often cut away at an oblique angle to give the archer a wide field of fire. To my mind this little opening is definitely an arrow loop, or *archère*. Could this cottage have once been a guardhouse for the manor, full of archers ready to slaughter would-be invaders and second-home owners?

A thick triangle of Delabole slate sits at the base beneath this tiny window, on which I now display my Beatrix Potter figurines – a collection started by my mother which I greatly treasure. Mummy would have been thrilled to know about Jeremy's family connection to Beatrix Potter, but it would be many years before Jeremy found out about it himself. Mummy identified each of Beatrix's characters with members of our family: my father was Squirrel Nutkin because he loved the autumn and collecting anything that might come in useful; Mummy herself was Jemima Puddleduck, who never wanted to sit on her nest but loved to travel about. I once asked Mummy which character was mine and she replied that I was a mixture of all three Flopsy Bunnies, because I had so many different personalities! Rory gave me a rare vintage Peter Rabbit last Christmas, which now has pride of place at the front of the others; I have decided, because Peter is mischievous, he is obviously Rory; Miranda is Mrs. Tittlemouse who keeps her home very neat and tidy and has a dread of spiders. Jeremy has to be Jeremy Fisher of course, if only because he used to go salmon tickling on the upper reaches of the River Dart in his misspent youth.

For the coldest months of that winter I spent each day at my table easel in the bedroom, wearing an old ski suit, complete with hat and fur lined cowhide après-ski boots bought years ago in Austria. But my hands were still aching with cold and it was hard to hold a paintbrush. I tried using some fingerless gloves, looking disturbingly like Fagin, but it was impossible to hold a small water-colour brush. So my left hand was permanently cold and the only solution was to run it under hot water to keep the joints moving. Fortunately the illustrations were bright and sunny subjects that reminded me of the warm summer months to come.

In the Spring following its publication I had sent a copy of *The Holiday – A Chough's Tale* to Lee Durrell, asking if she would consider selling them in the gift shop at the Jersey Zoo. The same year Lee, widow of Gerald Durrell, had flown to Cornwall to collect some choughlings that had been bred in captivity near Hayle; her plan was to start a breeding colony on Jersey. Imagine my delight when I was invited to Jersey for a two day book signing in July.

I had never been to Jersey before, so it was with great excitement that I boarded a little plane at Exeter Airport early one morning, just as the sun was rising. Jersey looked most alluring from the air; dark seas gave way to turquoise shallows that licked gently at swathes of golden sand; a castle on a promontory slipped in and out of my view, replaced by a patchwork of lush green fields dotted with farmhouses as the airport came into sight. An hour later several large boxes of books and a wheelie case with all the necessaries for my stay on the island were unloaded from my taxi at Jersey Zoological Park, where Lee met me. She suggested we had coffee in the Café Dodo before my book signing in the gift shop started. With her gentle, unassuming manner and soft Tennessee accent Lee was one of those delightful people you like on first sight, although I had been in awe of her for many years. As an academic who had spent two years studying the calls of birds and mammals in the jungles of Madagascar* for her PhD, Lee was a force to be reckoned with and a most worthy bearer of the Durrell name.

We chatted easily over coffee as if we had known each other for years; Corfu and mutual friends were the main topic of our conversation of course, Lee wanted to know about the years we had lived there on Sarava, about the tragic day we lost her and afterwards when we were building The Lion House.

"You should write a book about it," she suggested, before asking what had drawn us to Corfu in the first place.

"It was *My Family and Other Animals*, of course," I told her as she smiled and nodded knowingly. "When did you first read it?"

"At school when I was thirteen," I answered and she laughed. She must have heard this a million times before.

I showed her the mock-up book entitled, *A Greek Island Nature Diary*, which I had made, a *Blue Peter* version of what I hoped one day to get published as a gift book. Lee studied the illustrations carefully and said she loved my paintings and thought it would make a beautiful book. Before I knew it an hour had flown by and it was time to get to work. We walked together to the gift shop where I signed a copy of *The Holiday* for her as she had asked. Wishing me a successful day she left me to my customers. That evening the manager, Paddy, offered to drive me back to my hotel at the other end of the island. His car turned out to be a convertible vintage sports car and he agreed it was lucky I had a headscarf with

---

* Lee was honoured with an MBE in 2011 and is an Honorary Citizen of Corfu.

me; but he was more than a little puzzled when I asked if I would need to put on my wellies if it rained.

Paddy's car reminded me of the MG Midget I had owned for ten years, until Jeremy forbad me in no uncertain terms to drive anywhere with two young children unsecured on the parcel shelf of a tiny relic dating from 1961. When Jeremy had discovered its floor was full of holes, he had generously sent it to an MG specialist to have it stripped bare and completely rebuilt. Before its restoration I had needed to wear wellies to drive anywhere when the roads were wet, because water came streaming up through the rusty floor. On one rainy evening I was to be guest of honour as Miss Torbay at a ball at the five-star Imperial Hotel. Wearing my satin sash and sparkly crown with a glamorous long white Frank Usher evening gown beneath a red velvet cloak, I was still wearing my wellies as I pulled up at the main entrance and got out. The doorman knew I was expected and offered to take the Midget to the hotel garage. Gratefully I handed him the keys and walked towards the foyer.

"Er, excuse me Miss," he reminded me, "I think you might want to change your footwear …"

Back in the 1970s I did ask my local garage what they could do to repair the floor without major surgery; they told me they would use a kind of wire mesh padding, but the cost of such a repair was beyond my means at only twenty-three. It sounded quite a simple repair process, so I thought I would have a go at filling the holes myself. I raided Mummy's kitchen cupboards and found just the thing; I stuffed pieces of wire wool in all the holes in the floor and sills and was very pleased with my handiwork when I could no longer see daylight peeping through under my feet … until the first time I drove in the rain. Trailing along the road behind me was a wake of pink soapsuds, as a lather of foam rose about my shoes in the foot well. Only then did I realise that Brillo Pads were not such a brilliant idea.

Paddy collected me from my hotel the next morning and told me he had arranged with the keepers for me to wander around the park before it opened to visitors. I was so thrilled to see all the animals, have my own personal guided tour of their enclosures and to be told about the animals from those who knew them best. A young Western lowland gorilla called Indigo gave me a special performance, picking up a very long and leafy branch, waving it in the air like a pennant and running along the wire fence just to show off. Further into the grounds I found the lemurs, three adults sitting huddled together on a branch and staring at me with piercing golden eyes. Every few minutes I heard a sharp bang; wondering what this could be I followed the sound into a copse of trees. A few feet from me, halfway up a tree trunk, was a small wooden box. It wasn't long before a tiny red squirrel scampered up the trunk, opened the lid of the box, reached inside to take a nut and let the lid fall with a bang as he leapt away through the branches with the nut in his mouth. I counted about six other boxes as I walked on, watching more red squirrels, until a cacophony of bloodcurdling screams stopped me in my tracks. I ran back towards the sound to see the three lemurs standing upright on their branch, clutching each other like frightened spinsters, peering at the ground below and wailing hysterically for all they were worth. Their keeper was cleaning out their night quarters and taking no notice whatsoever.

"Why are they screaming like that?" I asked, having to shout to make myself heard above the racket.

"Oh, they must have seen a rat in their enclosure," he explained, "They come in to steal food and the lemurs are terrified of them!"

At the end of my visit Lee had confided that they always found it difficult to fund Durrell when so many of the larger charities could afford to promote and advertise themselves internationally, so gaining a far higher profile. On the plane on the way home I made a list of various things that I thought could be done to raise money in Jersey and beyond. I determined that I would include a page about the Durrell Wildlife Conservation Trust in my next children's book and would make personal voluntary annual donations to the charity. So it was that *Chesterfield Penguin the Butler – All At Sea* included a page about Durrell, which I hoped would help to raise awareness of such a worthy endeavour. Readers of all my previous books, *Butterflies, Swallows* and *A Greek Island Nature Diary* will have seen the Durrell pages in the books. I hope in some very small way, it has helped. I have been delighted to hear when readers of *Chesterfield* have taken their children or grandchildren to visit Jersey Zoo, simply because they had read about it in the book; others have generously sent donations too.

Similarly many readers of *Butterflies* and *Swallows* books have visited Corfu and Paxos after buying the books. They have kindly written to tell me about their holidays and how they have enjoyed visiting some of the places described in the books, as well as meeting some of the Corfiots we were lucky enough to count as friends. One lady from the USA wrote to tell me she and her husband had been so impressed with *Butterflies* that they had just bought a 56ft catamaran, had her shipped to Corfu and were planning to take their 10 year-old son to 'sail slowly around the Ionian, visiting all the places you wrote about in your book'. Then came the bombshell news that they had never sailed before! I was horrified. What a responsibility for me. Did she think sailing a large catamaran was like driving a new car? I wrote back immediately, strongly advising her to hire an experienced catamaran skipper for at least the first year. As Jeremy has always admitted – despite his many years at sea and thousands of ocean miles – the sea will teach you a new lesson every single day.

Lee Durrell has now restored a traditional and very elegant Corfiot house, where she lives for part of the year. She kindly wrote a wonderful introduction to my gift book, *A Greek Island Nature Diary†*, which also has a page describing the exceptional work done by the Durrell Wildlife Conservation Trust around the world.

Later that month I was able to fit in a day for a book signing at Mike's tiny bookshop in Port Isaac. Tuesdays were my usual day, unless it was raining of course as I had to set up my table outside. Mike was a long serving member of the local council and was always kind enough to forewarn me about anything that might affect my visits to the village. Out of the blue he had telephoned me the evening before.

"You might want to wear something special tomorrow," he said with a hint of mystery in his voice.

"Why?" I asked suspiciously, hitherto imagining him in the same fashion purgatory as Jeremy.

"Well I can't say who it is, my love, but some very important visitors may be coming to Port Isaac tomorrow morning."

I took the hint and wore my prettiest sleeveless linen frock, white with pastel coloured flowers, bought in Corfu Town and worn each year for Panayia Day in Kassiopi; my usual signing outfit – white cropped trousers and a blue and white sailor top was packed away in a dress cover for later. Arriving early at Port Isaac we could sense something was afoot. Gaily fluttering bunting lined the little streets leading to the harbour; even the courtyard housing the bookshop and two cafés was decked out with flags. It was already turning into a very hot day as Jeremy helped me set up my table and garden parasol before leaving to go home. Mike hadn't yet opened his shop

---

† Published by Unicorn in 2021.

so I wandered out into the road and noticed several secret police-men dotted around at intervals and desperately trying to blend in amongst the tourists and locals. (Secret? With their discreet ear-pieces, crisp white shirts and walkie talkies crackling somewhere inside their black trousers, they might as well have had blue flash-ing lights on top of their heads.). I approached one of them as he conemplated a hydrangea bush and asked who was expected.

"The Duke and Duchess of Cornwall," he answered.

My heart skipped a beat. I had just sent a signed first edition of my little Cornish book, *The Holiday – A Chough's Tale,* for Prince Charles to Camilla's sister, (a regular customer of *The Manor House Stories* for her granddaughter) who I happened to know would be seeing the Royal couple next time they visited the county. Amidst my excitement I was quietly fuming inside. Of all the days to have my face covered in a surgical dressing the size of a helicopter land-ing pad, why did it have to be today? A bee sting on my cheek had become infected and had required surgery, from which I was still recovering. As Mike eventually arrived to open his shop I began talking to the few customers in the courtyard, which was noticea-bly quieter than usual.

"Everyone's down by the lifeboat station," said Mike. "The Royal party are going to visit the lifeboat crew and meet the Port Isaac gig rowing team."

I went back to my friendly secret policeman again. It was swel-tering already and it was only 10.30.

"Do you know if Their Royal Highnesses will be coming up this far?" I asked as soon as he had finished talking into his collar.

"I expect they might well do, possibly," he said circumspectly, now looking at me more suspiciously as if I was a stalker at best or a terrorist at worst.

A couple of police Land Rovers were parked at the top of each hill that led down to the Platt and harbour; their drivers were watching me too. 'It's that wretched woman who planted a fake briefcase bomb for Prince Charles at the NEC and then tried to smuggle fireworks into The Palace of Westminster a few years back,' I could imagine them saying to one another.

A few tourists started to line up on the pavements, quickly joined by more until there was quite a crowd. I raced back to my table as fast as my kitten heeled sandals would allow and grabbed one of my books. The anticipation was palpable amongst the assembled visitors and locals as I stood on the edge of the road and waited. Prince Charles appeared first, talking to everyone he passed and shaking hands with many. Suddenly he stopped in front of me and smiled. I curtseyed and showed him the book, explaining that it was all about Cornwall.

"Oh how lovely!" he said, just as Camilla joined him in time to say how much she and her grandchildren loved my Manor House Stories.

I curtseyed to her, handed her the book and explained I had already sent a copy for Prince Charles via her sister.

"Oh yes! Thank you," she replied before turning to the Prince. "Annabel mentioned there was a parcel for you."

Neither of them were wearing hats and they must have been thoroughly overheated, although neither showed the slightest sign; it must have been a long trek up the steep hills from the harbour, Prince Charles having walked up one road and Camilla the other, each talking to people and shaking hands all the way. A photographer had been busily clicking away as we chatted; I was terribly embarrassed about the white dressing on my right cheek, although both Royals had expressed great sympathy after asking what had befallen me. Then the photographer very considerately crossed to the other side of us, from where my unsightly dressing would not be seen. The Duke and Duchess said goodbye and wished me a speedy recovery before making their way towards Nathan Outlaw's restaurant, where they were meeting the cast of *Doc Martin*. Luckily I was able to collar the photographer, who looked vaguely familiar, before he trailed after the Royal party.

"Hello, were you by any chance with the Torbay News in 1975?" I asked, "I'm sure we've met somewhere before."

"It wasn't me, madam," he said, rather taken aback. "But if you give me your email address I'll send you a couple of those photos. I think you'll like them."

I scrawled it in his notebook and followed him to the restaurant, where I joined the large crowd waiting on the road. After about ten minutes, the Duke and Duchess left in a gleaming black car, to be driven back to the helicopter that was waiting to spirit them onwards to their next engagement in Exeter. The actors began to file out of the door and several people asked for 'selfies'. Martin Clunes, the star of the series who plays the part of a cantankerous doctor, was one of the last to appear and I spotted my chance. I handed my phone to the lady next to me, walked over to Martin and asked if he would mind posing for a photograph.

"Not at all," he said, smiling charmingly. "Where's your camera?"

I pointed to the lady holding my phone.

"I *would* have this ghastly great dressing on my face!" I moaned as he put his arm around my shoulder.

"Just say I treated you!" replied Martin, quick as a flash.

By now my dress was clinging to me, but it had all been worth it. I walked on air back to Mike's shop and gratefully changed into my spare outfit, listening to the Royal helicopter flying overhead and wondering if Prince Charles or Camilla had any chance to do the same en route to Exeter; I certainly hoped so. The photos duly arrived by email that evening and I was thrilled to see that Camilla was holding my book in her hand as we talked. We printed the photo and put it in a silver frame; it has graced my signing table ever since.

Of course the photographer had most definitely never worked for the Torbay News or any such other; he was in fact Arthur Edwards, the most trusted Royal photographer *par excellence*. What a very generous man to give me proof of such a treasured memory!

Chapter 9

... and Other Animals

If you think you are too small to make a difference,
try sleeping with a mosquito.

The Dalai Lama

With the exception of mosquitoes and flies I hate killing anything. But there was one occasion, when I was just seventeen, about which I still feel very guilty to this day. I was staying for the summer with my Thai friend Addy's affluent family in their impressive house in a leafy suburb of Bangkok. It was the middle of July, one of the hottest months of the year in Thailand, just before the monsoon was due. Addy and his younger brother wanted to go hunting at a market garden the family owned in the middle of the paddy fields about an hour and a half from Bangkok. I decided to go too, thinking I might be able to do some sketches of the countryside. We were accompanied as usual by a chauffeur and a burly young Burmese bodyguard, sporting a tufty little topknot incongruously tied up with brightly coloured ribbon; he bore an uncanny resemblance to a younger version of Oddjob from the James Bond film *Goldfinger*.

Oddjob always slept on the floor at the foot of Addy's bed, huge knife at the ready; he never let Addy out of his sight. I was mystified why a bodyguard was needed at all, but apparently kidnapping children of wealthy families was commonplace. As Addy's father was prominent in the government and attended weekly meetings with the King, Addy and his brother were even more vulnerable. (But there may have been more to it, as a slightly silver-haired but just as muscular Oddjob was still diligently guarding Addy and his guests when my family and I stayed with him in Thailand nearly 30 years later. On a shopping trip to a gift market on the west coast of Phuket, eleven year-old Miranda and I had rather unkindly tried to see if we could shake off Oddjob by going into a stall one way and leaving from the back entrance. But Oddjob was already waiting for us there, arms folded like a djinn, having watched our clumsy deception with well-trained eagle eyes).

Early in that first visit to Addy's family home I had walked down the long drive towards the elaborate wrought iron security gates, hoping to go out into the neighbourhood to post a letter to my parents. Before I got half way down the drive Oddjob was at my elbow, gently ushering me back towards the house; he spoke not a word of English but I got the message when he drew his hand slowly across his throat. He alerted Addy who told me it was not safe for me to go anywhere by myself and that I must give my letters to one of the servants to post.

On reaching Addy's market garden we walked for about ten minutes through paddy fields, balancing precariously on narrow grass and mud strips that criss-crossed the water just a few inches above where the young rice plants grew. I found walking in the full sun on these slippery pathways very difficult and I was slowing up the hunting party to such an extent that Addy suggested I sat in the shade of a tree and waited for them to return. I sank down gratefully on the bank as the morning temperatures soared to a humid 98°.

"You better keep this with you, just in case," said Addy, handing me his extremely powerful hunting rifle before disappearing with the other men.

"In case of what?" I wailed after him in high alarm, but he just waved a dismissive arm and disappeared from sight without answering.

An hour passed as I sat in the welcome shade and did some sketches of the rice fields, bordered by forests of bamboo and distant palm trees, dotted here and there with large white egrets picking their way delicately through the watery fields in search of frogs and lizards. Then my eye was caught by something moving in the dry grass a few yards in front of me; the long stems were undulating gently. I reached for the rifle, very unsure of what was coming towards me. Suddenly, the biggest snake I had ever seen slithered out of the grass onto a patch of bare earth; it must have been about five feet long and as thick as my wrist. It had a triangular head, the colour was mostly pale beige with a regular pattern of distinct brown and black markings. I hesitated for only a second, hoping it would slip into the water and disappear, but it was heading determinedly in my direction. It was him or me, and him was likely to be more venomous than me, I decided. I lifted the gun, aimed and fired, almost tumbling over backwards with the recoil. I was shaking like a leaf and could hardly look at the snake, which lay quite still, stretched out like a stick. I dared not go near it in case it suddenly revived, but hid behind the tree trunk. Within minutes Addy and the others came running back, having heard the gun shot.

"What you done, Jani?" Addy asked.

Oddjob, Addy's brother and the chauffeur had guns at their shoulders, cocked and ready to fire at any unseen threat lurking in the bamboo thickets.

"I think I shot that snake," I answered, pointing to the lifeless body. "But I only meant to scare it away!"

The men looked amazed and examined the very dead reptile.

"Brimey!" exclaimed Addy. "Good shot Jani! You got him light thlough the neck!"

I think the Thai contingent of that hunting party looked at me with new respect from that moment. This red headed, freckle faced, pale skinned, skinny teenage English girl had more to her than they had imagined, even if she was badly in need of a brandy to calm her nerves*. The snake was taken back to the house where the admiring servants removed the skin and dried it in the boiling sun for a few days. Addy handed it to me, rolled up like a silk necktie, to take back to England as a souvenir. In the neck, just below the head, a bullet hole was clearly visible. I kept the dried snakeskin for many years as a souvenir, until our first marital home burned to the ground in 1983 and everything was lost. Addy only knew the name of the snake in Thai, which I have long since forgotten; I have tried to identify it on the internet and the closest image I can find is of the Malayan pit viper, one of the deadliest snakes in the whole of Asia.

Talking of animals, during the depths of the winter we spent ashore in Corfu after we had lost Sarava, the long dark evenings could be devoid of entertainment – our television only receiving Greek soaps, football and interminably long political discussions. Most of the tavernas and bars were closed and shuttered and the locals would be snugly closeted in front of their fires. Whenever Miranda was staying with us it was hard to amuse her when most of her Greek friends were away studying in Thessaloniki or Athens. As we only had a limited collection of our own videos, which we had watched until they were worn out, I resorted to taking her on regular trips to Acharavi where we had discovered a rental shop. Most of

---

*I was once Addy's guest at a formal dinner at the Thai Embassy in London. At the end of the meal the guests were asked to be upstanding to toast the King of Thailand. Addy was seriously allergic to alcohol, so I tried to stop him raising his untouched glass of Champagne. 'I have to toast my King!' he insisted, taking a respectful sip. He immediately sank to the floor, his face purple, and it took several minutes to revive him.

the current films were available to hire for a few euros and we had fun choosing from the shelves; although our tastes were sometimes different, I liked many of the films Miranda picked out. Very few were to Jeremy's liking, the exception being *Meet the Fokkers*, but he always had a newspaper or a history book to study if he really couldn't stomach the rom-coms we brought back to watch. The heaviest rains generally started in November, drenching the island in tropical downpours that flooded fields and valleys and caused torrents to run through the narrow winding streets of the villages until they reached the sea, staining the waters of the Corfu Straits with swirls of reddish brown gravy.

It always seemed to be raining on our sorties to Acharavi in the early evening when the shop opened; in the daytime the owner was out fishing, which partly explained the unusual odour in the shop. The winding road out of Kassiopi followed the coast and had to be negotiated very carefully when inches of water and mud covered the tarmac, over which Kamikaze motorcyclists sped towards oblivion; we knew of several who had lost their lives on this dangerous stretch. On one such evening the cloudburst was heavier than usual and the road became indistinguishable from the surrounding verges and fields as fat raindrops bounced a full six inches into the air.

"Mummy look out!" Miranda suddenly shouted. "There are huge stones in the road!"

I swerved to avoid one, then wrenched the steering wheel the other way to avoid another.

"They're everywhere!" I exclaimed, "I can't avoid them all, there must have been a landslide".

Then as I slowed to a crawl and raised the headlights to full beam, a horror show unfolded before us. Some of the rocks were moving! Slowly, some limping gruesomely, we soon recognised the lumpy shapes as gigantic toads. I slammed on the brakes and jumped out of the Jeep, hoping to move at least a few from the road where they were destined to be squashed by the next car and the next after that. One local truck was heading in my direction on the opposite side of the road.

"STOP!" I yelled, running in front of him, frantically waving my arms as the rain poured down and splashed on the knobbly backs of the toads, some still crawling awkwardly and others already flatter than pancakes on the road.

"Mummy, come back!" called Miranda. "You can't save them all! And don't touch them, they're poisonous!"

She was right, of course. I had no gloves and I knew glands beneath their skin exuded a poisonous secretion when they were threatened. The truck drove on as I climbed back into the Jeep; the driver probably hadn't even seen me or the toads and I could hear the sickening 'splat, splat-splat' as he drove over the poor amphibians. I swerved this way and that to avoid as many as I could, but my heart was breaking to think how many would be killed outright and worse, how many would be injured and die slowly on this dark road in the pouring rain. The toads were simply trying to follow a route known to them for centuries, maybe for thousands of years, to their chosen place for the 'winter sleep,' probably amongst the reeds that grew on the opposite side of the road near the beach. How were they to know that man had ruined their traditional pathway and built a road? This Common European Toad, the largest in Greece, is known as *Bufo bufo*; its name says it all and in my opinion, with a face only a mother toad could love, it is to be greatly admired, warts and all. They are remarkable creatures, nature's shape shifters who start life as jelly-like eggs, metamorphose into tadpoles then finally growing legs, lungs and a thick skin to emerge from their watery birthplace to breathe air and live a dual life above and below water. Toads in captivity have been known to live for fifty years, although their life span in the wild is usually about twelve years; in North East Corfu the chief elder of the entire clan is probably three years old at most. Christianity has been known to demonize both women and toads, attaching both to evil, darkness, sorcery, and poisoning – an obvious invention of a Patriarchy which attempted to control both nature and women. Well, that never worked. However the toad emerges in other mythologies as a powerful figure, a manifestation of the Earth Mother. I wish the Municipality of Kassiopi would build an underpass for these poor harmless creatures to save this mass carnage each autumn. From that evening on we made up our minds never to hire videos again when it was raining.

In retrospect rain seems to have played as great a part in our lives as fire. Having seen Venice sparkling in the sun from the decks of the Minoan Lines Ferries on our many journeys to and from Corfu, I was determined to tread its famous streets at least once. Eventually I won Jeremy over when he ran out of logical reasons why we shouldn't stay for one night on the way to Corfu for another perfect summer. Rory and Jeremy had swopped cars for the summer; Rory's growing events business meant he needed a bigger vehicle than his new Volkswagen Golf. It was rather challenging fitting our luggage into the small boot, but as we had no King Charles Cavalier with us that year, we adapted and filled the back seats with our bags of presents, which included a new tumble dryer for Antonia. Driving around the island that summer, we would gradually get used to hearing Greek boys and grown men gesticulating as we drove past. '*Koitá! Rho triánta-dio!*' they shouted, full of wonder as the car's crackling exhaust deafened everyone within earshot. Unknown to me, Rory's R32 really was rather special and certainly the only example on Corfu.

At Lake Garda, where we always liked to spend the night before catching the Minoan Ferry from Venice to Corfu, I visited the local travel agent to inquire about a room in Venice for the following night. I harboured sentimental visions of La Serenissima, mainly from my A-level history of art studies, travelogues and written accounts of the wonders of this fairytale city of gondolas, palaces and canals. But above all I imagined the beautiful depictions in the fabulous 1981 television adaptation of *Brideshead Revisited*, in which Sebastian and Charles visit Venice to stay with Sebastian's father, The Marquess of Marchmain, and his Italian mistress. Those Canaletto scenes of the boys visiting galleries, palaces, statues and churches, the shimmering sunlight on the Lagoon, the elegant linen suits and evening dress, the gondolas, morning coffee at Florian's and leisurely afternoons spent at the Lido were all firmly etched in my memory and I was certain Venice would be exactly as it had been depicted in the glory days before the second world war. My illusions were soon to be shattered like Murano glass falling onto marble. We had been urged to park the precious car – a magnet for Italian car thieves – in a secure underground facility for safety; we had already been victims to enough robberies in Italy, thank you very much. The car prison was at the Tronchetto, where we parked the car in a floor to ceiling cage of iron bars. Jeremy locked the prison and kept the key given to him by the attendant; for good measure, and fully expecting countless copies of the key to be for sale on the black market, Jeremy gave the watchman a fifty-euro note with the promise of another hundred if the car was intact the following morning. I felt so sorry for the dear little car as I looked back at it in its cage; it seemed to be asking what it had done wrong.

Sure enough the deluge began on cue as we boarded a *vaporetto* to take us down the Giudecca Canal to Saint Mark's Square. The windows of the craft were completely steamed up with condensation running down them in silvery streams, totally obliterating the sights I had so longed to see at close quarters. But I was still looking forward to our night in the luxurious comfort of the Ca' dei Conti, the four-star hotel the travel agent had so highly recommended and booked for us; with its fine view of the canal, yet only a few minutes' walk from all the great sights, it sounded perfect. At the time I was blissfully unaware that Italian hotels obviously went up to ten or possibly fifty-star ratings.

I was told it would be easy to find so we disembarked at San Marco, dragging our two small wheelie cases through the flooded streets. Our feet were sodden within minutes, the rain was coming down in stair rods now and we must have taken a wrong turning because there was no sign of the hotel. Fifteen minutes later we were getting more and more lost and Jeremy's temper was about to erupt like Vesuvius. He marched a few yards ahead of me, so I was trotting to keep up, every so often he would turn his head to give me the blackest of looks that said; 'This was all your idea'. I was getting desperate, I was drenched, cold and needed the loo. We then realised we had actually trekked through half of the Castello district and were back at St. Mark's Square again. The streets were full of people, so I stopped an elderly Italian and asked if he knew the hotel. Thank heavens he did; it was only a hundred yards away and pointed us in the right direction down a narrow alley.

(Jeremy has a flair for languages but, being a man, he would circumnavigate the globe in search of a destination rather than ask for directions; and anyway he has refused on principle to learn a word of Italian, so certain was he that a mixture of French and Spanish would always get you by. The German language is even more problematic for Jeremy because – as with many Frenchmen who find spoken English a source of hilarity – he finds its harsh, guttural enunciation altogether too ridiculous. Apart, that is, from one phrase gleaned from his father's pre-war copy of *A Motor Car on the*

Continent. So the next time our exhaust pipe falls off in Germany he will be able to say '*Mein auspuff ist geschwächt!*' with panache. The trouble is Jeremy finds this non sequitur frightfully amusing and has committed it to memory, opening any conversation with a German stranger by spouting it out with glee. Fortunately most of them accept it as an equally humorous icebreaker.)

"Damn it all!" swore Jeremy as the hotel came into view, "That's not a canal, it's a ditch! You couldn't float a Pooh stick in it!"

The small hotel was strawberry milkshake pink and picturesque enough, with its entrance over a miniature, ornately arched bridge leading directly to the front doors. But I had been led to believe our hotel would overlook the bustling waterway of the Grand Canal; I had been hoping to arrive with graceful dignity by gondola. Instead we had the inconvenience of negotiating a tiny bridge over a moat from Lilliput. We struggled up and over the seven steps with our unruly wheelie bags trailing behind us and entered the foyer, where we waited at the reception desk dripping all over the plush red carpets. I was about to take off my sodden shoes until I saw Jeremy removing his deck shoes and emptying a cupful of water from each one onto a potted palm in a corner.

Our room was dismally dark and smelt strongly of mildew, its elaborate furnishings and wall hangings having soaked up the previous winter's pervasive damp; heavy navy and gold curtains were half drawn across the only window, trendily draping several stained yards of their excess length onto the rugs with the sole purpose of stealing valuable floor space. I peered out to see the view of the canal that the travel agent in Lake Garda had promised; Jeremy was right, it was a stagnant narrow ditch and the ancient houses opposite were within touching distance, their windows looking directly into ours. No wonder our curtains were drawn. I could imagine the mosquitoes that would be breeding in the dirty water, busily plotting how to get in and feast on us during the night. I peeled off my wet clothes and shoes and took them to dry in the bathroom where the heated towel rail was stone cold. There were no radiators in the room either, in fact absolutely no means of drying anything. I unpacked without enthusiasm and tried to console Jeremy with the thought of an evening out and a delicious supper.

"But I haven't got a change of clothes or shoes," he replied miserably. "And I feel like a drowned rat!"

Then I realised I didn't have spare clothes either; for once in my life I had only been able to squeeze a nightdress, slippers, make-up, hairdryer and a bulging sponge bag into one very small wheelie case. In the luminous Venice of my imagination I hadn't dreamt that it could possibly be raining. I called reception and asked them if they had anywhere I could dry our clothes. 'No madam,' was the unapologetic answer. So there was no choice; my incandescent husband lay steaming on the bed in his wet clothes, his soggy leather deck shoes discarded on the floor. It occurred to me that since we were married in 1980 I had spent much of the time trying to cheer him up in one way or another when plans spun out of his control. Why did I make such an effort? Why didn't I just collapse in a heap and give way to despondency? It is hard to believe we could both be born under the sign of Aries, yet be so very different; perhaps this is why we have had a successful marriage, being so opposite yet sharing so many likes and dislikes. I left him to doze while I went into the chilly bathroom and had a tepid shower. I plugged in my hair dryer using the ingenious 'all territories' adaptor and made an attempt to straighten the frizz out of my hair, confident we would soon be sitting in an elegant Venetian restaurant and tucking into a delicious Italian meal. The electricity sockets weren't working. Putting on our cold wet clothes and shoes again was the only option available unless we ventured out in our nightclothes, which was actually quite tempting. We sloshed through the narrow streets again until we reached St. Mark's Square, now under inches of filthy water. I bought a cheap umbrella from a street stall but Jeremy refused to share it with me and strode ahead as if he knew where he was going. We peered through a few steamed up restaurant windows, but they were all crammed full, and in any case one glance at their menus convinced Jeremy we would not be entering.

"Good God! *Forty* euros for a plate of lasagne in this one!" he wailed each time until I was fed up with hearing it.

It was still raining and we were famished, so we plodded on until we found a tiny, dingy bistro in a scruffy back street that was half empty – probably a bad sign in Venice. We were shown to a table without as much as a *buonasera* or even a smile from the surly waiter, who tossed a couple of menus onto the table like a croupier dealing cards and left us to our gloom … a menu illustrated with photographs of its dishes is rarely a good sign. So for the remarkably reasonable price of sixty euros we reluctantly ordered our two dishes of lasagne and salad with a bottle of supermarket Barolo for a further extortionate fifty euros. Half an hour later our plates were plonked down in front of us: infant's portions of Lasagne with a wilting lettuce leaf hiding two slices of cucumber and a slice of tomato reprieved from the kitchen dustbin. Our Lasagnes looked remarkably like microwave meals and they certainly tasted suitably artificial. We hardly spoke a word through the miserable fifteen minutes it took to pick at the sticky pasta, demolish the unspoilable grissini and gulp down the anaesthetic.

Next morning I tried to make the most of what I knew would likely be our very last time in Venice. I suggested we could take in a gallery and a cappuccino at Florian's before liberating the car and heading for the ferry to Corfu. But to cap it all we had the variety of plastic breakfast you would expect from an English road house;

worse still, the picture window in our four-star hotel's dining room gave us an up close and personal chance to admire the full majesty of the bricklayers' art on the building opposite.

"Let's go quickly while the rain's stopped and we can at least see something of Venice before we leave," I said cheerily.

Jeremy paid the bill and, after asking the puzzled receptionist to point out the precise section of the hotel he had just bought, our wheelie bags were soon following us towards St. Mark's Square. I was horrified to see so much ugly graffiti on these ancient walls and monuments; this never appeared in *Brideshead* at all, but perhaps they cleaned everything before filming. Surely tourists weren't responsible for this desecration – unless Jeremy and I were amongst a tiny minority who didn't carry cans of spray paint about their person – which meant the finger of blame pointed at the budding Banksys of the Veneto. With optimism on the wane, I marched determinedly ahead of Jeremy towards Florian's.

The splendidly decorated Caffè Florian, situated under the *Procuratie Nuove* in St Mark's Square and known as the oldest café in Europe, is an enduring symbol of the city of Venice. It was opened in 1720 by Floriano Francesconi as *Alla Venezia Trionfante* (Triumphant Venice), although the clientele subsequently rechristened it Caffè Florian in honour of its owner. Its windows had witnessed the splendour and fall of the La Serenissima and the secret conspiracies against French and then Austrian rule; later, its gracious rooms had been used to treat the wounded during the 1848 uprising. Besides being the most famous coffee house in Europe, Florian's was the only meeting place of the time that admitted women, which explains why Casanova chose it as a hunting ground in his insatiable quest for female company. Despite such provenance Jeremy stubbornly refused to enter the hallowed doorway and stood resolutely outside.

"On principle I'm NOT paying ten euros for a coffee!" he announced, somehow forgetting he had willingly paid as much at a fashionable coffee house in Kitzbuhel.

"Well I'm going in! And anyway I'll need the loo before we go anywhere else."

I walked in and wove my way between six smartly uniformed waiters who seemed intent on blocking the doorway; none of them spoke to me or averted their eyes from surveillance of the Square in search of suitably blinged-up clientelle. There was only one other customer, an elderly but immaculately dressed Italian man sitting at a table by a window, reading his newspaper. I glanced at my reflection in an ornate Rococo gilt framed mirror on the wall; 'shabby' was the word that came to mind: soggy shoes, a very bedraggled navy Burberry rain jacket and frizzy hair courtesy of the only four-star hotel in the world without functioning sockets for a hairdryer. Oh well, there was nothing to be done. I sat at another window table and watched Jeremy standing outside with his back to me and waited. And waited and waited. After ten minutes Jeremy turned and gesticulated at his watch, indicating that time was fast running out to catch a *vaporetto* down the canal, retrieve the car and check in by noon for the ferry to Corfu. The waiters were still rooted to the spot by the door and hadn't come anywhere near me; this behaviour would be unheard of anywhere in Greece.

I still needed the loo, so I asked one of the statues in the doorway for directions. 'Ladies?' I inquired, washing my hands in heavily laboured mime – a handy trick that seems to be understood all over the world. Somehow the fellow summoned enough energy to point languidly towards the stairs. I went up and used the facilities, which were cramped and not a bit as smart as I had imagined, then came down again and left the building. Nobody even noticed. Next time you're in St Mark's Square I urge you to make free with

Florian's toilets; they're probably the best value in Venice.

Yes, we had had been desperately unlucky with our stay in Venice and our misfortune had clouded our judgement. I would dearly have loved to spend time in the little shop I had noticed on our way back to the canal, where you could have a perfume made to your own specifications. Nevertheless if Jeremy and I ever think of returning, it'll be The Danieli or nothing.

Chapter 10

Absolutely Fabulous

Doing nothing often leads to the very best of something.

Winnie the Pooh, A.A. Milne

I found these notes scribbled in a little notepad inside a summer handbag that hadn't seen daylight since we left Corfu. Somehow it must have been in England when Sarava was lost.

October 2002

'The Mediterranean Swifts have disappeared from the skies of Corfu; now they are somewhere between here and Africa where they will spend the winter. Corfu Town seems strangely quiet without their constant shrill whistles as they swoop and soar over the graceful Venetian buildings. Sitting alone at a table under the lime trees on the Espianada with the first of several cappuccinos, I notice the locals are wearing jackets for the first time since March. It's an early morning in October and I am still comfortable in cotton shirt and trousers on such a sunny day, even if there is a welcome hint of freshness in the light breeze carrying over the sea from the mainland. The scent of the town has changed since the last time I was here a fortnight ago; wafts of charcoal and woodsmoke fill the still air, mingling with the customary aromas of strong coffee and freshly baked bread. A vendor tends the glowing embers in the makeshift brazier on which he roasts chestnuts. Beyond him the strains of violins and a piano from the music school add to the magical autumnal atmosphere of an island that has at last breathed a sigh of relief and said farewell to summer for another year.'

I am scribbling these words on the tiny notepad I use for shopping lists. Two elderly Corfiot men are the only other customers at the Libro d'Oro, sitting at a table opposite me with their Greek coffees and glasses of water. They are watching me with interested innocence; I look up occasionally and smile at them as I listen to their unhurried conversation. They have no idea I can understand them.

"Look at the pretty foreigner … no tourists left here now. Do you think she lives here?" ponders one of the men as he twists the end of his moustache.

"I don't know. Is she American perhaps?"

"Or German, do you think?"

"Unlikely, she smiles at us."

"But why is she alone? Where is her husband?"

"Is she a widow?"

"Too young and she's not wearing black."

"What's she writing?"

"Postcards?"

"Maybe it's a love letter …"

"It must be an entire book!" interrupts the livelier of the two as they burst into raucous laughter.

This is a lightbulb moment. In my mind I am simply writing down my feelings and observations, as I have always done since we first came to this wonderful island. But here is an idea. Could these ramblings ever be strung together to make a book? I finish my coffee and wish the two of them a very good morning and enquire after their health in my very best Greek; they sit there speechless with open mouths and I chuckle to myself as I walk away.

A seed has been sown.

* * *

Just as mankind had the power to push the world to the brink, so too do we have the power to bring it back into balance.

His Majesty King Charles III May 2023

And there came upon the Earth a great plague …

Who could have imagined in those days of December 2019 that a horrendous disease born in China would so rapidly infect the entire world. The news reached us quite slowly at first, some cases of a lethal coronavirus occurring in the central Chinese city of Wuhan; it was thought to have started in one of those repulsive 'wet' street markets where fly blown raw meat and fish rub shoulders with un-mentionable body parts belonging to rare, endangered animals of which the Chinese are so revoltingly fond. We were drip-fed with whatever news our utterly trustworthy leaders deemed suitable for us to hear, as air travel gave the virus the legs it needed to thrive and common sense was consigned to the dustbin. The Bubonic Plague lasted for over four hundred years, mainly because it spread very slowly by sailing ships and donkey carts.

Scenes on the news bulletins reminded me of *Doomwatch,* a popular television series from the early 1970s, in which the opening scenes showed people around the globe disembarking from aircraft and collapsing dead on the tarmac. More recently *Contagion*, a feature film made in 2011, provided a chillingly accurate depiction of what actually unfolded before our eyes nine years after it was shot as hundreds of thousands succumbed to the disease. Many years before the pandemic struck, Prince Philip, The Duke of Edinburgh famously said if he were reincarnated he would wish to return to Earth as a killer virus to lower human population levels. He died in April 2021, so the conspiracy theorists can rest their fevered minds.

Our planet must have wondered, as the first lockdowns were introduced, if humanity had finally come to its senses. Dolphins and jellyfish filled the canals of Venice, suddenly crystal clear; in Turkey's Bosphorus, normally one of the world's busiest shipping lanes, pods of dolphins were seen leaping in the traffic free waters. Elusive, shy lions in the Kruger National Park lounged in the open, no longer concerned about hiding away in the cover of the veld. Wild boars roamed affluent residential areas in Israel; pink flamingos and pelicans flourished in the newfound tranquillity of lagoons in Albania. With the sudden absence of tourist boats, families of rare Dugongs swam in the shallow waters off Libong Island in Thailand; cougars strolled casually through a suburb of Santiago, Chile and closer to home, a herd of wild Kashmiri goats went window shopping in Llandudno, North Wales, munching their way contentedly through hedges, flower beds and window boxes. For the first time in a hundred years the snowy Himalayas could be seen from the streets of Bombay, as the smogs of pollution cleared.

Everyone reading this will know the catastrophic sequence of events that followed in rapid succession. This was the year the Earth stood still – at least it felt that way to us – and we were among the most fortunate as Cornwall basked in endless weeks of sunshine. Our walks with Dash across the moorland bordering our cottage were eerily quiet and peaceful, as if we had suddenly become stone deaf to anything but birdsong. We rarely saw a soul and never a single vehicle, except the occasional tractor; once we noticed an ambulance in the distance, urgently threading its way over the moors, its siren strangely silent. High above us the skies were clear of the cobweb of con trails; instead a profusion of skylarks took possession. Wild deer strolled past our five-bar gate at their leisure under the noonday sun, nibbling at the foliage in the hedges; garden birds lost their innate fear; rabbits, long horned Highland cattle and ponies grazed peacefully on the moorland turf and lay down in the middle of the lanes to absorb the heat of the day. Badgers trotted beside the hedgerows at dusk and confident foxes sat admiring the view on Cornwall's granite tors. Our presence was often so unexpected that Dash would inadvertently put up a woodcock, an egret, or a flock of oystercatchers – all far from their regular haunts – at a shallow pool concealed in a thicket of gorse.

Neither Jeremy nor I suffered with as much as a sniffle during the crisis, possibly because we washed or sanitised every single thing that came into the house; many of our friends were less fortunate, particularly those who had travelled by plane whenever restrictions were relaxed. Three very close friends tragically died of the disease and it was so very upsetting to be forced to watch their funerals on a website, instead of paying our respects in person. I was reminded of something my very first boyfriend's mother, the Comtesse de Contades, said at the doors of St. Honore d'Eylace Church in Paris, where the funeral of her old friend Christian Dior was taking place in October 1957. Gaspard told me that his mother, a former Dior model, had been invited to the funeral, but on reaching the church she realised she had left the invitation at home. Denied entry by a security officer at the door, she had the perfect answer ready: 'I have only come to pray for him and I can do that just as well anywhere.' Her words had remained with me ever since and they cheered me slightly as I watched those detached, impersonal funerals through the ether.

We did manage a few clandestine trips to Treyarnon Bay on the pretext of shopping at Constantine Stores, (where else could I find those essential tinned artichoke hearts in Cornwall?), and I enjoyed several swims in complete solitude. Jeremy wasn't at all tempted as the sea temperature was far below his feeble pain threshold, beyond which his fingers turned white within seconds. The beaches had become virtually free of plastic rubbish during the pandemic and the tidelines were made up solely of shells and seaweed, although Jeremy did find one sizeable Spiny Norman washed up on the tideline, after which he refused even to paddle at the water's edge. Spiny Normans (sea urchins to most people outside my family) were creatures from warmer seas we didn't miss at all. The name originated in a Monty Python sketch featuring a giant imaginary hedgehog; Jeremy and I had adopted it as a code to warn each other – without alarming our young children – whenever we noticed prickly sea urchins lurking on rocks. We rather liked the name, which joined a lexicon of family jargon largely indecipherable to outsiders.

As the lockdown was intermittently replaced by social distancing – a regime my agoraphobic husband found highly satisfactory – something unheard of began to happen around us: tables and chairs appeared on pavements outside cafés and bars, many with awnings or large parasols above them; marquees and covered terraces sprung up like mushrooms in pub car parks and gardens. Cornwall's spectacular coastline and countryside suddenly resembled the Mediterranean! What had befallen our supremely wise planning officers? Generally acknowledged as some of the cleverest minds in the world, they had suddenly concluded their citizens might enjoy sitting in the fresh air, sheltered from fierce sun or downpour, as they took in glorious views hitherto denied them from dismal interiors that at best boasted a single table with a view. Of course our elders and betters saw the folly of their ways as soon as the pandemic subsided and for our own good we were once again tidied away indoors. Wherever we found ourselves in the Ionian we never had to scratch our heads to think of somewhere to stop for an invigorating coffee, a refreshing beer or an appetising lunch. On the remotest island and in the highest hills we were invariably spoilt for choice; a kafenion or a taverna with a few simple tables set beneath a shaded terrace overhung with vines, cheerfully attended by the owner, was always around the next corner. We miss all that most desperately.

From my point of view, like so many millions of others worldwide, I was suddenly unable to sell my wares except through online websites. We were faced with a bleak financial outlook with no idea of when it might end. Jeremy and I never could bear to be idle, but overnight we found ourselves with a lot of time on our hands. Living on the very edge of the open moorland, Jeremy and I had been most fortunate to be able to walk in perfect isolation from the rest of humanity without fear of catching or spreading the dreaded plague. But we couldn't walk forever, so I decided the time had come to root out all the notes I had made during our years in the Ionian and try to turn them into a book. Of course my notes from the summer before the accident went down with the ship, but luckily I had brought all my diaries and calendars home to England each time we drove back across Europe from Corfu for Christmas.

With two hesitant fingers on my laptop keyboard I started to type up the notes that were left, whilst contemplating a suitable title. I remembered asking a friend's young twin sons for their opinions on titles when I had first contemplated the idea of writing a book about Corfu. They preferred my first choice, *The Butterflies Fly Backwards*, a phrase taken from something a Corfiot friend had once said to me; it sounded more unusual and more likely to attract curiosity. My family agreed as well, so the working title was set in stone like the Ten Commandments from then on. For the cover I would use my watercolour painting of the view from our favourite table at Taverna Agni, as it was in 2001; Nathan had used it as a menu background and had given me a few dozen prints of the picture, which he sold for me at the taverna. Rory offered to design the layout and help me find a Greek-style font for the title. This was quite a challenge as most of the available fonts were the stylized variety seen on Greek tee-shirts and menus for tourists. Ingeniously Rory found one that he could adapt by substituting a Greek 'e' and I chose scarlet for the font colour, hoping it would stand out in shops. I had never forgotten a comment made to me by the dour owner of the pottery in Stoke-on-Trent who had first produced my designs on bone china mugs. 'Red sells mugs' was the only critique he could muster as he studied my intricate design. Little wonder his company went bankrupt.

I was apprehensive about putting our glorious eight years with Sarava in the Ionian into words. Would I be capable of describing that idyllic period of our lives? Would I do justice to Corfu and the Corfiots? But the most worrying part was how I could write about the accident; after all I was not on board at the time. I was uncertain if I could persuade Jeremy to write about that distressing chapter, considering he could never talk to me about it. For years I had begged him to write a book about all our family adventures but he considered it far too private, unless it was written purely as a keepsake for the family. So I bashed away and the words seemed to flow faster than I could type, even when I graduated to three fingers; the memories came flooding back in torrents until I found myself watching a technicolour film of the events I was describing.

Any anxiousness about reliving our lives so publicly quickly vanished. Somehow the sunshine, warmth, colours, scents and flavours of the island washed over me again as if I had never left, dissolving my feelings of homesickness and loss; I think I was tugging on the invisible thread that connected us to Corfu. Instead I enjoyed being transported back over the decades and found it uplifting, comforting and reviving. I just had to hope the readers, if there were any, would feel the same. I persuaded Jeremy to read through it when I eventually reached 90,000 words, in the hope he would agree to write the last chapter. He wrote about the accident without further prompting. I cried when I read his account; it was the bit about Miranda's screams that really got to me.

A rough manuscript was mostly finished by March, although several months would pass before Jeremy had a fully edited manuscript ready to go to press. I took my courage in both hands and asked one of my favourite actresses to write an endorsement for the book. I wrote the letter, enclosing sample chapters and highlighting several passages from the book which I thought she might like – including one that featured some mutual friends. I didn't hold out much hope, knowing she must be permanently inundated with requests. However, a week after posting the parcel I received an email saying she was delighted to write a few words and 'would this do?'

> *Jani's descriptive prose beckons me back to Corfu, smelling the soft evening air and hearing the sea. Charming and amusing in equal measure, this is a book to cheer the saddest heart.*

> Joanna Lumley.

I couldn't believe my luck! I had been a fan of 'La Lumley' since my teens when she was a fashion and photographic model; when she starred as agent Purdey in *The New Avengers*, I copied her iconic haircut, along with half the girls in Britain. The whole world and I adored her as Patsy in *Absolutely Fabulous*; more recently her campaign to give British citizenship and permanent residency in Britain to the Gurkhas has won further praise. I sent a large bunch of scented Cornish narcissus for her in gratitude for writing the endorsement; she told me they made her whole house smell wonderful.

Once again I asked the Durrell Wildlife Conservation Trust if they could supply me with text and some snapshots of Gerry Durrell for a charity page to be included in the book. At last everything was in place and I could set a date for the book launch in May the following year at the Duchy of Cornwall Nursery, by which time two more titles of *The Manor House Stories* would be published.

In the meantime summer had arrived early in Cornwall and we were enjoying a spell of particularly hot and sunny weather. England was still in lockdown and I was missing the book signing days I had always arranged over the past five years, not to mention the income they had generated, all of which was earmarked for printing *Butterflies*. Then one morning I opened a card that had arrived in a silver envelope marked Special Delivery. As I read the words I squealed so loudly that Jeremy rushed out of the office in alarm, certain I must have either seen a colossal spider or broken a fingernail. I could hardly believe what I was reading: the letter came from a very senior member of the Royal Family asking modestly if I might consider undertaking a private commission for a whimsical painting, very much in the style of my illustrations for *The Manor House Stories*. Naturally I had done all the considering I needed within the time it took me to catch my breath.

My brief was very precise and colour photographs of the required background were quickly sent to me; sadly a site visit, as I had done with my Scottish commissions, was impossible during the lockdown. A unique tartan was required to 'dress' the characters in the painting, so I obtained a swatch by post from Scotland and proceeded to make the initial detailed pencil drawing. It was sent by courier for approval by my client, who luckily was delighted with it and gave the go ahead.

I painted at a table in the summerhouse where the natural light was so good, while Jeremy continued the long business of editing *Butterflies* almost to his satisfaction. Fortunately there was barely a breath of wind at the top of our sheltered lawn during the many weeks it took to complete such a finely detailed painting. By the middle of July the picture was ready to be professionally mounted, after which Jeremy packed it in acres of bubble wrap, rigid board and brown paper to prevent any damage. The rigmarole the parcel had to go through due to Covid was extraordinary. It had to be sent by designated courier to London, where it would be scrutinised by the security detail, then put into quarantine for two weeks before being sent by another courier to my client who was self isolating elsewhere. So it was almost three weeks before I received another Special Delivery letter from my client saying the painting was 'delightful,' expressing how pleased they were with it, adding that it had been sent for framing. Much later I received another letter saying 'Your painting now hangs proudly at ***** and is much admired.' This letter is now in a silver frame in our sitting room.

I like to believe this commission was, if not specifically an act of kindness, a very thoughtful way of helping me at a time when a considerate person would have known I was struggling in the lockdown. More importantly, a small proportion of my fee had enabled me to send the manuscript of *Butterflies* to the printers. We were utterly astonished when the first print run sold out within a few weeks; a larger reprint was ordered and once again our profits were swallowed up before we could enjoy a single penny from the fruits of our labours.

In January 2021, encouraged by the reaction that *Butterflies* was receiving, I contacted the editors of every glossy magazine I could think of to ask if they would include a review of the book. The only one of these high-end publications to respond was *Country Life*. The features editor spent nearly an hour with me on the phone, asking all sorts of questions; at the end of the call she said she would love to write an article about me and my books, although the final decision would rest with the chief editor. She had sounded so positive, saying my 'back story' and family connection to Beatrix Potter and the National Trust would be a perfect fit for the weekly magazine and a really interesting feature for *Country Life* readers. Sadly her editor (a man) didn't agree and the idea was shelved. It was the 'giant pumpkin story takes precedence' scenario all over again.

I also wrote to each editor of the seventeen 'county' lifestyle magazines, of which only two bothered to reply; as they expressed some interest, I sent a copy of *Butterflies* to each one. The editor of *Suffolk Norfolk Life* published a comprehensive review and described *Butterflies* as, 'A darn good read.' Freelance journalist Annette Shaw telephoned me to discuss a feature article she would like to write for *Devon Life*. The article, entitled; *A Remarkable Life*, duly appeared and led to further book sales. Annette also asked me what was happening about the gift book I had mentioned in the front of *Butterflies.* Of course I had absolutely no idea if or when my *Greek Island Nature Diary* would be published, but I hoped its mention might attract a publisher's interest; the cost of printing a luxury gift book, as I had envisaged it, would be way beyond my means. I already had over 50 watercolours of the flora, fauna and fascinating natural objects I had collected, and in most cases painted from life, during our years in Corfu and the Ionian Islands; I had also carefully kept the nature notes, pencil sketches and my own observations in various notebooks. I intended to add to these with further research on the medicinal, culinary and olfactory uses of the wild plants, as well as snippets of associated poetry, prose and references to Greek Mythology and folklore. After explaining this to Annette, I was pleasantly surprised when she suggested introducing me to a publisher. However, she warned, I would need to be patient, she added, explaining that the owner of the company she had in mind, Lord Ian Strathcarron, was invariably very busy and often out of the country; he would probably email me in a few weeks if he was interested. Our telephone rang at 5pm the same day.

Ian immediately said he was interested in publishing my book, adding that he thought my illustrations outstanding and explaining that he jumped whenever he got a recommendation from Annette. You could have knocked me down with the proverbial feather: it was the call every author dreams and fantasises about. We talked for about half an hour, mostly about sailing in the Mediterranean and Ionian. It turned out he had sailed around the Med on his yacht for two years and written several erudite histories of the area; serendipitously he now kept his yacht in the very same marina in Corfu where we had based Sarava for eight years. As you may imagine, I was jumping up and down as soon as I put the phone down. It was one of those moments in life where random pieces of a jigsaw seemed suddenly to fall into place.

"It was The Universe!" I told Jeremy.

"No, it was Annette," he replied, immediately looking up Unicorn Publishing on Google.

"I thought so," he called out from the office, adding a moment later, "they're vanity publishers."

To say my heart sank was an understatement; it fell through the floor and downwards to Australia. I couldn't believe this, it seemed just too cruel. I had to wait until Ian had emailed me a sample contract before I could call him to ask about the payment scheme, explaining that I would not want to go down that route. He leapt in quickly to assure me that vanity publishing was only suitable for some authors; in my case Unicorn would pay for all printing, editing, design and promotional costs in the normal way. In return I would receive royalties each quarter. Phew! Things moved quickly after that and I was assigned Unicorn's chief designer to help plan the 'look' and 'feel' of the gift book. The offices being in London, all discussions were by email or telephone, which involved a great deal of correspondence and patience. I had very specific ideas for the design of the book, but luckily it was plain from our first conversation that Felicity and I were singing from the same hymn sheet. I particularly wanted a padded cover, similar to a cookery book I had bought years before in Fiskardo – not because I enjoyed cooking but purely because the book had a tactile padded cover and the photographs inside of delicious looking dishes and Kefalonian scenes were fabulous.*

My other letter that day was to Lee Durrell, asking if she would be prepared to write an introduction to the book. Lee had already seen some of the original illustrations during my visit to Jersey Zoo in 2016. Once again luck was with me and she readily agreed. Her generous and lengthy introduction was eventually set opposite the Durrell charity page and included a charming photograph of Lee at Jersey Zoo's organic farm. Lee's words end with:

As I write these words … I am immersed in the magic of Corfu!

Come and share the magic by reading Jani's book – it will bring you straight here!

For the frontispiece and tailpiece I had painted the Greek letters *Alpha* and *Omega*, each embellished in the fashion of an illuminated manuscript. Below the first I included the opening lines of William Blake's *Auguries of Innocence*:

> *To see a world in a grain of sand,*
> *And a heaven in a wild flower,*
> *Hold infinity in the palm of your hand,*
> *And eternity in an hour.*

---

* *Classic Recipes from the Greek Island of Kefalonia* by local restaurateur Tassia Dendrinou, published by Livani Publishing.

The words perfectly describe how I feel about nature; by chance it also happened to be Ian's favourite poem – as he later told me. It would have been the first page of my submitted manuscript that he had seen, so I think it might have clinched the deal.

A launch party was arranged at the Duchy of Cornwall Nursery for November, shortly after the scheduled publication date. Early in September I received a message from Emma Fellowes who, being unable to attend my book launch, kindly asked if she and Julian could take us to lunch later in the month, when they would be coming to Cornwall for the weekend. I tried to insist we would very much like to treat them to lunch at a restaurant to save them driving across the moor to our cottage, as they had done the previous year, but there is no arguing with darling Emma once she has made up her mind about something. With typical thoughtfulness, she asked if I could recommend somewhere, so I suggested they met us at the Duchy of Cornwall Nursery which would be only a short detour from their route further south. I knew they would enjoy the restaurant and that Emma would enjoy browsing around the gift shop, the hothouses and the vast selection of plants. There were plenty of smarter options – you can't toss a pancake without it landing on a celebrity chef in Cornwall – but we invariably came away from these restaurants with the feeling their supercilious staff endured our patronage under sufferance. Moreover, as Jeremy observed, he never enjoyed stepping over the bodies of previous customers who had expired from starvation and regret, having just paid their extortionate bills for pitiful 'taster menus' that wouldn't satisfy the appetite of a mouse.

(On a hot day not so long ago Jeremy and I had both ordered Cornish lager instead of the outrageously expensive bottle of wine that should have accompanied our plates of seafood. The waiter must have taken exception to such frugality and brought out two bottles without glasses – obviously expecting us to drink straight from the neck as some of the young do. Funnily enough that episode was easily topped by the gin fizz I once ordered at a smart hotel on Lake Garda; the former palazzo had been a favourite stopover of ours for several years until it changed hands. When my gin fizz arrived flatter than distilled water I complained to the manager, who swore on his mother's grave that his recipe for the cocktail was correct. If only I had known the Italian for 'The clue's in the name, dopey'.)

I wanted to leave in plenty of time to get a good table before our friends arrived, as the restaurant is always busy and did not take reservations.† As so often happens, my dear husband refused to leave early enough, we got stuck behind a herd of cows, then a tractor and ended up arriving in a frantic rush. I careered into the entrance and was skidding towards the restaurant when I heard a familiar voice calling out from the other side of the shop.

"Jani! We're over here!" exclaimed Emma, glamorous as ever, with dapper Julian close behind her. She rushed over to me and we hugged.

"Look what I've brought," she said, opening her handbag and pulling out a large piece of paper. "I've written down all the questions I want to ask you about The Butterflies Fly Backwards," she laughed, "I just *loved* it but I need to know some answers!"

I astonished them both as I pulled out my own list of questions I needed to ask Emma and Julian; I knew only too well they would be forgotten as our conversations with these two lovely friends sped along like an express train. Lunch was a very jolly affair and we never stopped talking and laughing, Emma firing questions at me

---

† The attractive new Orangery Restaurant, recently opened by The Duke of Cornwall, now accepts reservations.

so that I could hardly eat my crab salad; I told her it was like being on *Mastermind*. By question number twenty-five I had to interrupt the men's conversation and ask Jeremy to explain properly what an *Admiralty Pilot* was; this gave me a much needed chance to finish my lunch. But Emma carried on saying she was determined to get to the end of her list when Julian petulantly interrupted, reminding me so much of Lord Kilwillie, the character he played so brilliantly in the television series *Monarch of the Glen*.

"Emma, *I* want to talk to Jani too! You've been talking all the time!"

At last Emma had finished her list and I started on mine; it was much shorter but the most important question was addressed to both of them. I wanted to ask if, knowing absolutely everybody as they do, they could suggest anyone to write an endorsement for my next book, *The Swallows Fly Back*, which was by now nearly completed. Tom Hanks was Julian's first suggestion, but Emma thought Tom might not want to be involved as he was a very private person.

"Can I write it?" asked Julian, much to my delight.

I hadn't liked to ask him as he had so kindly written the foreword to *The Manor House Stories* in 2013 and been so helpful in many other ways since then. A few days later an email arrived from Julian with his super endorsement:

This is a warm and funny demonstration of the triumph of the human spirit. Battered by almost every possible disaster, Jani and her husband come through them all, and keep you laughing until the end.

A friend of ours recently passed on some words of advice given to him by a mentor in his youth: to judge a person's character, one should look for the little things. Long before I had heard this, I had noticed Emma's expression as we left the restaurant together. The room was full of diners who had obviously recognised our well known friends, but were too polite to show any blatant acknowledgement. As Emma walked past each table she simply smiled her gentle smile at those watching her; it was a masterclass in 'how to be famous' without being either patronising or aloof. Such a pity more 'celebrities' don't follow her example.

For the cover of *Swallows* I painted a corner of The Lion House in the foreground, with my beautiful young Acacia tree in full flower to one side, (the one that the new owners cut down as soon as they had bought the house). Above the traditional Corfiot chimney two swallows fly near their mud nest, which is attached under the eaves. Falling away from the house the drunken olive trees cover the unspoilt valley, interspersed with slim Cypress trees, leading the eye to the glittering turquoise Corfu Straits, where a distinctive Minoan Ferry from Venice passes on its way to the New Port in Corfu Town. Beyond are the misty outlines of the sun kissed hills and distant purple mountains of Albania. Rory once again worked his magic on the design as with *Butterflies*, but on the spine he placed a small Greek flag. This was a nod to bookshops who display their books with only the spine showing, thus forcing customers to browse the shelves with their heads permanently and very uncomfortably tilted in order to make out the titles and authors. I was thrilled when Waterstones in Picadilly had placed *A Greek Island Nature Diary* 'face out,' as publishers call it, in the Travel section; it was particularly exciting to see it alongside Lawrence Durrell's *Prospero's Cell* and *Bitter Lemons of Cyprus*.

The old adage 'never judge a book by its cover' certainly doesn't apply to me; it is precisely the cover that attracts me to a book in the first place, the more attractive the cover the more I am inclined to buy it. I have rarely been disappointed, despite Charles Dickens' once asserting 'There are books of which the backs and covers are by far the best parts ...' The one exception was in an

Oxford bookshop many years ago, shortly before we were about to leave once again for Corfu, where I found myself scurrying around in great haste looking for some light reading for the ferry trip from Venice to Corfu. The first book to catch my eye was *Diplomatic Baggage* by Brigid Keenan. A contemporary cover illustration depicted the top of a globe and a typical British diplomat with a rolled umbrella striding ahead of a heavily laden luggage trolley, on which two young children sat with their glamorously dressed mother perched behind. The subtitle was *Adventures of a Trailing Spouse* and the endorsement – a single word in red, *Fabulous* – was written by Joanna Lumley. It was a good enough recommendation for me.

The second cover to attract my attention was an interpretation of a colourful embroidery sampler; the title also looked fascinating, *Mary Queen of Scots* by Lady Antonia Fraser. I am a sucker for anything to do with the Tudors, so this was definitely going in my basket. The special offer that week was a 'three for two,' so I quickly looked for something that Jeremy might like. This was far more difficult and I was fast running out of time, as he had given me precisely ten minutes before we had to leave Oxford to catch the ferry from Dover to Calais, after which our hotels through Europe and our cabin from Venice had been booked months in advance. I snatched a copy of *Captain Corelli's Mandolin* – and before my dear readers confirm their suspicions that I am an airhead, not just because I had noticed Hugh Grant reading it on the park bench with Julia Roberts in the last scene of *Notting Hill*, but because I knew the novel was set during the Second World War in Kefalonia, the stunning island we would be visiting again on Sarava that summer.

Diplomatic Baggage (or *Dip Bag* as Brigid calls it), was absolutely glorious, one of the funniest and most fascinating books I have ever read and it made me laugh out loud so many times. I began reading it when we were back in Kassiopi, having just been to Corfu Town to have a tooth out following an unfairly matched encounter with a particularly crusty baguette. Michalis, my handsome 40 year-old Greek dentist, had been trained in the USA and was brilliant, holding my hand at intervals during the treatment while a flat screen on the wall showed riotously noisy Greek chat shows. As I reclined in bed with the book on Sarava, being far from stoical when I am ailing, I was astonished to read within a few pages that Brigid had just broken a tooth! I loved the book so much I wrote to Brigid via her publisher, but I never received a reply. (We have since been in touch via good old Facebook and are now FB friends; she never did get my letter, so once again it rather confirms my lack of faith in most book publishers and agents).

Unfortunately my other choice reminded me of the dusty, fusty, dry history text books of my school days. I loathe to leave a book unfinished and will usually continue to turn the pages, positive it will improve as I plough on; but *Mary Queen of Scots*, despite being lauded by critics, utterly defeated me. If I had sought facts and dates I could have found them on Wikipedia, and in any case I knew most of the milestones in Mary's life – inheriting the throne of Scotland at the age of nine months, betrothal to Francis, Dauphin of France, (although I was never told how the Dauphin, or Dolphin, came by his title by my tedious history teacher, like all but one of our teachers at my boarding school, a grey-haired spinster clad in tweeds, twinsets, thick stockings and sensible lace-up brogues, who always referred to him as the *Door Finn*). I knew something of Mary's childhood in France, her three marriages and of course her beheading by a very clumsy executioner, who needed two swipes to complete the job. *I* wanted to know about her marriage at the age of sixteen to a boy two years her junior. Did she love him? Had his voice broken? Was he a spotty teenager prone to sulks and tantrums? What a wasted opportunity and what a misleading cover.

Jeremy adored *Captain Corelli's Mandolin*, so I read it after him and agreed with his opinion, although I have to admit to only really loving it after Corelli meets the beautiful Pelagia. Okay so perhaps I *am* a bit of an airhead, but I prefer to be called 'a romantic'. We eventually saw the film which I thought was wonderful, if only for the scenery of such a familiar island. Jeremy enjoyed parts of it too, but decided the screenplay was a travesty of the book; John Mortimer or Julian Fellowes, he insisted, would have done it *proper* justice.

So *The Swallows Fly Back* was printed in Wales and I already had hundreds of customers who had asked me to reserve signed first editions. (I wrote all their names on paper and attached them to the wall in the kitchen, never being able to find digital lists on my laptop, this was so much safer). These people were mostly readers of *Butterflies*; when we sent out the second print run I thought it would be a good idea to enclose a small leaflet with each book, a brief synopsis of *Swallows* and a colour picture of the cover. This paid dividends and many readers reserved copies of the signed first edition. As soon as the new books arrived in Cornwall, I wrote posts on various Facebook groups connected with Greece and her islands, as I had done with *Butterflies*, and orders came in to my website immediately, often as I was posting! One of the Facebook groups I had joined a few years earlier was for the old girls of my boarding school on the edge of Dartmoor. The first book had sold well through this group, but for some unknown reason my posts about *Swallows* were declined by the site administrators. I never did find out why. I had imagined that any old girl who had become a published author and illustrator would be interesting to former pupils, but maybe they thought it was too 'trade' in content …

On the other hand it may have been an exceptional year for giant pumpkins.

After the official launch at the Duchy of Cornwall Nursery in May, Jeremy and I embarked on a thrice weekly round of book signings and 'meet the author' days. We restricted our travelling to Cornwall; it was just too far to caper around the whole of England as we had done before. It was always hard work and occasionally downright unpleasant during inclement weather, but it was a direct sales model that worked well for me. On Tuesdays I was outside 'Buy The Book,' Mike's tiny shop at the top of Port Isaac, always busy thanks to *Doc Martin*. Thursday was my usual day to be beside the harbour in Padstow at the kind invitation of Elaine, owner of the Chough Bakery, famous for its prize winning pasties and proper bread. Here I should explain the reason I was not signing at the most obvious place for me in the village bookshop, a family business with outlets also in Falmouth and St. Ives. In 2016, when *The Holiday* was published, I had taken a copy into this shop to see if they might care to stock it, imagining the owner would be pleased to sell a children's book about Choughs and Cornwall. I was encouraged to see a table in the middle of the shop displaying books by local authors. The shop was empty apart from the manager who was barricaded behind the counter, safely hidden from any annoying customers who might require a grunt of acknowledgement from him. I explained that I lived nearby and put the tiny book in front of him. He picked it up and did a rapid 'card shuffle' of the pages, not reading a word or even glancing at the numerous detailed and colourful illustrations before putting it down again.

"I'll think about it," he muttered, having reassured himself the book did indeed contain pages made of paper.

So, with my tail between my legs and feeling very embarrassed and dejected, I left him my business card and the book and fled out of the shop, wishing I had never gone in. A couple of months passed and I heard nothing, until one Thursday when a lady rushed up to me as I was signing my books outside the Chough Bakery.

"I just wanted to say how sorry my colleagues and I were not to be able to sell your little Cornish book in the shop. We absolutely loved it and were so disappointed when the owner didn't order it; we could easily have had you signing your books in the shop," she enthused, explaining how she had worked there for several years and that her unhappy boss always behaved like that. Some people don't deserve to have shops.

Most Saturdays during the summer months were spent on the quayside at beautiful St. Mawes. Sales were exceptionally good in this new position, with locals and owners of holiday homes popping to the Post Office early for their morning papers before the visitors arrived. Then came the holidaymakers heading for the little ferry boats that took them across the sparkling water to Place and Falmouth; they all had to pass me on their way to the end of the quay where the ferries were waiting. We usually started packing up about 5 o'clock and by six o'clock, when the car was fully loaded, Jeremy would drive the few hundred yards along the quayside to the 'hole in the wall' fish and chip shop to order us a large box of chips to share as a late lunch and early supper. We were always starving hungry by then and the smell of the fish and chips wafting across the harbour was mouthwatering. In the picnic bag I always kept a couple of chilled drinks, some tomato ketchup and a bottle of oak matured artisan malt vinegar, from The Old Nuclear Bunker at Coverack.

As a very tiny child I always found the Sarsons Malt Vinegar bottle my mother hid in the larder, drinking it neat before she could stop me. Placing it on ever higher shelves was no deterrent; when

Mummy wasn't looking I can remember dragging a chair into the larder to reach the bottle. When I was about three Mummy took me to our family doctor who told her not to worry about it; he thought there must have been something in the vinegar my body needed, along with the beach sand I used to eat by the handful as a toddler ... I can still remember the satisfying crunch of it in my mouth. Extraordinarily I have since discovered that a deficiency of iodine is one of the causes of hypothyroidism, (an underactive thyroid gland), from which I have suffered for the past thirty years; one of the natural remedies is cider vinegar. No wonder I had always thrived on cheap Spanish plonk! My maternal grandmother and mother also had the same ailment and I remember Mummy being passionately fond of ginger – another natural remedy for the underactive thyroid, although she never knew that.

By that time I had almost lost my voice from talking to customers all day and was grateful to collapse into the car. Jeremy would drive us out of St Mawes to a vantage point on the road where we parked beside a five-bar gate with a spectacular view over the fields to the Carrick Roads, glittering in the late afternoon sun. Through the open window we enjoyed the fresh breeze coming over the water and watched a confusion of small craft puttering or sailing to and fro on the ruffled water. I can't describe how wonderful those chips tasted after a hectic day! Being surrounded by people in a bustling waterside village all day and selling books, the peace and quiet was so welcome. We have both decided those chips were the best we have ever eaten, crispy and crunchy on the outside and light and fluffy inside. There are worse ways to spend a day.

I was constantly surprised by some of the children's names I am asked to inscribe in *The Manor House Stories*; occasionally the grandparents buying the books were rather embarrassed and even apologetic when they told me the names of their treasured little darlings. Here are just a select few that have stuck in my memory like treacle toffee: Tallulah-Kiwi and her sister Autumn-Rayne, Beau-Brooklyn, Taya Moon, Arizona Sky, Aurora Cosette, Indiana Phoenix, Beauregard Trey, and Tigerlily-Tampa. It must be torture for those young children struggling to learn how to spell their names at nursery school. The first time I was asked to write 'Jensen' in a book I assumed it would be spelt like the car, an old flame having driven me around in a Jensen Interceptor, but was told by the puzzled parents it was after the racing driver, Jenson Button. I have had a few Portias too and always have to resist saying, 'ah yes, after the car'. Many of today's popular names, such as Meadow, Sienna, Willow, India, Savanna and Scarlett are names I wish my mother had chosen instead of plain Jane. When I frequently complained about my very boring name, Mummy called the more exotic names I longed for 'far too booky'; she knew Jane could never be abbreviated, but never imagined it would be embellished with an extra syllable. Thank the Lord for the lady who looked into my pram and asked Mummy my name; when she was told she exclaimed 'Oh, she's a little Janie,' which stuck. Bless her, whoever she was. I dropped the 'e' in the 1960's when it first became fashionable to end your name with an 'i' instead – hence Judi (Dench) Suzi (Quatro) Jimi (Hendrix) and so on.

The weather was not always with us, so we bought a small gazebo which helped to shade and shelter me and my display of books; one Saturday around lunchtime, a squall came in from the sea with torrential rain, so we dropped all four sides of the little tent and sat cosy and dry within for an hour, eating our picnic until it passed. On another occasion we were not so lucky. Jeremy always checked the weather forecast on the internet meticulously the night before every outing, specifically for each location. One Friday evening, after I had spent the entire day getting ready for a Saturday at St. Mawes, pre-signing a large quantity of books, making the picnic, picking and arranging garden flowers for my table, and refurbishing myself, he announced we could not possibly go when rain and gales were predicted. I argued that St. Mawes has its own micro-climate, as we had so often found; it could be tipping it down and blowing half a gale on Bodmin Moor as we crossed early in the morning, but on the approach to St. Mawes along the Roseland Peninsula, the skies would clear and the wind would subside to a gentle breeze. Even as the day dawned dark and forbidding, I managed to twist Mr. Grumpy's arm until he finally agreed to drive us to St. Mawes, where the flags at the harbour were being torn to shreds in the southerly force seven. It took both of us to put up the madly flapping gazebo as we hung on grimly to prevent it sailing over the harbour. Then the rain began, blowing in horizontally from the sea and soaking everything before we could attach the sides.

"That's it!" yelled Jeremy, "We're going home!," furious that he had just spent ten pounds on a day ticket for the car park. We drove home in stony silence.

In the middle of July, our busiest time of the year, I received a message from a lady who had bought all my books published to date, including a complete set of *The Manor House Stories* in one of the beautiful new presentation boxes that had recently arrived. She asked me if she could commission a painting of her family's favourite beach and taverna in Corfu, a setting Jeremy and I knew very well; I was astonished to see that her name was Miranda and felt it must be another sign. Jeremy helped me set up the summerhouse as a studio and as soon as my signing days were over in September I started working on the preliminary sketches. It was heavenly sitting peacefully in the charming little duck egg blue retreat, with every door and window thrown open to the birdsong; we enjoyed an Indian Summer that month and I could watch our resident swallows and swifts flitting to and fro, catching flies on the wing as fluffy white clouds evolved from one shape to another in the cornflower blue sky. After the intense record breaking temperatures of July and August, the fresher air was a tonic. Every morning I couldn't wait to open up the summerhouse again, often taking my breakfast with me.

Switching on Classic FM as I laid the first brushstrokes on the paper, the presenter played the opening track of *Adiemus, Songs of Sanctuary*; and from that moment I knew The Universe was with me. This haunting music had always been part of the soundtrack to our summers on Sarava, carrying me straight back to the colours, warmth, scents and sounds of the Ionian Islands. I had never quite summoned the courage to play the entire album since the accident, but on this day I turned up the volume and closed my eyes for the few minutes it played. Instantly I was transported to the foredeck of our beloved catamaran, feeling the sun on my skin and the delicious sea breeze as we sailed towards Paxos or Kefalonia; I swear I could hear the rush of the waves as they swept beneath Sarava's twin hulls.

Late in October I began the task of completing my illustrations for the final two children's books. The summerhouse was too cold to use by then, so I had to paint in the kitchen, with my cumbersome architects' easel facing the wall without any natural light. Rory bought me a special artist's lamp with different settings and a flexible head, which was a game changer. However it was challenging to be shut in the cottage for thirteen hours every day, starting around five in the morning and finishing in time for drinks at six. I made a list of the titles of the seventy-six pictures needed for the two titles and stuck it onto my easel. Each time I finished an illustration I would put a large red tick beside it; I can't tell you how daunting it was at the beginning of this marathon, with only one or two ticks at the top of the impossibly long list.

As I beavered away at my easel, I hardly noticed winter's fingers stretching across the Moor. The beaches of North Cornwall were deserted and decorated with interesting tidelines washed up by the storms. The leaves had been torn from the trees by the November gales and lay strewn in soggy piles on the lawn, above which the starlings returned in force and were greedily stealing the nuts and seeds from our bird feeders. The powder pink Camelia 'High Hat' Rory gave me for my birthday last year was flowering in the garden way before its time and there were buds on our hedge of rampant jasmine, its third flowering that year. The lemon tree Miranda sent me six years ago had doubled in size and was covered in sweet scented blossom and miniature green fruit. I doubted they would be ripe in time for Christmas, as they had been last year; the summer's early heatwave had thrown every plant into confusion. Six days before Christmas I finished the very last illustration, whooping with joy and relief. After ten years, and over five hundred illustrations later, the set of twelve books was now complete. Jeremy sent the files to our layout designer in Wales and I threw myself into preparing for another Christmas.

Chapter 11
Friends and Fiascos

Friendships between women are, as any woman will tell you, are built on a thousand small kindnesses ... swapped back and forth and over again.

Michelle Obama

It is quite extraordinary how a chance meeting can blossom into a close friendship; one of many such encounters happened to me the day I was asked to sign my children's books at the annual Riding and Heritage Day in Bodmin. It was 2016, a year that had already brought several surprises. I had set up my table in the main street, where various processions passed throughout the morning, culminating in the dragging of the shackled 'Beast of Bodmin' through the town, a macabre and sinister tradition. Bodmin Riding is mentioned in records as far back as the medieval era and was originally a celebration of St. Thomas Becket. The older celebration would have looked very different to the one we see today and included a group of horse riders carrying large flower garlands. As the final procession disappeared further up the road, I spotted a pretty lady on the opposite side, she was smiling at me and purposefully crossed the road to come to my table.

"Hi!" she said with a soft American accent. "I just had to come to see the lady wearing this lovely hat. I've just been in Venice and you remind me of the gondoliers!"

I was wearing my trusty boater, a Laura Ashley hat bought for Miranda when she was three. The American lady with the lovely smile introduced herself and we shook hands.

"I'm Kay, I'm from Chicago," she exclaimed, (taking me straight to Suzi Quatro saying 'I'm from Detroit and I don't mess around!'). "And this is Dave," she added, pointing to a tall man standing behind her. "He's my guide and is showing me around the area."

We talked a little more and Kay told me she was an extra in *Doc Martin*, where she had met fellow extra Dave, who thought she might enjoy seeing the Bodmin Riding Day. They were on a flying visit as they had to get back to Port Isaac that afternoon for more filming, but she bought a copy of *Chesterfield Penguin the Butler – All At Sea* and promised to keep in touch. During the winter months we exchanged news by email and on Facebook and she quickly became an email pen pal. I enjoyed hearing about Chicago and Michigan and she liked me telling her about Cornwall and the work I was doing for the next books. That winter she sent me photos of Michigan and Chicago in the snow and her boat house beside a frozen lake; I sent her photos of the windswept beaches of North Cornwall and our cottage decorated for Christmas. In 2018 Kay was booked to be an extra in Doc Martin again that summer and I invited her to stay with us for the few days they would not be filming in Port Isaac.

It was so good to see her again, we laughed until we cried at so many silly things, particularly when I had to sort out confusions between certain American and English words, which can be a cause of much misunderstanding. I had become familiar with obvious words such as 'restroom' and 'jello,' but others could be more problematic. Pantyhose, for instance, refers to a pair of tights and is not – as logical etymology might suggest – a discreet contraption to bring relief to the incontinent; rubbers are what we call wellies, a vest is a waistcoat, shorts are underpants and pants are trousers. Jeremy would be horrified to ask for suspenders – we call them braces – and I wouldn't care to find an exhaust silencer wrapped around my neck if I mistakenly asked to borrow a muffler from an American. Throughout America the pavement is the surface you drive your car on, whereas here in England … ah, not always so different in my case.

I took Kay to Pencarrow for lunch in the gardens, followed by a guided tour of the house and the chance to introduce her to Lady M. We also visited Trewithen, another lovely house and gardens nearby, where I had an appointment with Ross and Demelza, the two red squirrels who were part of a breeding program to reintroduce the species to Cornwall. As they cavorted amongst the leafy branches Kay took numerous photos for me to use as a guide in the illustrations for *Sgt. Simon Squirrel the Quartermaster – Battle of the Squirrels*, the September book in the children's series; she later became a sponsor for the book, as she had with several other books in the series. Each evening after supper Kay and I walked across the moor behind the cottage to watch the sunsets over the sea, a habit she found beneficial for her sleep; I am usually in my pyjamas by that time so this was a novel idea to me. The final series of Doc Martin was shot in 2022, so once again Kay flew over to take part.

We saw each other on her days off and one evening we took her to the Minack Theatre to see a production of *Twelfth Night*. This had been a long held ambition for Kay and the evening couldn't have been more perfect. I prepared a special picnic supper to eat before the performance; smoked salmon finger sandwiches, prawn salads, cocktail sausages, locally made pork pies and a chilled bottle of Champagne. It had been raining on the way to Penzance but as we headed towards Land's End the skies cleared and the sun sparkled on the calm sea, from which St. Michael's Mount rose like a mirage. The sight of Minack amazed Kay, as it does most visitors; she took photos constantly as we wound our way down the path through the stunningly landscaped clifftop gardens that form the natural amphitheatre. Here and there amongst the abundance of unusual shrubs and sub-tropical and salt loving plants were granite slabs with the names of Shakespeare's characters carved into the stone; I was thrilled to find a MIRANDA and took a photo to send to my daughter.

I had brought my warmest winter 'duvet' coats, bobble hats and gloves for Kay and me, and even some hot water bottles and rugs. The last time Jeremy and I had been at Minack was thirty years ago, when Rory and Miranda were very young, and we had seen a hilarious romp called *Daisy Pulls It Off*, which was perfect for the children. During that performance there was a collective gasp from the audience and a barely concealed murmur of 'DOLPHINS!' reverberated around the terraces. A large pod of dolphins was playing in the crystal water directly beyond the stage; even the actors in the wings watched until the animals sped towards deeper water, where a dozen gannets dived for fish, their wings folded tight as they plunged cleanly into the water. Our eyes were constantly drawn to the open sea, as if we were on the deck of an ocean liner.

My guest was enthralled from beginning to end, herself an actress and professional voiceover artist in Chicago. The crimson sun slowly slipped beneath the horizon and darkness fell before the end of the fourth act. It grew colder with every minute and we pulled the rugs tighter around our legs, thoroughly enjoying mugs of hot chocolate from a flask with some Scottish shortbread. It was a truly magical experience and as we climbed our way back up the fiendishly steep path Kay said we had made a dream come true – how lovely.

I needed the loo before the long drive home, so I made for the little stone building in front of us while Kay waited outside with our rugs and coats before taking her turn. Whether it was the effect of the bubbly, or simply my tendency to ignore signs I can't say, but I bypassed the long queue of women and walked straight into another open doorway, beyond which I could just make out a line of people with their backs to me. I had almost closed a cubicle door in the dimly lit room before I realised they were men standing very purposefully facing the wall. I shot out as if I'd seen the Devil himself. Kay greeted me with a fit of the giggles, which started me off too. All too soon I found myself wishing for a fully operational 'pantyhose' in my 'shorts' as I queued for the 'restroom'.

Is it just me, or do such idiotically daft things happen to other people too? I think it must run in the family. My Auntie Pam had once been caught short whilst on a long walk through some remote Devonshire countryside; imagining nobody could see her, she communed with nature in the middle of a grassy meadow. Just as she was in the middle of relieving herself, knickers around her ankles, a steam train emerged from a tunnel and chuffed by within a yards of her. The driver blew the whistle and waved cheerfully at her, swiftly followed by all his jeering passengers in the carriages.

Another fortuitous meeting happened quite by chance in Kefalonia, where we had moored Sarava in Fiskardo for our first visit of that particular summer. Only Miranda was with us for some reason, and as she and Jeremy were happily getting everything ship shape after our sail from Corfu, I decided to reacquaint myself with the picturesque village. Usually we had friends staying with us and I would be busily preparing afternoon tea or cocktails before changing for a relaxing supper ashore. It was mid afternoon and the temperatures were touching 35°C as I walked across the passarella onto the quayside, wearing my lucky white swimsuit with an ample white sarong and an even larger white straw sunhat. I hadn't gone very far before discovering a tiny jasmine and bougainvillea covered alleyway leading up steep steps to heaven knows where. Following the sweetly scented jasmine and picking a couple of sprigs as I passed, I climbed the steps and eventually came out on a road with a sign pointing further up the hill to the Fiskardo Nautical and Environmental Museum. Every ornate balcony and roadside verge was a riot of colour; deep blue morning glory wound rampantly through scarlet, magenta, cerise and orange bougainvillea and powder blue plumbago; competing for the most beautiful flower award were the tiny white star flowers of jasmine. Each of the traditional Kefalonian houses I passed was painted in pastel shades, set off perfectly by the backdrop of the ultramarine Ionian Sea. Rounding a bend I came upon the museum, an attractive old building with a pillared colonnade that had once been the local primary school. I walked up the steps into its cool and dark interior, where I spotted the finest pair of suntanned legs I had seen in years stretched out beneath the reception desk. Old leather flip-flops lay discarded on the floor and as I looked upwards for the owner, I saw a young man with blonde curly hair slouched back in a chair and almost asleep. I walked up to him and asked in Greek if I had to pay to get in.

"Er …" was his response. Pairing his handsome tanned face and china blue eyes with a distinctly laid back manner I knew he must be English, so I repeated the question.

"Oh thank goodness, I don't speak much Greek I'm afraid!" he replied, grinning as he got up to shake my hand. "I'm Simon."

Assuring me I didn't have to pay to get in to the museum he began to show me around, explaining he was just finishing his gap year before going to university. As a volunteer with the Nautical and Environmental Club he loved the days out on the diving boats, observing and documenting the marine life of the area, but he dreaded the long days he had to be on duty at the museum. When he added that he was from Exeter I nearly dropped through the floor; we were still living on Dartmoor at the time and it soon turned out we had many friends in common, including his best friend who was the son of one of my fellow British Red Cross Events Committee members. We had last seen that fellow in Kassiopi when he had sat down on a glass topped table and gone right through it. How had he ever become head boy at Simon's public school in Dorset was beyond me. When the telephone rang on Simon's desk I nipped outside and took the opportunity to call Miranda.

"You must come up to the museum right away!"

"Not likely, it's far too hot! I'm not leaving the boat."

My pleas of *'There's someone here you would really really like to meet, so jolly well get up here now'* fell on deaf ears. What to do? I felt they had to meet each other, especially as Miranda, at just sixteen, was getting understandably bored with only having her parents for company during our stay in Fiscardo. I went back inside and asked Simon if he would like to join us for drinks on Sarava as soon as he went off duty.

Back on the boat I excitedly told Jeremy and Miranda that I had met a handsome young man and invited him for drinks later on, quickly adding that we had friends in common.

"What on earth did you think you were doing?" asked my husband, "Picking up unsuspecting young men? What ever must he think of you!"

"I bet he'll be some fearful swot if he works in a museum," moaned Miranda, as she and her father continued their swabbing duties.

A few minutes after six, I heard a voice hailing Sarava from the quayside; Miranda burst into my cabin before I could open the door.

"Mummy! He's gorgeous!"

My reply of 'I told you so' went unheard as she dashed back up to the cockpit to welcome this Adonis on board. Naturally Jeremy and Miranda fell into easy conversation with our delightful new young friend and by the third round of drinks Jeremy asked him to join us for supper at a taverna on the quayside.

"You decide which one, Simon," Jeremy suggested, although we had our favourites. "You'll know them all from a local's point of view."

Later Simon returned and soon he was guiding us to a small taverna at the nether end of the harbour, which he assured us served the best food in Fiskardo. We sat at a table beside a tiny spit of sand where the water lapped at our feet; and as the moon rose over Ithaca and the calm black sea before us, the setting became perfection. As Simon had promised, our plates of fresh sardines and red mullet were excellent and all too soon it was time to ask for our bill. Peering at the slip of paper by the dim light of the candle lantern on the table, Jeremy was puzzled.

"Why are there only three main courses on here?"

"Oh, I paid for mine earlier on," Simon replied. "I didn't want you to think I was taking advantage of your hospitality."

"Well, you really shouldn't have," said Jeremy, suddenly quite impressed. "We wanted you to be our guest. To make up for it, why don't you come sailing with us tomorrow? We're heading down past Sami for the day."

As it was Sunday, Simon had the day off and appeared first thing in the morning with his swimming things and a grin like the Cheshire Cat. We had a wonderfully relaxing morning swimming from Sarava and chatting in the shade of the awnings; we ate a lunch of perfectly ripe melon, sliced juicy white Italian peaches, wafer thin prosciutto bought in the little delicatessen in Gaios, parmesan shavings, balsamic vinegar and freshly ground black pepper, served with Jeremy's speciality Melba toast, all washed down with ice cold Gentilini.

On board Sarava we had an electric fly swat, shaped like a tennis racquet. Simon discovered it and spent most of the afternoon leaping around the decks trying to swat wasps with a series of impressive strokes, until one particularly energetic volley on the aft deck tumbled him into the water, the zapper flying into the air and landing in the cockpit. Pride comes before a fall, even for a young Adonis. That was probably the moment Jeremy teasingly christened him Able Seaman Simon – ASS for ever after.

Simon became a regular visitor to Sarava and his family became friends of ours. A year later I was able to use him as a model in a fashion show I produced for the Red Cross. It was particularly amusing to cast Miranda as the bride in the finalé, with Simon as her groom. He took to modelling like a duck to water and looked marvellous in morning dress for the wedding scene. During the rehearsals, one of my fellow committee members had overheard how we had met Simon in Kefalonia.

"He said you were all dressed in white!" she exclaimed. "I imagined you were in some sort of splendid Arabian garb and thought it didn't sound at all like you!"

Memories of our enviable years in the Ionian still sustain us through the English winters. Corfu, after all, was for us a place where every other chance encounter slipped so insouciantly into firm friendship. Our short days in Cornwall are occupied with long walks on deserted beaches, where the wild Atlantic surf fills the air with salt spray as we search for sea glass and shells on a falling tide, or sometimes with sorties onto the open moor, leaning into the gale as we make our way past herds of unconcerned ponies and gentle Highland cattle. Dark evenings pass quickly after such bracing exercise, as our minds turn to the friends and places we remember from a very different climate; from the comfort of these musings we cling resolutely to the remaining traces of exuberant Greekness we had so willingly acquired during our lives in Corfu.

The thaw will eventually return to Cornwall and before we know it Spring will have burst upon the county again. Daffodils nodding their heads in the stiff March breeze and the tiny pink cyclamen flowers peeping bravely above their Corfiot corms will flourish as the vast North Cornish skies again revert to a more familiar cerulean blue. Buzzards soaring on the thermals and skylarks singing over the moorland heather will proclaim winter over for another year. Then the swallows will return once again to fill our hearts with joy.

Epilogue

There was a time when a book could be sold purely because its author had been to distant climes and returned to tell of the exotic sights he had seen. That author was Marco Polo, and the time was the thirteenth century.

Howard Mittelmark

The most extraordinary and totally unexpected things have happened since the publication of *The Butterflies Fly Backwards* and *The Swallows Fly Back*, particularly the Facebook messages and emails that arrive daily from readers all over the world. I should have been prepared; as Louisa Durrell said: *If you live long enough in Corfu, you cease to be surprised at anything!* I never thought for a single moment that anyone would bother to write to me, but the response has brought me new friends from every continent. Jeremy Just Chaplin and I have been invited by many kind readers to visit them if ever we find ourselves on their shores; we have even been invited to Katmandu, where an elderly Gurkha soldier and his wife have asked us to stay. I have always wanted to see the Himalayas.

I find myself at a bit of a loose end as this series of books is completed; I have enjoyed writing them so much. But I have had an idea swirling around in my head since we first moved to North Cornwall, a yearning to revisit and complete the story of the year my family spent in Spain. *The Road to Poor Jesus* will trace the many close shaves and delights that marked our precipitous dash to the sun in 1987. Jeremy and I began writing alternate chapters five years after our equally hasty return from Jesús Pobre; we even sent the first few chapters to various publishers and agents. Without exception they replied that our efforts were well written in an agreeable style, informative, humorous and interesting; but they warned that autobiographical travel books were never going to be a popular genre – and this after the astonishing successes of *My Family and Other Animals*, *A Year in Provence*, *Extra Virgin* and *Driving over Lemons*, to name but a few. At the time I asked the owner of the very successful Dartington Bookshop in Totnes if he agreed. He replied, pointing to the prime position right by the door where they were all prominently displayed, that true life travel stories were his best sellers. As soon as I can find a moment I will return to my little summerhouse in the garden and bash on regardless – after all, I am almost a very big and important publisher now!

As for our beloved Corfu, we have always hoped to return one day. 'Maybe next year,' we have consoled one another ever since we returned to England; but since *The Manor House Stories* called to me from their little suitcase in the attic twelve years ago, the books have completely taken over our lives and left no time for holidays. Jeremy thinks precious memories are best left alone, but I am determined to go back one day to see all our friends, especially my goddaughter Antonia Julia and her family. I will leave the last words to her, written on a recent phone message.

JANI MOU, COME BACK!

Roasted garlic and beetroot dip

3 whole heads of garlic, the 'real' pink skinned garlic from farm shops or any Mediterranean country is best, rather than the small white variety from China you find in supermarkets
3 medium sized raw beetroots (unless you are buying a Greek beetroot, the size of a large onion, you may need 4 if they are rather small!)
250g cream or ricotta cheese (I sometimes use organic Greek Feta)
2 tbsp virgin olive oil
1 tsp sea salt and a generous helping of freshly ground black pepper

Preheat oven 200C.

Slice the top quarter off each head of garlic but do not peel. Remove tops of beetroots, wash and scrub well but leave skin on. Quarter beetroots and place on baking tray. Pour some olive oil on garlic heads, sprinkle on salt, pepper and loosely wrap in foil and place on same tray. Add olive oil, salt and pepper to the beetroots and bake for 45 minutes. The garlic should be golden and crispy and the beetroots soft.
When cool enough to handle (I use my Marigolds as I can never be bothered to wait!) squeeze the garlic gently out of its skin into a bowl or food processor.
Add beetroot and cream cheese and blend until it becomes smooth and creamy. Chill for a couple of hours and serve with toasted or charcoal grilled pitta slices or crusty bread. This can be made 24 hours in advance.

Durrell Wildlife Conservation Trust

is an international charity working to save species from extinction. Headquartered at Jersey Zoo in the Channel Islands, Durrell's vision is for a wilder, healthier more colourful world. Established by author and conservationist, Gerald Durrell, in 1959, Durrell's overall aim is for more diverse, beautiful and resilient natural landscapes in which species can thrive and people can enjoy a deeper connection with nature.

Their approach concentrates on the rewilding of animals, the rewilding of ecosystems and the rewilding of people.

www.durrell.org

Photographs of Gerry as a boy in Corfu and in later life at Jersey Zoo reproduced by courtesy of the estate of Gerald Durrell

The author contributes voluntarily to Durrell